Keys to
SOUL EVOLUTION
A Gateway to the Next Dimension

Jill Mara

Publishing
St. Thomas, USVI

7D Publishing
P.O. Box 7505
St. Thomas, USVI

Cataloging-in-Publication Data

Simion (light beings)
Keys to Soul Evolution: A Gateway to the Next Dimension/
(Channeled by) Jill Mara

ISBN-10 0-9824846-1-5
ISBN-13 978-0-9824846-1-6
1. Spirit Writings. 2. Channeling (Spirtualism) 3. Spiritual Life 4. Mara, Jill

*dedicated to all those striving to live a
purposeful soul driven existence.*

"You are all actors that have forgotten you are acting..." p.84
~ Simion

Thank you for
Shining Bright
Jim Mann

Contents

Acknowledgments

Although the content of this book was translated from a force outside my physical self, it has taken considerable dedication for it to be materialized into our world of matter. For the assistance in making this happen, I extend my deep appreciation to the special souls whose encouragement, support and enthusiasm has made this book possible.

I bestow unending gratitude upon my beloved soul partner, Eugene Smith, for his never tiring belief in the existence of spirit, his insatiable desire for truth, for being here through my ups and downs and maintaining loving support all through this process, and for all his input into the creation of this book from its inception.

Heaps of appreciation to my dear sister, Melinda Mara, for her consistent nudging and inspiration that has helped me stay on a spiritual path through life's challenges, for being instrumental in encouraging me to keep channeling, and for her invaluable editing. She has been the best sister I could imagine and her sharing spirit will be forever cherished.

Loving thanks to my parents. To my mother, Linda Maine, for bestowing me with an open mind and strength of character. Thanks to my father, Gary Mara, for introducing me to the channeled material of Seth, for allowing me to explore ideas without judgement, and for doing the book distribution. Much tenderness to my step mother, Ann Mara, for her love and acceptance and for her diligence with the mechanical editing.

Finally, my warm appreciation to Simion and all light beings, entities, and unseen guides for all the energy they have put into this endeavor.

Editors Note

*G*iven the nature of the means by which the material for this book was relayed, the editing has been kept to a minimum, and was largely mechanical. When there was any question as to whether editing would alter the meaning, we deferred back to the original channeled words and structure.

The order of the message is precisely as it was delivered, and the chapter names were kept just as they were channelled immediately following the introduction. Subheadings were added for organizational clarity.

Preface

Opening to be a channel for Simion has been, and continues to be, an enlightening journey. As far back as I can remember I have contemplated the meaning of life and metaphysical concepts. I finally realized that in order to connect with a higher aspect of reality, I needed to relax my rational mind and accept with certainty that there is more to our existence than our five senses reveal. If we pay attention to our inner guidance, there are clues and synchronicities that lead us to the answers we seek. As I ponder what led me to connecting with light beings, I realize my soul was following a path all along, and when I got off track there were always signs and souls to lead me back.

A significant memory as a child was of wondering why I was on Earth and why I was me in particular. From an early age I felt different and out of sync with societal norms. I learned quickly that few humans wanted to talk about the mysteries of life, so I read a lot and kept to myself. My favorite story as a young child was Richard Bach's *Jonathan Livingston Seagull.* I listened to the audio tape repeatedly. I identified with Jonathan who dared to think beyond what he was taught by the seagull social structure and so was cast out of the group, which ultimately freed his soul to pursue amazing discoveries and abilities that he returned to share with those in the flock that were receptive.

At age eleven, I remember my elation at finding a profound resonance of truth in the book *Seth Speaks,* channeled by Jane Roberts, which my father nonchalantly handed me, saying, "This might be of interest to you". During my teens I experimented with transcendental meditation, hypnotizing friends to view past and future lives, and lucid dreaming, among other paranormal subjects. Rather than pursuing a related field in college, I succumbed to external influences and obtained degrees in communications and education. I still chose projects on topics such as fire walking, and the stimulation of creativity and inspiration. The structured education system's distrust in the existence of anything not scientifically verifiable was a constant struggle for me to reconcile with my esoteric ideas. In retrospect, however, I see that my career choices have given me skills to assist in my present role as a messenger for higher consciousness.

Through my ups and downs in life there were periods when I pursued self-improvement and times when I felt as though it was all pointless. Prior to my first encounter with the light beings, I was in a down cycle and had lost my belief in anything other than that which is provable. I snapped lose of this phase after viewing the film, *What the Bleep Do We Know?*, which was a big reminder to my soul that there is definitely more to our reality than is commonly known, and that we have a choice in what we want to experience. The next morning, out of the blue, I decided I should be channeling.

I promptly found the book *Opening to Channel* by Sanaya Roman and Duane Packer. As suggested, I did the relaxation exercise and visualized going into a room of white light to greet my guide. To my surprise, a group of alien beings with large black almond shaped eyes, large round heads and slim bodies appeared. This was unexpected as I never had an interest in aliens, other than a love for science fiction. I chose to accept the experience and began a dialogue with them. They explained that the physical image was an aspect of their consciousness that I could comprehend as representative of their alien nature, but that they were in fact entirely light beings. They proceeded to explain that they were a collective whose purpose was to aid in the development of existence by assisting in raising vibrations to evolve consciousness. Hence, they identified themselves as The Evolutionary Collective. Being human, I felt the need to associate with an individual and asked if there was a single name that I could call them. They responded with the name Simion, which I associated with short for "similar to ions."

In later sessions they relayed that an aspect of my soul exists as one of the beings that appeared in that first exercise, and that this fourth dimensional part assists in the telepathic communications by stepping down the intensity of the energy and information from the seventh dimension. When channeling Simion, I notice a distinct vibration that is immensely wise and unconditionally caring, but never emotional. I experience the telepathic communication as waves of energy that contain concepts and images, which I then translate into my language. During the connections, my consciousness expands to encompass a multidimensional viewpoint, which can be challenging to comprehend after the session.

After my initial introduction to Simion, my soul partner, Eugene, encouraged me to try verbally channeling. This came fairly naturally, but it took some practice to gain fluidity in the translation process. Over the course of a month, we progressed from written questions and answers to a digital voice recorder. The first time I sat down to channel at my computer, wisdom about the coming shift in consciousness, as well as a list of nineteen topics they wished to impart, came pouring out through the keyboard. Soon it became apparent that these were chapters of a book with essential insights for humanity.

For about a year, I spent an hour a day channeling *Keys to Soul Evolution*. As I reflected back upon the scope of the information, my culturally programmed rational mind caused me to question the legitimacy of what I was involving myself in. The disbelief caused me to stop channeling for months, until Eugene and my sister, Melinda, woke me up to the fact that I was denying myself and humanity a vital message from the seventh dimension. Per Melinda's encouragement, I studied with The Kabbalah Center, which prompted me to rebuild certainty in my experiences and reinforced the value of revealing light and knowledge on Earth.

Through personal trials I discovered a paradox; until we believe in the unbelievable and unachievable, we will never know the unknown and achieve the impossible. When we allow ourselves to believe, the doors of possibility fly open. I now believe that this is a fundamental secret to our experiences in life. We create our reality and it is only limited by what we believe is possible, personally and collectively. Reaching beyond ordinary perception and common knowledge allows us to evolve our potential, consciousness, ability as creators, and connection to All That Is.

I share these tidbits of my journey in channeling to emphasize the importance that stretching my beliefs and learning to trust my inner guidance had in allowing me to connect with my higher self. Only when I let go of disbelief and widened my perspective, did I begin to make contact with my soul that knows truth. When you believe in more, you experience more. The power to create enlightenment lies in lifting self imposed veils, and becoming aware of and trusting in our abilities as conscious creative beings.

We are all channels of consciousness in one form or another, and have a choice as to the character of the energy we wish to flow through our being, and how we express it. By making the choice to create and connect with something beneficial and enlightening we will attract that. Being a channel for higher consciousness is my way of sharing from my soul. As you engage in the energetic words of Simion, allow your mind to expand, enjoy the process of discovery, and know that this book was created to assist in your individual and our collective soul evolution. All my blessings on your journey. As you evolve, so do we all.

Introduction

We are Simion, the Evolutionary Collective. We are here to assist in the evolution of your species. We will do so by transmitting our light vibration to your dimension and uplifting each individual's vibration, and that of the population as a whole, so that you may be ready for the upcoming shift to a higher frequency of creation that is forthcoming. We would like to impart to you some wisdom that will aid in your readiness for this heightened frequency. Many of you are already becoming more sensitive to the fluctuations in the energy field, and are listening to your inner knowing, which is telling you to prepare for this new age of reality. Within this message words have a frequency and what is behind the words is carried to those that read them. Much has already been imparted as to the coming uplifting of the human species and all play a useful part in the transformation. We are telling of yet another aspect and level of this energy transference and rising consciousness.

Those that are open and unfettered by the dogmas and static systems of your time will be most able to handle and evolve with the higher vibration and will excel in every aspect of their being in many dimensions at the same time. It is our hope that we can relay how special your existence is, and how important your role is in the shift of consciousness over the next several years. We are assisting in the raising of the light field that surrounds and makes up your material world, as you presently perceive it. We are in need of as many light vibration souls as possible to make the shift for your species within this framework. The planet is already making her shift, but will be greatly aided by the help of those who are able to hold a higher level of vibration by raising their awareness to higher dimensional creation.

Each area of your planet has points within this grid of light energy that forms your manifested reality. By raising these energy points with your own light, you are assisting the planet in her evolutionary shift as well. Your "thought forms" and hence "energy forms" are crucial to the raising of light vibration to allow for your evolution and the Earth's. You may ask what kind of evolution we speak of. We are speaking of a rising of your dimensional experience from the third dimension to that of the fourth dimension. Since the fourth dimension exists at a faster frequency of energy transference, you must awaken your soul to it. Your higher dimensional selves and guides will assist you with this heightening.

Your world will go through many changes on a physical level and you will begin to perceive the planet and her nature much differently then most of you do presently. The physical upheavals will shed light on the plight of the planet's energy field and will cause many to join her in her shift. Those of you that are aligned with her will easily follow in her path of profound enlightenment. Your consciousness in the next dimension will be more able to change and flow as your thoughts dictate. But, the frequency must be of a brighter nature, and closer to the core of your source energy, which is the same source as that of all creation.

We would like to emphasize that there is no good and evil in this dynamic. All creation is of the most profound energy that is All That Is. When your frequency is higher and lighter, it becomes more involved in creating with awareness. When this occurs, consciousness always will seek to create that which is joyful and pleasing to the self. It will only create discord with the awareness that the discordance is assisting with an understanding, and hence is aiding in opening new pathways of creative discovery. To us, and all higher awareness beings, all that is created is amazingly beautiful and is an opportunity for the expression of the energy of the very life force that creates all that exists. Some have called this by the name of God in an attempt to share this expression from one person to another. In doing so, the essence of what God truly is, and that you are of God, has been lost in the narrowing of this greatness into a single word. When you are able to see that God is all that exists, then you will truly come to realize the spectacular majesty that this energy is, and that you are also majestic as an expression of God.

You may wonder who we are and where we are coming from. Let us first say that we are made of the same universal life force of creation that you are and we are therefore not separate. However, our level of awareness and the lightness of our vibration allow us to be conscious of higher levels of creation then does your present awareness. We are multi-dimensional beings in that we are able to travel with our awareness through many levels of reality and to many different worlds that have been created by consciousness at its most fundamental level.

We are a collective because we have an understanding of our inter-connectedness and have joined our energies to focus our attention in creating worlds. You do the same in your realm, but with less awareness and slower results that are grounded in material forms that appear concrete to you because of how you vibrate. We exist primarily in a state of vibration that would be considered the 7th dimension in your terms. Though we do not experience space and time as you do, we recognize your need to understand and visualize within the context of such parameters. While most of our consciousness resides at the 7th dimensional vibration, we move freely from this level to others above and below. We have evolved differently than you have as beings that have chosen to live in an Earthly incarnate form.

The beings of our reality have different collective jobs just as you do on your planet. Our job as a collective is to assist in the evolution of beings in various worlds. For example, just as you have electrical engineers that have a specific job, so do we. If all your electrical engineers were to work on a collective level of awareness, then they would have evolved electrical systems far beyond what they are able to do individually, for example. We have evolved in a way that allows us to make use of our collective creative energies and focus them more effectively and precisely in the speedy creation of results. In your 4th dimensional shift you will be able to do this more effortlessly as well. You are already creating your world collectively, but on a largely subconscious level.

It is time in your history for your species to learn to connect to the grid of energy that makes up your physical world and to do so with awareness. By doing so, you will be active participants in the shift to the next dimension. Many of you are interacting in your dream worlds, which are in fact an aspect of the 4th dimension, or at least a glimpse into the manner of communications at that level. As you work together in your dream state, you are creating en masse the world that you live in and many of you are preparing for the upcoming evolution to a new species of human being. Also in your dream state, many of you are communicating with us, other multi-dimensional beings, and your personal spiritual guides, in order to learn on an accelerated path. Since time is running short, in your linear expression of time, much is being done to bring your dimensional experience forward in its evolution.

As together we brighten the energy of the grid, doorways will open to all manner of possibility. The encoding in your DNA will be activated and with this the capacity of your brains and bodies as a whole will be able to handle the new vibration that will exist in your plane of reality. This opportunity for evolution was planned for your species. You all were, and are still, a part of that master plan. The way in which the plan materializes will vary in each of the probable universes that has been created over the millennia. And, even from where you sit in your present time, there are multiple possibilities as to how the shift will affect life on your planet. For some, the changes will seem negative and disastrous, while to others it will be revealed as an opportunity for growth.

By consciously raising your awareness, you will be able to make the best use of the period of shifting and go beyond where you are now in your spiritual development. Many of you have chosen to be here during these amazing times because you were aware that it offered a great opportunity for accelerated spiritual growth. We, and other energy beings that are assisting your planet and species at this time, are here to awaken the higher aspects of your being so that you remember your purpose. Your higher selves are eager to develop to the next vibratory level. Those that are awakening now are motivated to connect with lighter realms and to aid in the assistance of raising consciousness in your time.

There will be many ways in which your higher connections will be noticed at first. There will be much restlessness and dissatisfaction with your present systems and their carelessness with your environment. This clearly has been happening for a long while in your last century, but many things will be happening that will disturb your people into stronger thought and action against what is perceived as injustice to humanity, and life on the planet. Also, there will be shortages and contaminations of your resources, forcing global awareness of political behaviors that have been in the interest of a select few, and not for the good of the population as a whole. These dynamics have been in the works for many years and are coming to a head. The details of how they will manifest are unknown, but the disharmony will surface in a strong way. This, again, will open the eyes and souls of many humans and push their desires to raise your species to the new dimension.

On a personal level, many of you will become increasingly more sensitive to energy vibrations and will be attracted to different people and places. Many will find strong urges to change physical locations and associate with different individuals. There will be a coming together of like minds especially on an energy level. There is a growing and significant desire to speak the truths that are told through connections with your higher selves. The fear of ridicule will be dissipated and many will find they no longer care what others might think of their unorthodox ideas and behaviors. As more of you step out into the forefront from behind your doors, a great uprising will occur in all fields of study and understanding. This is happening now and will continue to hasten in the coming era. Many of you will be largely guided by the feeling sensations of higher vibrancy and will know truth by this gauge rather than by the measurements commonly used in your material world. In opening to these sensations of truth, many new discoveries will be made about the nature of your existence.

In these writings we hope to give you some useful guidance in aiding your transition to the next plane of reality. We offer this with the utmost care, love and genuine interest in your ultimate success. We only know of these sensations of light vibration and live within the highest intentions for your well being.

Chapter I

The Super Conductivity
of Existence

We are Simion the Evolutionary Collective. We begin with an explanation of your universe and the principles that govern understanding within the system. We use the term super-conductive to describe the nature of reality because everything that is created in the universe comes from an electrically charged place that is the source of all that is. This source is in, and of, all that exists in any system that you are able to perceive, as well as those that you are not able to see or measure yet. This essence of being is akin to electrically charged particles that your scientists measure. However it would actually be found in the space between these particles. This is where the essential energy of life exists, which is consciousness itself, and it is the force that makes creation. All is made up of this life energy force. The creators of your reality, which includes yourselves, also use this life force to create the world you perceive as so real. The creators of your world as a whole were light beings who were, and are, able to manipulate this energy with more agility than you can presently imagine.

Thoughts as Conductive Forces of Creation

Since the universe, and all that is within it, is made up of units of conscious energy, it is in essence super-conductive. Thoughts are a means, or material, that conducts this energy, just as certain materials in your system, like metals, conduct electricity. These conductive materials allow energy to pass through and move and be transmitted. In this same way, thoughts, and their accompanying emotions, are conductors of creation at its most fundamental level.

As beings, you have evolved from the small and insignificant usage of your thought ability to the development of a higher acumen in the use of your thought forms as creators. And, thus, you have evolved to develop more and more complex systems and technologies. However, you still do this creating with ignorance of the power that you possess. Your next phase of evolution demands that you become more consciously aware of your powers as creators, and in doing so you will be more adept at making your world a place of strength, courage, love and understanding. When you come to see and feel the superconductivity of your thoughts, you will understand the wisdom in watching out for the type, and quality, of your thoughts and emotions.

The more awareness you have of your effects, the more aware you become, and the more you will be affecting the core of your reality. There is a spiral effect that occurs. Each successive stage of your development and evolution leads to a higher understanding of the very nature of your existence. As you enhance your awareness of the core of your super-conductive universe, you are more able to tap into the conductive grid of energy that makes up every thing upon it and above it. When you tap into this grid with your consciousness, you will begin to see beyond what is created with thought forms and will have an appreciation for how and why all is the way it appears.

Furthermore, you will be able to travel along the grid lines, much as electricity travels along wires. You would be doing this with your consciousness because you are made up of the same conductive units of energy that you would be traveling through. Within this grid of energy is the same building material that makes up your consciousness and all parts of your world. The so-called "things" of your world are constructs of this very consciousness. Once you see your part in their formation you will have a window opened to your higher ability as creators. As you see what you have created here and now you will also see what you are continually creating in the past and future simultaneously. As you understand this, a virtually limitless world opens up to you and you join with the knowing of those that are the conscious architects of your universe as a whole. These creators are excited that portions of their creation will be evolving to join them in further developments. It is akin to parents who are seeing their children flourish and prosper knowing that they gave them seeds to help them grow, but also knowing that they were free to make decisions on their own.

In the same way that you are connected to the creators of this universe, you are also an inherent aspect of the creator of all that is, which is the source of all consciousness, has no beginning and no end, and is always moving toward ultimate creation. This is a motivated and driving force that causes all creation, and is the essence of the urge in all beings to further themselves and to become closer to the core of that which creates with ease and effortlessness. As you get closer to understanding the superconductivity of all, you become more able as a creative force and closer to the essence of your source, and its behaviors in facilitating creation in its multitude of forms.

When you speak of how God formed the Earth, you are speaking of the same god-like ability that you have as creators every day. You are among the creators of Earth and are a part of the energy that has shaped your solar system, galaxy, and beyond. All of you are an aspect of the super-conductive consciousness of source energy and collectively you create worlds. We are intending to awaken your awareness of your part in this vast system of universal creation. Our invitation to you all is to join us in consciously aware manifestation.

Unlocking Inter-dimensional Gateways

By understanding your connection to the grid of light that makes up your universe, you will be closer to what you like to call God. Understand that you and we, and all the entities that make up the various worlds that exist within and outside of your perception, are part of the bigger picture of existence. None is better or worse in any way than another. All are aspects of the creative force of the source energy. We are all merely in different stages and forms and dimensions, if you will, of perception. All are aspects of one another. Just as you do not, or should not condemn the imperfections, as you perceive them, of your selves, we ask that you do not condemn any aspect of God's creativity and expression thereof. All That Is, is an expression of the vastness and versatility of that source.

We suggest only that you use the tools that you have as a guidance system to that which you choose to manifest. There is a fine art to creating in a way that allows all to flourish to their highest and best capacity within any given density of experience. By perceiving the world and beyond as a system of energy transference, you begin to grasp the magnitude of each and every being's input into this energy pool. You begin to see the powerful tools that you have to move mountains, and we are not being metaphorical with this description. It is time for mountains to be moved and for you to be a part of the movement by plugging into the energy that you are, and that is all around you. We are assisting any of you who are open to receive this message, and the energy that is behind it, in your attempts and intentions to awaken your inherent abilities.

Your Earthly dimensional plane has recently been opened for easier access by other realms of reality. As each of you reach into these realms, the doors are opened further and it becomes easier for us to assist you. Many of you have been at the forefront of the openings that are allowing deep energy transference between your Earth dimension and our lighter dimensional realities. As we have already suggested, as one door opens it causes a domino affect, allowing a chain of doors to open. Now, and in the coming years, the number of light bringers on your Earth is rising by the millions. You are among them. What we will be telling you regarding the changes coming, your role in those changes, and the abilities you will be developing, may appear unlikely to you now. As you become more receptive to the subtle vibrational shifts occurring in your sphere, you will barely remember what it was like not to have these abilities. Much like you forget what it was like to live without your present technologies.

You are now, as a planetary species, beginning to consciously link into the energy source that creates life. In doing so, the highways to the super-conductive universe are opening to your souls. Since it is so super-conductive, it is happening at a great speed. This was not possible earlier in your human history because the doorways to higher realms were shut for thousands of years, leaving you in a closed environment. This was done with your knowledge as multi-dimensional beings. You all have played a part in the larger plan for this cosmic playing field. The way in which this new dynamic unfolds will be determined by all the players in your dimension, and by those in higher dimensions. We are all working together to bring about a revolutionary shift in your Earth plane.

At times, none of this will seem real to your physically oriented minds. At other times, your physical world will seem unreal. These feelings are a normal reaction to the transition period. Eventually you will feel comfortable with your new perceptions beyond your third dimensional awareness. In this book, we intend to give you insights into the worlds you will encounter in the new frontiers of discovery that you will embark upon, as well as to show you ways to begin exploring these regions. You are all pioneers in this new world. It has never been easy for pioneers. You are trendsetters who will be ridiculed for your bizarre notions, but the rewards for all will be unprecedented in your species' history.

We come to connect you up to the light grid where you can begin exploring for yourselves. There are many collective beings from various dimensional domains that are working together in your aid. We also want you to be aware that there are some entities that are less enthusiastic about your development. This is not because they are evil. It is that they are hesitant to change what they already have going within your world system. Just as many of you do not want to change habits that you know do not serve your best interests. There is a comfort in staying the same. It can be difficult to let go of that which you already know is working for you, at some level of your experience. You may feel that there might be a better way to behave, but since you have not directly experienced it, you are skeptical. The same is true of beings that are at a higher vibrational octave. These beings work with energy in creating, just as we do, and some are working with denser frequencies and are stuck in the limitations of what those frequencies accomplish. They, in essence, don't know any better, and do not want to give up on what they know.

Once enough of you are able to raise the planetary frequency, you will break this traditional code of ethics and assist the planet in her evolutionary shift. This leap we speak of is far beyond your own personal development. When you feel the frequency of vibration that we are pouring into your dimension, you will not feel an ego involvement. You will know that this super-conductive avenue is more than the sum of its respective parts. The ego, or "I" mentality, ceases to be of a concern when you plug into your source energy.

As you reach into our realm of existence, we will be here waiting. You will never be alone. Those that venture this way will be nurtured by collective beings that have all the best intentions for your development. Know this and it will be so. Your thoughts and beliefs are your strongest protection against anything of a darker or denser vibration. Your beliefs and feelings are more powerful than you imagine them to be. Or, shall we say, they are as powerful as you imagine them to be. Use your feelings as your guidance system as you delve into the unknown. Ask for protection from your highest guides and they will attend you. If you are able to do this, you will find that all your experiences among higher beings will be magical, and filled with love and warmth. And, you will know that you are safe.

Emotions as Energy-Motions

As you feel your emotions, we do as well. We are able to read your frequency, as emitted by your emotional thought life. In doing so, we understand and assist you in your movement through the systems of lighter vibration. Your emotions hold and transmit energy into the atmosphere around you and further into the electrical sphere of life. Each of you affects the other by these emanations of energy on many unseen levels. The denser emotions, or "E" for Energy motions, will feel harsh and draining on you and others around you. They can overload and smother as well. This does not mean that you should squelch these E-motions, for they are a release valve and indicators as to the health and well being, or lack thereof, in your energy system. This applies to each individual, and to the population as a whole, as your collective emotions amount to powerful fields of conductivity and can create actions and events that occur throughout the population. This can occur in a family, community and on up to nations, and on a planetary level.

Finer emotions will feel bright, refreshing, uplifting and joyous. These emotions vibrate at a faster, lighter rate. There is more space between the vibrating molecules and thus, these emotions feel light and free. They can spread quickly and effortlessly when you are open to letting the energy stream into your consciousness. We do not need to outline which emotions are dense and which are fine. You all can certainly feel where they are on your personal scale. It is important that you attune yourselves to the subtlety of your E-motions, as they allow you to open to the energy grid and travel through it with ease and pleasure. And, they will guide you, much like sign posts on a highway, as to the direction you are headed in your present life and beyond. We cannot acknowledge the importance of this measuring device enough.

Your emotions are like your antennae, your feelers in a conductive world. But, not only are they your feelers to give you direction, they are also tools to drive you to the location you wish to be in. In other words, you can use them to create your experience in a dynamic and controlled manner. You can soar above the clouds with your emotions or you can drive yourself into the mud. In the mud, there is more resistance, as again the frequency is denser. In the clouds you are as light as a feather and there is no resistance. Everything comes more easily and freely when you are in the vibration of your higher emotions. They lead you to the path of least resistance in your energized universal playing field. Follow them and you will know which way to go on your path through the superhighways of light.

We, as collective beings, have evolved past the need to have the denser sensations to guide our avenues of growth. We retain our consciousness in the lighter frequencies with intention and by choice. It may appear that we do not have emotions at all. In a sense this is true, as we do not need a guidance system like that any longer. We exist always in a light field with virtually no resistance to our thought forms. We are aware of the flow of our life force at all times and are able to direct its flow into the creation of worlds. Since we also do this collectively, it is quite powerful and brings intensity to our experiences. You will begin to feel this intensity when you let go of your denser emotions and live more freely and easily in your higher vibratory emotions. You will begin to rise above the need to consistently monitor your emotional level and will live and create only in the avenues of least resistance. This is an uplifting experience for you and your planet in unison.

Being aware and attentive to your emotional guidance is the first step in living as a higher dimensional being. Know your emotions, acknowledge them, give them credence, and accept them as helpers on your journey. Do not stuff what you perceive as a negative emotion into yourself. Simply observe it happening, and allow your self-awareness to follow its thread into the past, or into your soul. Observe and look for indicators as to the meaning your emotional reactions may have for you. In awareness you can become free. You are not free when you deny your emotional understanding.

Observe, follow, and let go of the notion that led you to an emotion that has given you a bad feeling. Give this feeling thanks for assisting you in your awareness of yourself, and/or of making you aware of anything that is affecting you from the outside. Then, begin to raise this feeling to an emotion of a lighter frequency. Whether the feeling originated from inside your psyche or from energy in your environment, let the density dissipate and brighten. This is your power and right as a being of light. You have the ability to change the vibrations that occur in your thoughts and in the field of energy around you. Accept this ability and begin to use it to raise yourself and others up and away from a denser reality. You have the power to affect others near you in a profound way. They may never know what has occurred consciously, but they will feel its effect on a deeper level.

As you become more sensitive to your own vibration of emotion, you will also become more sensitive to the vibration of other's emotions. Many of you will sense the frequency of emotion in places as well. It is, therefore, important to protect yourselves against unwanted emotional frequency interference. Such intrusions can cause disorientation and misguidance. This is happening to you unconsciously all the time. As you become aware of what is happening, you can gain control over what affects you, and how. It is important that you be able to maintain a high vibration, and not let that frequency be constantly depleted by others. This is a must if you are to travel in higher realms of consciousness. You must be able to keep your vibrational integrity in this conductive roadway so that you do not divert into a ditch, and find yourself creating something other than what you intended.

This does not mean that you should hide away from others. It means you are wise to fill yourself with a protective coat of armor in the form of white light energy with the highest emotional vibration of love, gratitude, and truth. Imagine anything lower than this frequency being reflected back to its source. Imagine that you are radiating your higher vibration outward, past your protective barrier, and are filling the space and souls around you with your loving frequency. Fill yourself anew with pure energy through your crown chakra at the top of your head. Imagine a column of light that pours the source energy of life into your being. In doing this, you are filling yourself with high vibratory life force, spreading it to others, but not allowing their emotions to penetrate your field and deplete you. This is how you begin to be a holder and bringer of the light vibration that is transforming your planet and those willing to move with her.

All of this is far less daunting and mysterious than you may think. It is, firstly, a matter of being willing to accept your role and of asking for assistance. It can be as simple as your imagination will allow it to be. Your power in transformation is in using your thoughts and emotions, and in allowing your imagination to take you places you had not thought possible previously.

The Power of Imagination and Tuning Your Thoughts and Emotions

The Imagination is your most amazing tool and yet it has been the least used to any great effect. Those in your culture who have managed to free their imaginations and follow the paths that they have been led to with their visions, have seen greatness in many capacities. All creativity begins with the imagination. One can only get beyond the standard way of viewing anything by stretching his or her imagination. This is easier said then done for most human beings, as they have been terribly programmed to see reality with limitations. These limits have been energized in the field of your planet, and therefore are strong vibrations to break away from. It is not just that you were taught certain things and only see them, it is that what has been taught has a life of its own, and is easy for unconscious thinkers to plug into and perpetuate.

The same domino effect that can get you higher can also keep you down, as these limited belief patterns get larger with each added human thought. This is why it matters what you pay attention to. This is why advertising and media in general works so well and can control a society. Unaware consciousness takes in all the vibrations of thought directed its way, and unknowingly follows and feeds that thought form further. Soon a snowflake of thought becomes a snowball rolling down a hill, and you have an icy mass of energy going down with power. The only way to break out of this trend is to protect yourself from unwanted input, and to spring ahead with the use of your own imagination to make snowflakes with new purpose and meaning.

When you begin to see thought forms being created you will readily accept them as energy. You will feel the vibration they emit and sense what they are creating. This is an ability you all possess and can develop using your imagination and your feelings as guidance. Thoughts and imagination are energy forms powered by E-motions. The "oomph" a thought has is determined by the intensity of the emotion pushing it. If the thought is fueled by lighter vibratory emotions, then it will move quickly and smoothly to its creative destiny at a speed equal to its intensity. Little effort will hinder its movement in space and time.

If a thought is fueled by dense emotions it will impede movement and keep the thinker just where he or she is. Or, if the negativity is strong, it will attract a seemingly unrelated event that is on the same wavelength. In other words, what you think you get. But in the case of thoughts powered by denser emotions, the resistance might not allow the thought to make it to its intended location. Instead, it may produce results that are similar, as the frequency finds the closest match. This is why events that you perceive as bad occur, even though you, of course, were not thinking about these events. You were, however, thinking of something that vibrates at the same frequency, and thus attracted the unwanted event into your experience. This happens less often with positively charged thoughts. The guidance system for lighter vibratory thought is more accurate because there is less resistance, and therefore less interference preventing the manifestation of each thought.

You are more successful as creators when you maintain your vibration in the path of least resistance. This is what we have learned as collective creators. You can learn the same by becoming observant of your feelings, thoughts and imaginings, and by tuning their respective frequencies to the highest and lightest energy of creation. You can practice this in your everyday life from moment to moment in every 'now' that you exist. It is simpler and more elegant then you may imagine. Start by imagining that it is simple and elegant and you will be connecting to the energy consciousness that has already found this to be true. Imagine that it is possible for you to sense, see, and direct your thoughts, feelings, and emotions. Envision what your daily encounters would be like if you were more sensitive and aware of the life energy of everything around you. Your imagination is an incredible tool that opens doors with minimal effort. Once the door is open, you can choose to enter an enlivened world, touched by the essence of who you really are. Your imagination is the key to that door.

Awareness, Density, and Dimensional Octaves

We will touch upon the subject of emotions and imagination again later. Now we wish to relay a deeper understanding of the concept of dimensions, as we see that your minds have a need for placing the unseen worlds in a linear structure of some kind. We have mentioned dimensions as levels merely for your sake in visualizing realms of perception beyond your own. Dimensions, as we speak of them, are realms that vibrate at a certain speed. There are multiple frequencies of vibrations or densities existing within each dimensional vibration. The best analogy to use from your world is that of musical notes and octaves. Each note has a frequency at which it vibrates to create a material sound. There are several notes with various frequencies within each octave. Jumping up or down to another octave of musical notes, would be similar to switching dimensional perspective. A note from one octave will resonate with the same note in another octave and hence one dimensional frequency affects another. All of the vibrations within each dimensional experience have their own energy signature and state of consciousness. All in a given realm has a certain level of awareness that is unique to it.

In your third dimensional vibration, you have consciousness that exists in a variety of types and magnitudes of awareness. A cell, for example, is less aware than a plant is of the world beyond itself. Animals are aware of their surroundings for survival, for example, but not much more than that. Humans have awareness beyond themselves and their survival. And so it goes with levels of consciousness. The cells within your own body are conscious 3rd dimensional beings, but they have limited awareness of how they fit into the bigger picture of your entire body and that they are in fact a crucial aspect of that whole. Similarly, your conscious mind is only somewhat aware of how it fits into a larger planetary system and beyond, and how important your energy is to the health of that whole. If your cells are unhealthy, so are you. The same is true for your influence on the natural and energetic systems that you are unknowingly an aspect of. This is true on a physical 3D level and on the energy level that creates the 3D.

Many of you wonder, then, what other dimensions are like. You should firstly acknowledge that any description of other dimensions must be filtered through the dimension that you are presently experiencing in order for you to comprehend them. In filtering, you will always have a distorted view and any attempts to explain them will come with obvious limitations. We will attempt to give you a sense of the concept of shifts in vibration that occur when changing dimensional octaves. To switch octaves requires a leap in consciousness and hence a leap in awareness. So, in a way, dimensions can be considered steps into a new way of perceiving. Since everything is an aspect of All That Is, it does not require a change of what you are, but rather, it requires a change in how you perceive and assimilate that source energy. Evolution is the means by which beings of consciousness move into higher realms of dimensional perception.

The reason we do not find the labeling of dimensional levels with numbers accurate is that the switch to a higher vibration of perception is not always so cut and dried. There is not necessarily an exact point of dimensional awareness change. For example, many of you in the 3D are able to cross over to 4D in your perceptions. Does that mean that you are leaving your reality? This simply means you are tapping into another vibrational octave. You have changed your perception and awareness level to include a lighter frequency dynamic. You did not need to go anywhere to sense this change. You only needed to expand your perception to include higher vibratory existence.

Vibrational consciousness that is denser than you, has limited perception of you. So the lower frequency dimensional realities may not experience humans at all, though you are influencing these frequencies when you resonate together. Within the lower dimensional realms there are also varying frequencies, and those that are less dense have more awareness of systems surrounding them. There is dispute among us as to where the line is drawn for the lower dimensional worlds. But, they are in the molecular world of consciousness and are fundamental to the reality of all. Without the first levels of density there would be nothing after. In other words, the first levels of awareness are building blocks of all existence.

Many have referred to lower density beings in your realm, such as animals or plants, as lower dimensional beings. However, we see these beings as a part of your present octave of vibration at a denser state of awareness. And again, we reiterate that all of this, to us, is a matter of semantics, as we are all of the same source energy. We prefer that you view the differences as changes in conscious perception. All these worlds exist at once in the same space and are experienced in one way or another, based on the awareness with which they are being perceived. So, when we refer to various dimensions, understand that it is only for the simplicity of reference to indicate a shift to another level of perception of consciousness.

Enabling the Available Accelerating Energy

We are here to guide you in the new era. It will assist you to know that you are living in an incredibly dynamic world that is created by your flow of consciousness. This consciousness is the energy that makes up your universe and it is super-conductive. The sooner that you accept this and allow it as the fundamental understanding in your society, the easier and more fluid will be your transition to the next stage of your evolution. If you stop to look around at what is happening in your sciences, technologies, and spiritual and philosophical disciplines, it will be apparent that a revolution is occurring that will be looked upon in the future as the turning point to a new world.

It will soon be commonplace to speak of, and experience, the realities of other dimensional realms of perception. As your sciences are discovering, so shall you begin to verify with your own personal awareness, the existence of dimensions beyond what you currently perceive. All that is being discussed and researched regarding the upcoming shift in the frequency vibration of your planet is preparation, a platform, if you will, to mentally and physically enable you to handle the new levels of energy transference as they continue to accelerate.

If you find yourselves feeling tingling sensations in your hands, or anywhere in your physical body, you are beginning to retune to a new sensitivity that will become a natural occurrence in your sensory repertoire in the new era, in which you will travel your super-conductive universe readily and simply. What this means for your consciousness will be explored in more depth as we continue. Know that it is inevitable and necessary, and that you are more ready than you currently accept. The preparations have been going on for a long time, in your terms. Much has been happening behind your common sensory awareness. But, unconsciously your soul is profoundly aware of what is needed and how. Therefore, this writing is actually a reassurance and further aid in what your soul knows will be its future. As we have said, you intended to be forerunners in this dynamic evolution from the start. We are helping you awaken what is available to you now, that previously was not. The energy frequency is accelerating so rapidly that even those who are opposed to change will be enveloped by the strength of the movement. All will be well within it.

You can each assist in the uprising now by simply believing it and imagining a world that reaches beyond your five senses and your limitations of space and time. These are constructs that you agreed to live within in this aspect of your multidimensional selves, and you are ready to expand as a species to encompass more sensory and dimensional awareness. This is not by any means the first such giant leap that your species has gone through in its history, and it will not be the last.

There is so much more to evolution than survival of the fittest. True evolution can be found in that which mystifies, that side of yourselves that innately senses that you are more than a physical reaction to your environment, that senses the profundity of all that is alive, and seemingly not alive, in your amazingly intricate, yet simple reality. It is this deep, inherent knowing that is the basis for creation itself, and the drive for its expansion. This inner knowing is the core of what you are and what everything around you is made of. That consciousness represents the actual building blocks of All That Is.

Acknowledging and Sensing Creation Frequencies

When you sit with yourself and quietly allow your mind to travel inward away from all the constant input you are bombarded with on a daily basis, what you are left with is the essence of you as a conscious creator. When you quiet all the programming that your environment has placed upon you, you find the core of your simple, yet elegantly creative, consciousness. When you allow this quiet in your mind and senses, you can feel only the simple greatness of creation. That is why you must always check within before seeking answers outside. You created what is outside in the first place, so to find out the intentions of that creation, you can only look inside your quieted sensing self. You may say that if you can get past the wild fluctuations of your thinking mind, then you only sense nothingness. And we say, that is impossible, because nothingness does not exist. There is always something, because the universe you are in is always in a state of creation.

Try it. Quiet your sensory input and feel your creative consciousness and its frequency of vibration. Be still and feel your consciousness creating a frequency. You should be able to sense a vibration. Is it fast or slow? Can you feel the pulse of yourself, of your consciousness? Can you slow it down or speed it up? Whatever this frequency is will determine what your consciousness is currently creating. Does it feel separate from the physical world around it? Can you feel the vibration of sounds and sensations in your environment?

You feel and sense what is around you because you are filtering each thing's frequency through your senses. You see colors as their vibration is picked up by your visual sense. You hear sounds as you pick up the vibration through your eardrums, and so you sense objects as you filter each frequency through your third dimensional awareness. There are many physical frequencies your science has measured, that you do not readily pick up on a conscious level, such as X-rays and Ultraviolet, for example. It stands to reason, that you have yet to measure other frequencies in your environment as well. The point is that you are living in a vibrating world, and you are vibrating along with it. You agreed to bring your soul's frequency to a level that could exist within your present sensations. You agreed on the scope of the world, and on what awareness you would work with inside of it. This is an amazingly beautiful reality that you and all the consciousness therein, corroboratively and continually create.

Why are you a part of this vibrational world? You are part of this world for the sake of creation. You have developed virtual reality games in your culture so that you can be immersed in an experience. You place yourself in the position of a character in the game, and the goal is to be in that world as if it were real. You try to forget who you are and become the game player while you are there. This is what you have set out to do in your present consciousness. You put yourself in this wildly interesting situation, with the hopes that you could play as the character and enjoy the creation and interaction within that reality.

Just as a video game would be no fun if there were no challenges, you have put yourself in situations that would allow opportunities to experience the uniqueness of a vast amount of options. This is not to trivialize your life and say it is just a game. It is of course whatever you perceive it to be, but ultimately it is about experiencing, creating, and expanding the creation so that you have more to experience. By evolving to the next level, you are giving yourselves more awareness, and therefore more to experience and create. This, again, is the driving force of All That Is.

In a sense, we are collaborators in the movement of your consciousness. We are a higher part of you. We are a part that is more aware of its part in creation. We are looking forward to your joining us in moving your world perspective into a vibration that sees, senses, and creates more profoundly, and with greater intention. When we say that it is easier now for you to touch different dimensional realities, that does not, however, mean that it will require absolutely no effort and intention. It requires a great deal of attention and intention, but once you give it that, the rest will blossom in a way that was not possible until now. So, any attention goes farther than a lot of attention once did. And a lot of intention will take you into those places that you only previously acknowledged in your dreaming state.

Firstly, pay attention. Sense more, and beyond your usual limitations by intending to do so. Your effort to feel outside the usual sensory input will trigger your inherent and hidden capabilities, and will get the attention of your guides and selves from other octaves of reality. With that attention, you will receive an influx of energy to open your sensory channels deeper. A little thought toward your heightened sensitivity will go a long way in enhancing it.

We ask that you not only read these words with interest, but that you believe that what we say is possible, and give some attention to this growing aspect of your developing consciousness. Once you notice changes in your psychic and inter-dimensional sensitivity, do not hesitate to share this knowing with others. As you do so, you are aiding in the opening of their centers of receptivity, and can very well be helping them to acknowledge what is already happening in them.

There is so much for your sciences, and all your areas of intellectual and spiritual thought, to discover about the nature of your reality and its energetic qualities. By combining the thinking from various disciplines, you are beginning to open before unfathomable doorways of possibility. You are altering the previously held doctrines that kept you from seeing your fundamental role in the creation of what is around you on a material and experiential level. You are now connecting sciences with spirituality, and Eastern thought with Western. This communication, and melding of ideas, is a large part of how your species is awakening, and is allowing the frequencies of advanced sensations to occur.

It is the seeming complexity of life that confuses. But, in actuality, it is all poetically simple and dynamically creative in a continuous now. Everything you think about matters. And what you think follows and affects all levels of creation, from the smallest particles to the widest spaces. Everything that exists is consciousness, otherwise it would not exist. All consciousness creates itself every moment and is constantly changing in response to the ebbs and flows of the frequency surrounding it. Within those fluctuations, probabilities are playing out or not, they are chosen or not, all exist as a soup of potential from which to draw or subdue. And thus, an ever changing motion of life unfolds in every instant.

The super-conductive nature of consciousness is the answer to all the questions of reality. Once this is understood in its utter simplicity, doorways fly open and possibilities unimaginable to you now become mere ways of being. We would like to assist you in opening your awareness beyond what has been programmed into your brain and senses from the beginning of your civilization. You all have access to the libraries of knowledge that exist in the frequency ranges of your planetary system, and can learn to delve into that information for your own personal growth and to assist with the heightening of your fellow beings.

Chapter 2

Tapping Into the Energy Field of Your Planet

Believe it or not, all the information from your planet is stored in its energy field. Everything that happened since its creation, and every bit of consciousness that has joined Earth, has an energy marker in the planet's field. All of this is readable, like a book, if you know how to tune into the language of conscious reality. There are many among you that already do this quite successfully and others who are merely glimpsing the sea of probabilities.

When one tunes into the planet's energy field he or she will feel the sensations of conscious energy and sense the flow that it is directed towards in your present moment, and in the past and future. All are changeable, but there exists strength in those probabilities that have been given conscious focus. Psychics, and generally sensitive individuals, connect with the energy matrix more easily and naturally than others. They may not realize what they are connecting with, but they sense, feel, and/ or suddenly know things that they cannot explain logically. This is the start to developing the ability to read the astral library that surrounds your planet.

Thoughts Enhance the Earth's Energy Field

In the coming age, having this kind of knowing will be quite useful.

We intend to aid you in your personal discovery of the records of time, and probable time, and give you assistance in learning how to play within this field for your collective development. The more aware you become of this field of endless information in the form of thoughts, images, sensations, emotions and all the mediums that you use to create reality, the more able you will be at doing just that....creating reality. You can do it even more effectively. Your species, the form of life that you have chosen to exist within now, is ready to leap ahead and be a stronger creative counterpart in the creation of its now. Keep in mind that the physical reality you are living within is one that a collective consciousness has created. It now has a life of its own and new probable realities unfold from it.

Some of you presume that what you do and think does not matter much in the scheme of it all. You are sadly mistaken. You are the creators of your world and what you do as a whole affects worlds beyond yours as well. As you develop into more able creators, you will be formulating new dynamic probable realities. All of this is you being the expression of All That Is, or God, if you prefer. What kind of realities do you want to take part in creating? Which threads of consciousness do you want to experience and uphold? Which way will you influence the energy field of your present probable reality? Does it matter? If what it is that you and the other conscious forms on your planet predominantly experience matters to you, then it does.

Everything that has been thought and felt exists in your planet's records. If it has not been thought or felt, then it will not be there. As you see, that leaves quite a range of choices. The only probabilities that exist are those that have been given thought energy in the past, present or future. As you continue to think about a given probability, you give it more power. And, if you add lots of feeling to your thoughts, it is as if you have fed that option some growth hormone.

24

All the conscious life on this planet can be accessed at any time. You can connect with anything to which you can tune your vibration. All of your past lives on this Earth are stored in exact detail in the many ways they played out according to the intentions of that life and those surrounding it. You can read those stories and further enhance or diminish aspects of them when you add your present energy to them. In doing this, you may be affecting the souls that lived that life with you, and may also be living with you today. Do you see the potential in all of this? We are only scratching the surface, but you can start to imagine the potential this knowledge will unleash. Understanding that these records exist and that you can tap into them to aid your evolution, and that of the species, is crucial to your advancement in the coming decade. Start by believing it. You must be open to the possibility in order to start exploring it.

Become Aware of Your Energy Field

The ability to tap into the archival energy field lies wholly in shifting one's awareness. You must be aware of yourself as a multidimensional being that is constantly connected to everything that exists. Start by being more aware of your own energy, and the vibration of your individual field, otherwise known as your aura. This is your personal Akashic record. Like the planet, you too have your own energy record of all that you have ever thought, felt, and experienced, and even of what you considered. You can become aware of what lies in that field, and of how it interacts with the auras of others, and of the planet.

We cannot accentuate enough that your intention to have this awareness, and your trust and openness to this energy, is all that is required. You may believe that this is much too simple an answer. Yet, for so many of you, these are the most difficult things to do, as they require a letting go of all your previously held restrictive thinking that has been ingrained in your mind from birth and fed through repeated advocacy. Yet, this is all that is necessary.

Allow yourself each day, even for a few minutes to start with, to accept that you are energy, and can feel the energy of your soul and its shield. By practicing this you will be strengthening your ability to feel your aura. Let go of disbelief for those few minutes and imagine that you can sense beyond your physical self. By doing this you are adding to the belief that you can in fact do so, which is all you need in order to actually do it. Trust your feelings no matter what they are. Always trust your own inner sensations and acknowledge them as valid aspects of the vibration of who you are and of what your thoughts have made you. This is your reality. You are presently what you have created with your own visions, and the world is the collective vision of the consciousness in your sphere of reality. You are not entirely what you eat, but you are certainly what you think, feel and in turn do, and all of this is held as energy in your aura.

The first step then in connecting with the auric field of your planet, is to connect with the energy patterns of your own aura, which holds all the energy vibrations that you have ever created. It is quite fantastically beautiful if you take a moment to think on this concept. You are all that you have ever fathomed. What you have given the most energy to, you are, and so it goes for your species as a whole. Many will say, okay, I have heard this in some form or another already. But, have you taken the time to feel this and be truly aware of all that you are? The more aware you become of yourself and the frequencies that you emanate, the more you will be able to read and affect the frequencies that surround you. Give yourself this gift of open awareness every day. Eventually, it will be your natural way of being and you will be able to flow through the energy fields of life.

You may wonder how all that you have ever felt or experienced could possibly be stored in a field of energy around your body? It is not much more amazing than is the process of storing data in a tiny computer chip, really. You do not see this information until you access it from the appropriate program in your computer system, after you have turned it on using a power source. That information then seems to be miraculously revealed once you find the correct file to open. This stored information can be changed at your will when you are aware of how to use the respective program that controls it. It is much the same with your collective data banks of stored experiences. Once you know how to access that data, you can open the appropriate file and change the experience at will. It is a matter of tuning your consciousness. Firstly, you will need to turn on your power source and learn to read the energy output.

The computer is a very useful analogy as it is a way of life for many of you, if not directly, then you at least have an indirect understanding of how a computer system operates. Let us begin by turning our conscious power button to the "on" position. We do this by acknowledging our own source of power. That power is the life force itself. It is what makes you walk and talk and move your bottom every day. It is what motivates you to continue. The power is not the food you eat. However, the food and water you consume is a part of the cycle of being in a physical world, in which energy is constantly exchanged from one form to another, in a miraculous web of life further enhancing the inter-connectedness of all that exists in your plane of reality. You are not limited to the physical exchange, however. You have an even more dynamic and life giving exchange that takes place with the cycling of thought and emotional energy, as we have discussed. This is the higher, finer aspect of the life force, if measuring in the scale of densities. So your "on" button is always "on" really, but you may not be aware of how to find your stored files.

One way that you have already discovered, as a species, to tap into memories from your energy files, is to slow your brain waves to a frequency used in hypnosis. This slower, alpha brain wave automatically eases the access to your memories of past and future probabilities that are based on your current time/space positioning. In meditation, you are also slowing your frequency to be able to access parts of your consciousness, and its surrounding energies, to allow for awareness beyond your normal active waking state. In a dream state, your frequency crosses over to the astral plane and accesses your personal, emotional, and thought energies and communicates with those energies in others.

It is time to make these connections the norm rather than the abstract. If you were to do this over one night, however, it would make you a bit batty. Your conscious frequency would not be able to handle the sensory input that you are able to access. Therefore, conscious control of these frequency levels requires that you ease into it and practice. We assure you once again, that your dream states are filled with connections that are constantly elevating you and assisting in preparing you for the added influx of higher energy that is steadily rising in your plane of existence. In the next several years, you will be seeing an acceleration that is amplified exponentially. Where your thoughts are, will govern which spiral of energy you are sucked into. Be aware of where you are now in your thoughts, as this is where you will be flowing and growing as you mix with those frequencies of like mind.

You can use an enhanced connection with your own auric field to clear and reprogram old patterns that no longer serve you. If you are able to raise your frequency, which you can easily do by quieting your beta brain into a calmer alpha or theta wave pattern, then you can see what is ready for change in your mental realm. Allow yourself to feel your own blocks of old patterns and thoughts. Acknowledge how patterns have taught you lessons regarding how to be more aware of your place in this world, as a soul experiencing your chosen life. Then, set your thinking and feeling energy on the path that you wish to go.

Clearing and establishing new pathways by rewriting your files with new energy is easier with the incoming frequencies, and will go far in propelling your consciousness into the new era of human evolution. This re-scripting of your energy field is not difficult. It only takes a bit of attention. If you are willing to take a few minutes of your precious daily routines to tap your storehouse of data and reprogram it, you can see tremendous change for the better in your life, and the lives of those around you. As we have said, everything you think and feel also affects everyone else around you and beyond.

Take a few minutes a day, or more, to relax your busy mind and allow your thoughts to flow to a particular feeling you have about yourself now, in your past, or in your potential future. You may want to follow the thread of that feeling to its source in your energy field. Acknowledge the source, and always give thanks to the feeling or experience for the lessons it has brought you. Then decide if this feeling about yourself is one that you wish to enhance or let go. If it is the former, then give the feeling more by adding to its energy with more appreciation and images of its continuation.

If you have a feeling that you are ready to move on from, then give it thanks, and decide how you would like to feel or be instead. Give this new vision a few minutes of appreciation and follow a thread of energy to the probabilities that already exist for this avenue in your aura. Allow this probability to flourish by giving your attention to it. Do this all in the state of joy for creation. This is your right as a conscious being. You are learning to be a conscious intentional creator of your reality. Revel in it. This is your destiny.

We are here to assist in the transformation of your souls, as part of the one soul of humanity. In order for your soul to transform itself you must trust in its ability to do so. Your connection to the auric energy of your soul, and that of your planet, will allow you to learn of your personal soul's nature and that of your collective soul. Lessons to be learned in this lifetime, and simultaneously in other lifetimes, can be accelerated at this moment in your evolution as a species.

Efforts to tap into the space between the material aspects of your world will reveal all the secrets of your personal existence and of the race as a whole. All your aims are ultimately the same. Each of you represents a part being played by your collective soul. As you become more aware of the energy of your actual self and how it intermingles with everything and everyone in its environment, you will see the inter-connectedness and synchronicities that have allowed you to be as you are today. Seeing these connections from past lives, and in this present life, will open door-ways for your soul to elevate its vibrational level further, and become an active and conscious member in the collective evolution of your species and planet.

As you recognize your place and its importance, you can fulfill the goal of your soul from its inception, and all your lives present, past, and future will evolve accordingly. By tapping into the energy of your multi-dimensional being, you are becoming a truly dynamic creator on multiple levels of reality. All of your lessons are available for you to acknowledge and appreciate. Together they make up an amazing being of light with much to share. The lessons of your present existence are only a fraction of your potential. Why is it time to be conscious of your multiple lessons? It is time for your soul to expand itself to a level of consciousness that lives inter-dimensionally with a deeper understanding of its role in creation. This is something that you have earned collectively.

Your Frequency and the Energy Field

Take a moment to imagine and feel that you are one with everything around you and that your molecules are intermixed with your environment. Feel the atoms of your body and mind bounce around to the matter around you. Exchange electrical particulars with the furniture, with your pet, with your computer, and with the trees. Feel the food that you eat and the air that you breathe. All of these seemingly separate and different materials are all of one cosmic energy source that creates them. You are an aspect of the vibration that creates you, and all that surrounds you, in every moment. The more you can allow yourself to feel the energy field of what you are a part of, the more you will recognize how your consciousness is involved in manufacturing this reality.

When you think of something or someone, you are creating a bridge between you. This is a real circuit of energy that creates another link in your web of connections. Again, the level of the thought's frequency will determine how quickly it reaches the target and how it will affect you both. Bright, high frequency thoughts and feelings will be received immediately, if both are on the same octave. If thoughts are directed at you, which are of a lower vibration, then you will not receive it as long as your frequency remains higher. If you lower yourself to the same level it will affect you adversely. It is believed, by some, that a lower vibration will always take away from a higher. This is untrue. Darkness cannot take away from the light. However, if you allow your consciousness to be affected, you can lower yourself by, in essence, turning off your light, and turning into the shadows to be enveloped by the darkness.

Staying in light energy is simply a matter of conscious direction. The more light there is among and within each of you, the easier it is for everyone to connect. It is hard not to see the light in a room filled with lamps. It is more difficult if there is only a single candle in a corner. If a room is filled with joy and elation, it is easy to join in. Likewise, if you walk into a funeral where all are sad and depressed, you can easily be overwhelmed by those feelings of despair and become that yourself. The goal for all is to keep the joy and elation alive in all aspects of your lives, so that it is inviting for all to become the same.

Understanding your interconnected relationship with everything around you, and how your energy affects everything around you, is a key first step in being able to change your consciousness and why to do so. Perceiving your soul's link to your past and future selves will allow you to open the portals to manipulation of your soul's development, individually, and en masse. Once you are able to change your own past, present, and future, you can begin to partake in the recreation of your species past, present, and future. This can only be attained at the high vibrational energy levels where intentions flow freely.

Lower frequency mass creation yields results that are so slow and untargeted that complete chaos occurs. Nothing is created as it was originally intended when you are trying to create in a pile of mud. Much of what goes on in your world today is the result of this unconscious, lower vibrational, instinctive, reactive, fear based, chaotic and undirected level of creation. It is time to move the entire game field to a new octave where you can be what you are meant to be.

Those that seek this understanding will intuitively know that it is true. This writing is meant to speak to those that are ready to change their consciousness and raise the level of your species to a new awareness. With your change, everything will change, down to the molecular level. All life, and seemingly inanimate objects, will be transformed along with your mass soul's consciousness. Your imprint as beings on this planet, and its energy field, is much more profound than you yet realize.

Utilize Existing Pathways
and Choose Your Energy Links

Those of you who are reading this are likely to have always felt that you are in some way special, or that you had some special purpose in this lifetime. You may have wondered for some time what that purpose is, and many have still not found it. It is time for that inner knowing to be awakened in you, if it has not done so already. You are here to assist in the transformation of the one soul of your planetary existence. An important part of the awakening is the realization that you are not separate. Others are with you in the game as a part of a collective soul. While not all souls will awaken as readily as some, all will follow when the pathfinders have cleared the way. You are the pathfinders.

The path has already been forged by the efforts of the One Soul through your history. Individual souls that have managed to acknowledge the truth of what they are have elevated their consciousness and created openings, or links that have made the frequency of higher dimensions and information in the Earth's energy field, accessible to you today. These links have expanded with each successive effort, so that finally there is enough light revealed for more to see. Now all you need do is follow the pathways created by these great souls. This is a fine place to start on your journey to connect to the astral light of your planet to enlighten your soul.

We are not here to reinvent the pathways. They are already open to you. In fact, we are able to communicate this message through a pathway that was created thousands of Earth years ago at the beginning of your recorded time. As others in history found the path it widened and is now available to anyone who asks with their consciousness plugged into the same intention. It can be easier for you to walk these paths if you are with others that have the same worthy intentions, and are connecting to the purest form of the original source of the opening. Pathways can be diffused with cloudy motives, and over time lose their ability to flow powerfully. We liken this to wires running through several machines before they get to the socket in the wall. It is always best to plug directly in. When you find pure sources, the well water will flow and you will recognize the energy behind it, if you allow yourself to be open and trust your inner knowing.

The sources that are most conducive are different for various individuals. While we are all one, in essence, we have been living as divided parts of that whole for millennia. Your souls have grouped and obtained various creative connections to the source. What resonates for each of you will be different. When you resonate with a pathway, you will have found your soul group. Those that have followed a given path throughout the history of mankind will gravitate toward it in consecutive lives, as they were originally part of the making of that link to the light. Does this mean that one path is better than another? Absolutely not; but, be cautioned that some paths are corrupt and diffused. The closer to the core you can go, the purer your connection will be.

For example, many of you will identify with particular religions. Be aware that most religions were founded based on the connections made by one enlightened soul who was able to impart truths to a group of listeners. If you want to find the essences and pure truth of that pathway, go to the core of the teachings. Be wary of the factions that have used the conduit for political or personal advantage, as this link will be leading to more darkness. Those religious dogmas that have gone astray are more dangerous than no path at all, as they have diverted the pure way into one of delusion and destruction. To follow in the footsteps of that delusion will only lead to further chaos in the world.

You will recognize all truth as similar or the same if it is truly connected to source energy. The words will be different, but the energy will be of the same vibration. It does not matter which path is taken, as long as it is the direct opening created by the soul with the original intention to raise the consciousness of humanity. Such souls were not only religious figures. They were musicians, artists, scientists, philosophers, spiritual channels, athletes, authors and even a few political leaders. You can connect to high levels of energy in your universe through pieces of music, works of art, and certain writings that are expressions of direct avenues to the highest realms.

How will you know which way to tread? You will know when you open your heart to the intentions that are radiating the same. If your soul is in sync with the goal of creation, then you will attract and recognize that in others, and in expressions that connect you to it. Can you connect without associating with a particular pathway? Yes; all you need to do is ask for the connection. It is helpful and will accelerate your growth and the growth of others if you amplify existing approaches so that others may find them easier as well. By assisting with others you are exponentially increasing your ability to hold more light. We will delve into this deeper again, as it is another important key. But, firstly, you should find your own connection so that you are sharing light from a high source.

If all the knowledge of the universe is available to us, then why don't we just reach out and grab it? For the one simple reason that you are not on the same frequency that it is stored in. When you touch the frequency, you touch the data that is stored there. You have all sorts of information stored on your computer, but until you actually turn it on and search for the correct file, it is not going to show up in front of your face. This is also true for the planet's records and your soul's records. When you are able to turn on the power that activates those records, and understand what and how to search for information therein, a whole world of knowledge will open to you. Not everyone will connect to everything. You will connect to that which is of interest and benefit to you. Just like you do not do internet searches for topics that are not of interest for some reason or another, you will not be connecting to the planet's knowledge if it is not a part of who you are in some way.

Once again, what you choose to connect to is what you will manifest. Our goal is to encourage you to connect to the highest possible state of consciousness so that you can manifest a higher level of creative awareness for your species. If you connect to the astral knowledge of war, you are filtering more destruction onto your planet. Just by thinking of war you are already doing this. You can connect to this and create more of it. But what we are aspiring to is that you change that story into a new adventure of harmony and peace, where all have the means of expressing their inner light, absent of the negative forces so prevalent in your world.

Cleanse Your Energy Field to Aid Your Connections

You are all too familiar with the distractions that get you down every day and keep you from expressing the greatness that you are. Imagine if you could dissolve these distractions and be free to express the best of all that you have worked for in your lifetimes. How freeing it is when you are the best you in every moment, without feeling all the blockages and garbage piled up in your mind. If you can remove the damaged filters, and connect to the pure truth of who you are, you will be a giant step closer to changing this world. It is as if you are walking around in a gray, or even black, cloud. All you need to do is wave it aside and walk out of it to see the light, but you are convinced that you are trapped like an animal that has been caged all of its life and does not escape even when the door is opened. His mind has him convinced that there is no way out and therefore he does not see it when it comes. You are a lot like that. That black cloud is what you think you are, but none of it is real.

Its smoke and mirrors. The cloud is what you have been told by others, or assumed, based on what you perceive around you.

The reason why so many of you suffer from low self-esteem is that you are not even looking at your real self. Of course it looks bad to you, because it is not even you. It is not even real. What you are seeing is the negative energy that you have connected to in this life and others. It clings to you and you keep believing in it, and repeatedly reconnecting to it. It is actually a separate entity of low vibrational energy. All of this can be pushed away, which would allow you the freedom to be the light being that you really are. In that state it is impossible to feel badly about yourself, or anyone else, because you are a completely creative vessel of source energy and can only flow that light.

Thus, another important step in making your connections to the energy grids of your universe is to first clear away the cobwebs of your own soul that fog your vision. You can clear the cobwebs by first seeing that they are there and need to be swept away. If you think you are already dust free, then you will see no need to get the duster out. Unfortunately, you will be missing your opportunity to see clearly and instead will continue to see the world through a fogged lens. You must be willing to look at yourself and everything that you have chosen in your lifetime. There are no coincidences. Everything is there as you made it, according to your intentions. Now it is time to assess the attention you have given to all aspects of your life, and decide what should stay, what will go, and what can still be learned from. If your race is to continue in an upward direction, there is no more time to repeat the same patterns again and again until it dawns on you. You must seek the answers and clean your own house of the grime.

Be painstaking in your search for the areas in your life where you remain in the mud. Where do you have lower emotions taking control?

In what areas do you need to transform into the real you? Where are you hiding from yourself and the world? Where do you have fear and uncertainty? These are the areas where you have an opportunity to reveal your true light and share with the universe. Clean up your own energy field and you will be able to radiate the vibration that will connect you to the higher realms, and assist in cleaning up your planet's energy field. How can your frequency connect if it is shrouded in a vale of darkness? Your brightness is hidden and waiting to be set free. Only you can do this by choosing awareness.

The Link Between Frequency, Connection, and Creation

In order to transform the world, you must transform yourself. Getting rid of your own negativity will allow you to assist in getting rid of the negativity of others. By radiating light you are able to fill others with the possibility of revealing their own light. What is in them that is light will recognize what you are radiating, and it will open a doorway for them. The more garbage you can clear away from yourself, the easier it will be to stay connected. This means that all your karmic debts and contracts should be welcomed as opportunities to clear your energy field. You can transform your soul by changing your reactions to challenges. Challenges are giving you a chance to see who you really are, and to then alter yourself if necessary. The goal is to transform lower frequency vibrations into higher vibrations so that you can become a better director of your creative reality.

Some of you actually worry that the world would be no fun without the negative side. It is believed that good cannot exist without evil. Without a comparison it is thought that goodness could not be known as such. You think this way because it is your familiar comparison to have these highly contrasting levels of energy. This is designed to teach you the difference in frequencies in the extreme. It is a playing field that allows drastic choices to be made in one direction or another, with eventual consequences related to that which you generate. This is important to learn as a creator. You are learning to navigate with these big obvious building blocks, as a conscious being within a limited sphere. The more you can control the output of your consciousness, and are aware of the inter-connectedness of all the things within your reality, the less need you will have for drastic good and evil contrasts. It is a matter of fine tuning.

As you fine tune, you no longer see reality as good and evil, but rather as flowing or stagnating creation. You will see the energy of various levels as aiding creation, or slowing it down, so to speak. Negative energy becomes a hindrance to your goals as a conscious creator. This is not a judgment, but is simply an understanding of how creation works. As we have said, destruction is part of creation, but it is ineffective. It does not go the way you intend. It falls short and becomes a chaotic mess. There is no judgment regarding good and evil acts. There is only the recognition of the effectiveness of a soul's ability to transmit energy as a creator. The higher the realms you connect to, the more able you will be to create your intentions. The only way to reach those levels is to vibrate on the same frequency. The only way to do that is to transform low vibrations into lighter more conductive frequencies.

So, how can you tap into the energy field of your planet and attain knowledge of your soul?

1. Raise your awareness of the super-conductivity and inter-connectedness of everything in your universe.
2. Clean up your own energy field to begin raising your vibration.
3. Seek avenues that already exist to assist you in connecting to higher levels of source energy.
4. Use your imagination as a tool to connect to the feeling place

of what your evolving soul knows to be true. Imagine how an evolved soul would perceive the world with more awareness from beyond your physical dimension.

All of these topics will be discussed further as we progress, as they are key elements in your success. Much can be said about each concept that will aid you in realizing the meaning of your soul mission. At this point, we hope that you are becoming aware that you have the potential to be more than you presently are revealing to the world. And, that once you recognize that which you truly are, the doors to a new universe will be open to you. It is a world filled with possibilities. It is a world not of drastic measures of good and bad, but one of endlessly refined creativity. It will be filled with exciting new challenges that encourage more of your light to shine with the power of creation.

Chapter 3

The Coming Age and Your Place in It

*T*here is much hype on your planet about the coming era and the shift that is expected to take place. Many cultures throughout time have predicted the age that you are entering, and much is being surmised as to what was meant by these predictions. Some have called it the "End of time itself," or "The end of the world as you know it". They see much turmoil and distress. Some believe it is a time of resurrection for the righteous souls. There is much confusion about this transition, as it is a new territory as of yet not experienced, and has been described from the point of view of the consciousness that made the predictions originally. You may have observed that there are many prophets and advanced ancient cultures that point to specific dates or events as catalysts for global change. What does all this mean for your planet? We would like to shed some light on what all the fuss is about and what it means to each of you individually, and as a race of beings.

A Multi-Dimensional Perspective

When we look upon your history, we see much more than you do. We see the energy dynamics at play from beginning to end occurring simultaneously. We view your world beyond the confines of linear time. We know this is difficult for you to fathom, but it is important that you at least contemplate what that means. You should immediately see that with this perspective, there is nothing concrete. Nothing is set in stone or predetermined. There is not a destiny; instead there are parameters of possibilities that are ever changing. It has already been suggested that you can change your past and future in the now. This is of critical value to understand.

What your prophets and visionary societies have passed on to your present consciousness is the result of your state of minds now, as much as then, and in your future. It is all a dynamic creative movement of consciousness. It may appear rather complicated to your limited view, where you presently sit. But, once you begin to delve into various levels of probability, you will be astounded at the beautiful synchronicity of this flexible creationism. You are so bound by your linear and physical reality that this may be overwhelming to contemplate. But when you are in the flow with the light field, it is all seen as poetically simplistic and truly eloquent.

We invite you to participate in creation at this level of awareness. Soon you will be able to see what science is becoming aware of on a mathematical and theoretical basis. You will be moving your consciousness between the electrons and viewing the universe from multidimensional angles instead of simply the three that you see within now. Your awareness will be attuned to the space that cannot be seen with the limitations of your five senses. For the present, take our word that there is much more to comprehend in the universe than you currently perceive.

The Current Cosmic Bulge in Space/Time

Based on the vibrations emitted by your species throughout its existence in all time frames, your present position is like a culmination. It is a swell in the fabric of space and time. This coming age is a climax created by what is being vibrated in the past, present, and future in multiple probabilities. Mayans, many Native American cultures, prophets in Europe, ancient Chinese mystics, etcetera, were able to glimpse this climactic period and send messages through time. Some are still being revealed as the energy amplifies and continues to affect those still feeling the vibrations in those respective pasts. Each time/space probability folds over another continually, and thus perpetually reaches into your present perception.

It is inevitable that great change will occur on your planet in your lifetimes. The nature of the probabilities that you will have the pleasure, or displeasure, of experiencing is still being created on multiple levels, but they will undoubtedly be dramatic. Again, we know this because we see the bulge of energy being created from all directions in space and time. We also see the potential that the energy bulge elicits. It is truly exciting for us as orchestrators of evolutionary development. This is why we are adamant about dipping into the candy jar at this time. It is our hope that we can assist with raising the vibration even higher by taking the bulge and spinning it in an upward spiral.

Think of a potter's wheel. The potter's hands can shape the outcome depending on the pressures placed at different locations on the ball of clay. Bulges in the clay represent heightened energy levels in the fabric of time. The shape of the vessel can be manipulated from both sides of the clay as it spins. Pressure from the bottom and top affects the middle, and the ultimate shape of the piece is experienced at the moment the wheel stops. When you are placed in the linear time expression, you are able to experience the results of the wheel at the time of stopping, in essence. You experience one possibility of the many that the vase could have been, and is.

The energy dynamic that is occurring now, in your linear existence, has the potential of pushing your soul's vessel into an entirely new shape. It can become something beyond its present limited parameters. It can become a vase that holds more types of materials, for much longer, to use the pottery analogy. When your vessel grows ours grows as well. We expand along with you, as we share our light with your universe. This is why we have a vested interest in your world. When we help elevate your soul, we elevate our own.

We are infusing your history with the pathways necessary to raise your present consciousness. Ancient methods are coming alive today because they are being opened now more than ever. They were largely dormant, but sustained by select souls who came with the purpose of protecting the knowledge. Now those doorways are being opened for everyone, which is what will allow you all to elevate to your new vessel. Many of the predictions were signposts from the past designed to awaken your soul's potential as never before. Much in these ancient connections have encoded messages that actually affect the frequency of your DNA allowing your vessel to hold more.

Management of the Energy Influx Will Determine Your Destiny

Since you are rooted in a physical realm, the actual matter that makes up your body must undergo its own transformation, in order to be able to hold the influx of energy that will aid your soul transformation. As your DNA is mutated on a frequency level, it will also be altered physically. Whatever occurs in your energy field is reflected in your physical self as well. The more you can expose yourself to source energy, the easier your physical and soul transition will be to the next level of your evolution. It is vital for you to be aware of what you are connecting to as the coming era draws near. You will experience that which you attract in a

44

big way. As we have said, the strength of the transition period is quite powerful and will be noticed on multiple levels. Where you maintain your consciousness will determine what you will create and experience, as an individual and en masse.

You should comprehend, at this point, that a shift will occur on your planet, but that the extent and nature of the result depends on whether your mass consciousness produces dense vibrations of chaos and destruction, or those of enlightenment. The amplified energy level is available to be used in either direction. In other words, this is an amazing chance to transform into lighter beings that are more connected to creation in their daily existence in unison with the progress of planet Earth, or to slide down the slippery slope of negativity and lower your soul status, creating an even denser reality.

The verdict is still out as to whether your kind will push ahead or destroy themselves. This is not meant to scare you. It is meant to wake you up. The help is all around you. All you need to do is ask for the assistance and it will come. No one said it would be easy. It is an opportunity to become something else, or die. Many of you will have, or have had, the feeling that you do not want to be here now, or that you would rather leave now than continue on. This is a natural reaction to what your soul is aware will be happening on the planet if you do not do what you came to do. You are all here with a very important purpose that you must fulfill. It is a great challenge, but the outcome can be spectacular if you put forth the efforts.

You, naturally, want to know what will happen during this shift that is so dramatic. What are the probabilities for your future as a race? You can see the probabilities yourself if you tap into the aura of your planet. If you let your imagination envision the scenarios, what does it tell you? What do you envision as the best possible transformation, and the worst?

If all the energy put forth by your human consciousness were to come to a head in the near future of your history, how do you think it would climax? You may see war, famine, and death, or you may see cooperation, peace and everlasting life. The truth is that all the scenarios that your human consciousness can portend can become your reality in a very short span of time. The energy is expanding exponentially to allow your consciousness and that of Earth's to create what it desires through intention. What will your intentions be? What are they now? All the warning signs are out there. What will your species decide to do with the indicators?

The openings to enlightenment are everywhere, as are the doorways to destruction. Never before on your planet have all avenues been so readily at your disposal. If it sounds like we are leaving the future up to you, we are, and it is. The difference in this coming era is that the planet is shifting with or without the human race. If you go with her the rewards will be plentiful. If you go against her it is to your detriment.

The Earth has a consciousness of her own, just as you do. If you are in sync vibrationally with her, then you will elevate to the next dimensional awareness together. If you remain in a lower vibration you will no longer be able to sustain a reality in line with her existence. If this sounds drastic, that is because it is. The soul of the planet is also a creator. She too is capable of gathering light and sharing it just as you are. She is bursting at the seams in her evolution. She is in a process of shedding her negative vibrations and revealing more of her connection to the Creator or the source of All That Is. Will you be a part of her that is revealing more of creation or a part which she is releasing? The decision is entirely yours. If you do not continue with her to the next dimension, your soul will not die. But, you will have missed an opportunity for more life.

When we speak of more life, we are talking about the ability to regenerate and perpetuate the creative force of creation. When you elevate your soul, you come closer to the core of creation, and therefore are imbued with more of the spirit of life itself. The further you are from that source spark, the denser and more harmful your existence becomes to the sustenance that perpetuates existence and the farther you are from God's true nature. The denser frequencies, ultimately, become the waste product of creation. The wasted energy is not lost; it is infiltrated back into the system as something else, feeding the cycle from the bottom up. Nothing in creation is ever lost completely, it is simply reformed. What your soul transforms into in the coming years is up to you. And, whether the human race continues as a species on Mother Earth is up to your collective souls to determine.

Infusing Life with Conscious Awareness

We are well aware that all of this may appear much larger than your daily life routines permit. But, it is exactly what you do with those daily moments that will add up to the bigger picture. All those mundane activities that you do every day can be transformed into activities of higher consciousness, should you decide to open your awareness in every moment of your life. You each can be connected to the deepest profound level of creation by simply changing your awareness. If you are to experience a revived soul in the years to come, then you must become alert and revived throughout your life, and consider the ramifications and consciousness that you infuse into each miniscule second. Each of your thought processes will add to a whole, and intensify the experience for your soul and all those connected to you. Put forth the conscious efforts now and your coming era will be filled with a new, seemingly magical, quality of fulfillment.

Think of the times in your life when you felt as though you were in a special zone where your mind was focused and invigorated, and you moved with ease and grace through your challenges with a sense of deep satisfaction. You have all had glimpses of this feeling no matter how short-lived they were. Imagine that to be your usual state. Imagine how much more meaningful life would be. These are moments when you actually understand the meaning and purpose behind your existence, accept your place within it, and revel in its creation. This is the state that you can live within as a people. Imagine it, believe it, and create it with your own life now. That will allow your coming era, and your place within it, to be exuberant and deeply fulfilling.

In that case, your place within the new era would be that of a purposeful member of a unified soul consciousness that has the intentions of the whole One Soul in mind with every thought and action. This is pure and simple, purposeful creation for a higher goal. Everyone can have everything they ever dreamed of without harming another. In fact the more the cooperation and the higher the intention, the more fulfillment is felt by all. When you are in this state of existence, negativity is a nuisance and simply not tolerated, as it is not conducive to the creative goal of the whole. Will there be no individuality in this dynamic? Ironically, there is more individuality. Each individual spirit, at its best, cooperates to make a better reality for the unified soul. The creative essence of each individual part is what makes the whole unit stronger, and more potent as a force of creation.

Conformity Versus Individual Truth

As humankind lives now, individuality is largely squashed in a sea of conformity and into a mass consciousness of sheep that feed a few greedy self-interested few. It is the very act of diminishing the individual spirit that allows such negativity to flourish, and the soul to be so shrouded with darkness and death. True life is the freedom of each soul to be its own spark of the creator in unison with the spirit of the One Soul. This is why it becomes so much more fulfilling to be in a light vibrancy, as your soul is uncovered from the ego that has succumbed to the dictates of society.

When you shed conformity, you become the real you that is a beautiful being of creative flowing light. When that light flows into the river of the unified soul, then it becomes a powerful force. When you are conforming to the desires of some social demand controlled by the ego, then no light of your own is being shared. You become a carbon copy of a dead self that feeds the lower frequency of disunity and destruction. You give nothing to the soul living beside you, except more of the same self-serving essence you paid for when you bought into the shiny silver car that is better than the neighbor's car. This is not individuality. It is the destruction of the life force of the soul. It is a dead end that leaves the soul devoid of meaning and depleted individually, and en masse. This kind of self-serving interest is not individuality, it is conformity. We are only truly ourselves when we are sharing our personal truth which is the bright light that we all seek to emit from our soul. When you feel that sense of fulfillment, you are being you. When you are being you, you have something worthy to add to the collective soul that enriches.

As each of you transform, you give an exponential opportunity for those around you to change. You each increase the potential for the whole. Every small step creates a wider step for others to join. Your coming age will offer increasingly accessible stairways to heaven, if you will, based on the efforts you each put forth in your every day encounters and intentions. There is no such thing as a small act. Everything is bigger than usual at this time. If you each make the best of this increase in energy, there is much hope for your world in the future. We can see the levels of probability for your planet and its inhabitants, and are aware of the effects you are having on that future with all of your intentions.

Remember that you cannot destroy the light of creation, but you can always reveal more of it in your plane of existence. Your coming age has the potential to be lit up with the movements of your creativity as a more unified soul, with each person playing an elegant role in dynamic change, filled with poetic synchronicities of meaning that offer insights, and further improvements, that are fulfilling on many levels.

Imagine an existence where the majority, if not all of you, are at a level of awareness which inspires meaning and understanding. What if you were to all recognize that your current position could offer you continual enrichment by the flick of your consciousness? The cooperation between you would be on a level that you only glimpse today. It would not be the systematized cooperation that you use today. It would be on a much deeper scale of awareness of one another's contributions spiritually. All interaction can be on a level of knowing that some of you are just beginning to touch upon as you seek meaning in all moments and interactions with others. Every meeting and memory has meaning. When you develop your sensitivity to the exchange of energy in your actions with the world around you, this transference can be more finely tuned for the benefit of all the beings in your reality.

The Evolutionary Leap Through Vibrational Change

We see a future for you in which your greatest minds, and most developed souls, are the leaders, not those that have the largest egos. The lowest levels of vibration in the next octave of reality will be what you presently experience as among the highest. That, of course, leaves no room for anything lesser than your best intentions. The low frequencies in your present experience will not exist in the dimension that your soul is transforming into. The planet will not support those vibrations. As we have discussed previously, and your scientists are at least fundamentally aware of, everything in your physical world has a certain vibration that gives it a form that you each perceive with your consciousness, as filtered through the physical vibration of your brain. You experience your physical life through these limited material filters.

As you change your consciousness along with the planet, you are expanding the frequency capacity of your body and mind in tune with the Earth's change. This is happening on an energy level that affects your biological and material building blocks of life. This is always occurring on some level, and is what allows evolution to occur. Evolution now has a chance for a giant leap. This is not the first time that this has taken place on your planet, as we have mentioned. Since this is not a history lesson, suffice it to say that it is completely natural for your planet and its inhabitants to make evolutionary leaps of consciousness, which in turn cause drastic physical change as well.

How the physical material will be altered on your planet is up to all of you, and Mother Earth. We are only giving you extra energy as you ask for it by connecting to it. As we have said, we are all one. So in connecting to us, you are, in essence, tapping into an aspect of creation that is vibrating at a higher frequency, but is still part of the same source. The more you expand your awareness, the more you can handle from our realm of consciousness.

Cooperative Energy Will Inherit the Earth

In the coming age there will be no competition between each other. The competition will be experienced as a group desire to better the whole. A dog-eat-dog mentality will not exist. This cut-throat system of gaining power will be replaced with a group motivation to produce results for all concerned. The only way for all to succeed to their fullest capacity is for each individual to cooperate in the aims of the higher good. Instead of fighting for resources, you will join forces to share in the production of greater wealth for everyone. This will not be accomplished with a political system, such as communism. But will be afforded, rather, by universally raised consciousness and natural motivation to make existence more fulfilling, and enriching, for each soul as an integral part of the one.

In such a reality there is deep appreciation for the contribution of each individual's unique abilities, and an understanding of the strength of many to transform material forms. Experiments have already been conducted in your world that demonstrates the power of combining many minds with focused intentions on a particular goal. For example, group consciousness has been able to directly alter crime rates in cities simply by praying for the change. You can do this with anything, at any time, if you are able to join together in common goals that vibrate in the lighter super-conductive frequencies. In your new dimensional reality it will be commonplace to attract like minds and use that attraction to develop projects with success. Obstacles will be more readily overcome and redirected as needed for the most positive results. Again, when you are living in higher vibrations, energy flows more freely, and reaches its target more precisely. Creation in these frequencies of light is joyful, enticing, and engaging. When in this involved flow, there is no boredom, worry, or fear. There is rather enthusiasm, excitement and anticipation. When there is a hurdle to overcome, it is viewed as a new, engaging dynamic that can be redirected to a potentially better situation, or is seen as revealing new insight.

Think of a video game. Obstacles that pop out at you are what make the game fun! The monsters in the closet give you an opportunity to test your coordination or wits. They make you laugh and try again. They make you motivated to be better and make the next level. If you are playing against the machine, then you are your own competition. If others could join your game as characters to assist in a mutual mission, then you would be thrilled to work together to beat the computer. The coming age can be like a game that you work mutually to create and play, with the goal of becoming the masters of the universe, by all succeeding in becoming better game creators. You become more like the creator by creating. You are much better creators when you share your energy with one another, towards a common focus.

It may be hard for you to imagine a world of cooperation when you look at what is going on around you today. But we are here to tell you that it is possible to exist in a reality that is a balance of receiving and sharing, so that all are winning, and none are lacking in personal enrichment. The personal fulfillment would still be different for each individual, but together, everyone is encouraged to reach their best potential, because all are working for the same objective. If someone is left out or behind, they are picked up by the team because the team needs the heightened energy of each member to do well. You would work together to keep the energy high for the whole. By helping others, you help yourself. This is crucially important, because any negative energy on the team will degrade the whole. When you raise your sensitivity to energy levels, it will become more obvious when a part of the whole is out of sync, or in need of a boost.

As you evolve to become a cooperative being, those that do not follow suit, and remain motivated solely by self-oriented gain, will diminish. They will not be able to compete with the collective power of those connected with a universal mind mentality. Those who develop the skills of mental and spiritual cooperative energy exchange will begin to inherit the Earth. An exchange of energy will occur, between all life forms, on a molecular level, with a creative common goal to flourish. The give and take is comprehended, on a deep level of understanding, as beneficial to each being in the relationship. This dynamic interchange requires a sensitivity to the tone emitted by all living beings, and their underlying flow of atomic particles one to the other. As you exchange energy, you exchange life particles that also hold a consciousness. These units of conscious energy flow through one larger life form to another in a spectacular dance of vibrational movement. When your consciousness is of a higher, lighter vibration this exchange is effortless, and each flutter is poignant.

Deepening Layers of Communication

You are gaining a deeper appreciation for the potential energy exchange that can occur in words, sounds, colors and physical movements. The frequency of the flow of energy can be elevated or subdued by the use of these means. Volumes of universal energy and meaning can be transmitted in symbols, sounds, and colorful images simply by transferring the intentional energy into the form through focused consciousness. This of course, is what music and art is all about. However, much of your present expression in these areas lies in a lower emotional vibration, and is not used to its greatest capacity for transferring vast amounts of consciousness. Also, you will learn to detect the meaning, and extract the most from the message, as you become more attuned energetically. It is possible to extract whole lifetimes of knowledge and understanding from a piece of art work that was imbued with this information, through conscious connection with the source energy of that knowledge.

There have been many people in your history who have managed to grasp this concept of imprinting images and music with transferable energy, and those pieces of work will continue to affect the viewers, or listeners, on a soul level. If the recipient is open to the frequency, they will connect directly to the original intention manifested. There are pieces of art, music, and written words on your planet that have tremendous power to connect an open mind to intentional source energy. These pieces of work have soul altering abilities if the reader, or listener, is able to resonate on a similar frequency. There is a protective factor built into such transmission so that each soul grasps what it can handle at the time. That is why deep, spiritually connected works can be read, viewed, or listened to many times, and each time the work may reveal something new, depending on the awareness of the consciousness attending. Having such understanding of the use of various means of communicating energy will be of fundamental importance in the coming phase of your evolution.

In this new stage of evolution, you will each be less obsessed and limited by a self-interested perspective. Your ability to relate and synchronize with others will become increasingly acute. Your sensitivity to each other's emanations of intention will govern your interactions. You, thusly, will communicate more profoundly through various forms of energy transference. Each communication will take on more significance, and the consciousness behind the transmission will be detected on a core, soul level. It is that core essence that you each will respond to. This is how you will determine which souls to continue associations with and how.

Many of you will be communicating with thousands of other souls by means of your particular form of transmission. The more that is received by others, the more you will be able to obtain further. When you relate to another on a more personal level, one to one, the interchange will be oriented toward how you can become better together, by continually assisting each other in taking each other to another level of understanding. This requires great sensitivity, and interest in another outside of yourself. It puts you in a position of giving in balance to receiving, and thus, creating something new and powerful in that middle ground.

With these skills of cooperation, and mutual understanding of balanced energy for the benefit of the planet, and its beings as a whole, anything is possible. You will find amazing new challenges with worthy aims, and you will understand that the goals can be accomplished. You will be able to see the world that you wish, and you will be able to create it.

There exists abundance on all levels for everything. Your new challenges will be creating together in many unique manners of manifestation. There is no one solution. There are multiple avenues to accomplish what you desire as a species. The fun is in cooperating to creatively find the most beneficial means for all to succeed. As your consciousness advances in its awareness, the inherent abilities to create fulfillment will be available to each of you more readily.

The Evolution of Methods, Solutions, and Extrasensory Perceptions

The environment resulting from your species' advancement in consciousness can be discussed for quite some while. And, of course, there is no one absolute picture that can be painted. Once you reach the critical mass of individuals to bring about your species continuation into the next realm of reality, there are multiple probable worlds that you may create with your new consciousness.

Whatever you can imagine as a team, you can create. For example, you can envision a world where you each learn to self heal and have no need for medicine. Or you can create a world in which you depend on well trained healers that use the manipulation of frequency to cure ailments. It could be a combination of both, and there are many possibilities as to how healing can be mastered as an art form. The same can be said for all other aspects of your culture and community needs. There are many ways to obtain necessary services for life that are far from your present financial institutions, and the way they presently manipulate the flow of material wealth. Your understanding of wealth will so drastically change that the old system will eventually cease to have any meaning at all.

You can, and will, feed the world many times over with quality, energy producing methods. Your developed awareness will lead to a deeper appreciation of the energy inherent in how food is produced. And, the intentions injected into the molecular structure of the food will increase its nutritional value by many fold. Many in your world are coming to understand the importance of this. But, once your sensitivity to the energy of food is heightened, it will not be an intellectual knowing, but rather a deep feeling of the quality of energy being consumed, and its affect on your physical system. You are, after all, consuming energy when you eat. The appreciation for the quality of that energy has been lost in your time. The Native American, and other early tribal cultures, had a better understanding of the importance of the intentions, and level of appreciation, they instilled in the life forms that they hunted, gathered and consumed. In your coming age, you will re-learn their knowledge and take it to the next level of understanding to ensure a high quality of energy interchange between all life forms.

As we have indicated, your old systems are presently in a process of breaking down energetically. They will no longer be supported by the next octave. You are already seeing a shift in the old patterns as they are internally rebelled against. The rebellion will become a revolution as the masses refuse to follow the dictates of an energy dynamic that has only the depraved interest of a few egotistically governed groups in mind. The shallowness of such self-interested perspectives will not be tolerated, and will begin to lose whatever steam remains. The trends you see in all aspects of your economies and cultural structures that appear fringe and outlandishly idealistic will gain a powerful momentum in the coming years. Each of you will play a roll in the strengthening of new approaches to old dilemmas and in the diminishment of static systems that feed on low frequency vibrations.

As you make these advancements, you are transforming your species into more light connected beings, closer to the core of creation. This is a process that takes time, but is presently on an accelerated path. If you get on the path, you will move quickly along it, and reach higher heights. You will also pull others along, like a magnet pulling on metals. If there is anything electrically similar, it will be affected in those around you. Each of you has various levels, types of sensitivities, and talents. Again, you are not all the same.

Many will start to develop skills and awareness that was previously hidden. Perceptions that you now consider extrasensory will become commonplace, and certainly accepted. Some will have sensitivity with sound, for example, while others will have clairvoyant images, and others will have better manipulation of material forms. It is much like your varying types of intelligences as presently understood, but they will reach into the unseen realms, which are vaster than your physical plane. Many of you are already experiencing the increased sensitivity. If you are, begin to cultivate it. Be open and give the ability credibility by acknowledging it and asking for more. If you are not yet aware of any heightened ability, then, after reading this passage, you will have opened the opportunity if you allow it. These abilities will amplify in you as you give them attention, and as the energy begins to shift more considerably.

When and How the Transition Will Be Experienced

Many of you are eager for signs, and specific time frames, in your linear understanding. We can tell you that it is occurring as this is written, and, in the time it is published, the energy shift will be double. Much is spoken about the year 2012 as a marker for a transformation. The fact that it is believed to be such will have significance in itself, but the timing is not limited to a particular date. It is up to you all as to when you will make the final leap, or if you will at all. Many will not make the leap. It takes a certain mass of consciousness to move forward, but that does not mean that all will go. Do not feel bad for those left behind. You all have a choice. Some will not be ready or willing to alter their limited perception. They will experience what their consciousness has created for them with an intense boost of force. As the energy increases, whatever and wherever your intentions have been, and are, will be amplified. If your life has been about greed and egotistical satisfaction of desires, then those energy patterns will be increased, and will attract those of like mind until it is all consuming. Ultimately, the denser frequencies will self destruct on your planet. Systems that are based on such motivation will destroy themselves from within.

Again, what some will see as horrible and destructive, others will experience as invigorating and freeing. If you have been a part of a business that takes advantage of human spirit, then life will crumble around you. However, if you have taken part in the liberation of human spirit, then life will awaken around you. These diverse realities will coexist until one overwhelms the other. How long in your years this takes can vary. But, again, you are heading toward a climactic push from the cosmos. We are telling you as much as we can without interfering with your own creative process as a species. We can assist you, but the doing is your concern.

You will discover interesting cosmic anomalies in the coming years that are connected with the physical representations of the shifting frequencies. Your scientists may or may not comprehend the impact these cosmic events are having on your world. And knowing about them does not change what will happen. It is the need of the planet and your species that will cause physical events that accelerate change. Together you will decide what is necessary to move you from chaos to calm and from lack of focus to concentrated creation.

For some, 2012 will be an ending and for others it will be a beginning. Which it will be for you depends on what you are creating with your consciousness. The same laws always apply, but with added strength. If you are an addict, you will likely be completely consumed by your obsession. If you are violent, you will likely experience a violent end. If you are petty, you will be in a world of pettiness. If you are fearful, expect to be frightened to death. On the other hand, you may be filled with love and tenderness and will experience more of the same. If your energy expands outward to others and the planet, you will receive much blessing and protection. If you are restrictive and self-absorbed, you will implode.

You need to give out more energy than you take in, for it will be too much for your limited vessels to maintain. You can do this with your thoughts and feelings alone. Just thinking and feeling outside yourself will release energy and allow you to take in more. Releasing is important. If you do not let the energy expand outward, then it will consume you and burn you up inside. If you send positive attitudes and intentions to others and the planet every day, you will find great glory and an expansive satisfaction on many levels of your soul.

Affecting Potentials and Probabilities

The year of 2012 was precisely calculated astronomically by the advanced astronomers of the Mayan culture as a turning point for the planet Earth, and hence all life upon it and around it. They were able to determine that the potential existed magnetically for the Earth to make its next great leap, presented physically as a possible reversal of magnetic polarity. The calculations they made indicated that the planet had the likelihood of reaching the central position of the Milky Way Galaxy, and the Galaxy has the possibility of reaching a significant position in relation to surrounding systems on a larger universal level. The Sun, it was seen, would also be placed in a strengthened position of power relative to Earth, and the other planets of your solar system. However, there are factors in the cosmos that affect these universal dynamics and can alter results.

Just as your butterfly effect theory implies that the flap of butterfly wings causes a chain of events that may affect the formation of a hurricane across the globe, so can movements of conscious energy affect the movements of planetary systems. So, while the predictions have high probability factors of occurring, there are minute energy shifts that can alter the final events in ways that can change your future significantly. We can see many alternative outcomes depending on various fundamental probabilities. There are numerous large events that can play out in a reasonably known number of ways. Then, within these large events, there are endless small realities created by individuals and en masse. With this understanding you can see why offering exact predictions is impossible, and irresponsible.

You should be aware that you have a great potential to change the world as you know it and redirect the potential energy. How you play your part within this dynamic of shifting power is for you to determine. Each of you has an influence on the whole. You each have butterfly wings. The pattern of your wing beats in unison will affect the type of events and their impact on Earth that occur in 2012 and the potent years that follow.

The remainder of this book will discuss how you can prepare your soul and assist the one soul of your species, and the planet with all its life forms, for its evolutionary shift, so that the outcome will be of the highest vibrancy for all concerned. We have already begun to explain how you can practice getting closer to the knowledge that is available in your planet's energy field, and how to start using your imagination and emotional life to connect to frequencies that will elevate your consciousness. It is now time to get down to the serious business of raising your vibration so that you can handle the light that will be accessible as never before.

Chapter 4

How to Raise Your Vibration
and
How It Will Affect Others

*T*his is probably the most important chapter, as it is the foundation of everything to come. Learning how to bring your energy frequency to vibrate in tune with the next dimensional octave is absolutely the key to forward movement. This chapter contains many exercises and mental dynamics that you will need to practice. But, you are not left alone. Each attempt is accompanied by an energetic support system. Higher vibrational beings, and those of like spirit on your planet, will connect with you every time you make an effort. We suggest that it certainly will not hurt you to try, even if you must pretend at first that we are real, and that you could seriously benefit from the simple mental exercises we present.

Awareness of Your Energetic Filters

You may, at this point, want to go back to chapter one, to remind yourself of the super-conductivity of the universe, as that is what makes the simplicity so profoundly powerful. Remember that your thoughts, imaginations, visualizations, fantasies, and emotional life are all energy forms that create what you experience. If you use these faculties beyond the limited way you have used them in your life, then you will bring yourself to a new state of awareness. Think bigger than you have perceived yourselves to be. You are bigger. You actually do expand beyond the dimensional space that you perceive yourself to be filling. Your energy field, even within a space/time perspective, extends outward, and from there, all your thought energy extends endlessly.

Even the visualization of this can begin to awaken your connection to everything around you. However, there is a reason why your physical system has filtered out all the energetic pulses of life that exist in your sphere. It is too much for you to process at once, and much of it you do not want to process. In other words, it behooves you to be aware of what you connect to, and how.

If you have ever done psychedelic or other mind altering drugs, you are aware of how the elimination of certain mental and emotional filters can be eye opening and also disorienting and frightening. Chemically induced connections are merely the dissolving of particular emotional and mental filters which may offer temporary glimpses into other ways of seeing, but do not offer a real connection to other realms of reality. They could be used as a glimpse, but that is the extent of their benefit. If something significant is discovered while the filters are down in this way, they have no meaning until acted upon by the real changing of your connections. You would have to change your frequency through your thought energy to actually make something real of what you think you saw or understood.

Mind altering methods of touching beyond your normal perception have been used for millennia, and to great effect when used with guidance from those that have obtained a higher level of understanding. Drugs are not used with consciousness in your society today, and so are more detrimental than productive, and certainly unnecessary. They do offer a fine example of how a good thing can seemingly turn bad, and how important it is to choose what, and how, you connect with the unseen worlds.

Vibration Protection Methods

The first tools that you will learn are for mental and energetic protection. Again, there is no such thing as bad and good or evil and holy. There are only levels of vibration, some of which make you soar as creators, while others make you sink and get stuck. Higher vibrations are connected with the source energy of creation, which is where we all prefer to be if we can. Everything that exists actually is this source energy, but most are shrouded in mist and are unable to see it. This is by design.

Evolution is a process of continued awareness, as we have discussed. It is a constant awakening. The animals, plants, rocks, and minerals of your planet have their own evolutionary awareness taking place. They exist in a different octave of dimensional awareness than your own, but they are all an aspect of the one soul of your universal plane of reality. None within this system and around it are better or worse. But, part of evolving is choosing what you want to connect with, and how much veil you wish to have around your experience of what you are.

Using mental methods of protection are simply a means of choosing what you will connect to. It is you, as a consciousness, deciding to stay with the highest realms possible for your vessel to contain. Protective mental processes send a signal like your radio tuner, so that you dial into music that will be pleasing and not disturbing. Once you set the station, you can freely enjoy the music being played. Using protective methods are a way of setting up your playing field, if you will, with intention.

We suggest that you create your own mental images, thoughts, emotional behaviors, or symbols that bring you to a state of adherence to the higher realms. In other words, find something that is meaningful and will elicit the correct emotional activation for you. It is most important that the symbol bring about an emotional state of security for you. However, there are images, rituals, sayings, symbols, etcetera, that have the power of protective connection inherent in their vibration. This is because their original creation was imbued with this intention. All the souls of your planet then add to the power of the protection by enlisting its use. Every religion and belief system has symbols or methods that are designed with the idea of protection. Some are ancient and some quite modern. The power behind the methodology is dependent on the purity of the original inception, and of the continued sincerity added by conscious beings through time.

You may have a natural affinity to one saying or image over another, because of your past life or present beliefs. If you do not already have something in mind for your protective ritual, then we recommend that you find something that resonates with your soul. The possibilities are many. You can imagine a protective shield of white light, or picture the Virgin Mary, a favorite saint, Buddha, or another religious figure watching over you. It could be "The Force" that protects you or a quotation from a revered author or religious writing. It could be ancient symbols from long departed cultures or languages. What matters is that it has a personal connection for you. You can even make something up of your own. Though, that method might not have the direct power of historical or group intention, it will still connect with the energy of protection because that is what you intend.

Before embarking on any journey physically or mentally, use your personal protective shield to ensure the highest connections possible for your endeavor, and to dispel any lower forms of energy. Always go forth with this consciousness. Use your shield with everything you do and it will begin to strengthen with use. Say your prayer, imagine a coating of white light, touch your cross or star pendant. Do whatever it is that feels right to you, and do so with intention. It is important not to do this out of fear, and not out of sheer habit. There must be life force behind it every time. It does not take a big effort or a lengthy amount of time. It can be a flash of a second to connect you to that protection, as long as it is with the right state of mind.

You may want to cement your symbol, at first, with a deeper meditation or visualization, to create a sort of post hypnotic suggestion that will bring that feeling and connection back at the thought of your personal symbol. For some of you it will be best to stick with your own made up symbol because you have negative feelings about religious or cultural ones, which would connect you with the corruptions of those ideas instead of the intended protection. So again, we hope you understand that the most crucial factor is the feeling and intention that you have. That is what gives it the real power.

Of equal importance to intention is your feeling of certainty. You must allow yourself to completely trust that your protection is foolproof. Nothing can penetrate your force field. This knowing is the strongest force you can ever have. It opens you to the realm of anything is possible. We will discuss this more later, but for now, begin by knowing without a shadow of a doubt that the forces of the universe are called upon to protect you when you summon them. And so it is.

Elevate E-Motions to Deepen Fulfillment

Once you make it a routine with consciousness to prepare your soul with a protective connection, you can open your doors to the world that is not experienced by your five senses. You have created a filter system of your own, and can now direct your thoughts where you would like to go. Since the goal is to raise your vibration from its current status, you will want to make thoughtful decisions regarding your aims. Aim high.

"What is high?" you ask. Remember your guidance system. Remember your E-motions. Aim for the highest energy-motions. Aim for your most elated state that is lasting. And the lasting part is critical. You will want to aim for that which gives you a sense of fulfillment and becomes an aspect of who you are. Seek the type of fulfillment that makes you feel good about yourself and the world long term.

When you think of who you are today, it is your accomplishments that will stand out. It is the obstacles that you have overcome and the actions you have taken to improve your life, and the lives of others, that make you a fulfilled soul. You each came into this world with a certain amount of accomplishments from previous existences, and also from those you have not lived yet in your consecutive view of time. In this life, you are a composite of certain chosen aspects of your soul, expressed in a particular way this time around. In this life, you are seeking fulfillment in the areas that you have not yet experienced. You are branching out and expanding your soul.

In order to raise your vibration, you need to stretch your frequency. You were already born with some veils lifted. Those are not the areas you need to raise or reveal. The aim for you will be different than it will be for your neighbor, parents, or siblings. And believe us, it is not the new car that raises your vibration in the long term. It may be what you had to do to get the car, depending on where your consciousness was in producing it, that will brighten you, however. It is not the material things possessed that will give your soul satisfaction. It is the process of challenging yourself to transform that will truly give you the elation you seek.

Lots of temporarily enjoyable things, one after the other, will give you pleasure no doubt. But, the satisfaction is fleeting. It only lasts as long as the input lasts. And it does not make you a better person. For example, if you eat chocolates, you will likely get a wonderful sensation of happiness when eating it. This is all fine, but you must keep eating them to maintain that sense of satisfaction. On the other hand, if you were to work out your body and get in good physical condition through concerted regular effort, you will begin to feel a truer, long lasting sense of fulfillment. You have overcome something and created a better, brighter you, as a result. You are here to be the brightest you possible. You are not here to simply enjoy chocolate, although there is nothing wrong in doing so. If you can find a way to eat your chocolate with more consciousness, then it could be more enriching as well. Raising your vibration is about revealing more of your light source. It will not happen if you play at pleasing yourself with no personal change.

Transforming Personal Obstacles to Reveal Light

As you overcome obstacles in your life, you become a brighter person and soul. You become more than you started with and express more light of creation, as an expression thereof. If you stay the same, you are not conveying more of your soul potential. By continually growing and expanding yourself, you brighten your representation of All That Is. This does not mean you must run marathons or be a president. The meaning in movement is individually determined. For one person, simply walking out the door and overcoming a fear of the outside world may be such a giant leap that it transforms his or her soul forever. For others, it may be speaking their minds, or loving their mates no matter what their faults. For some, any small act in those directions will reveal more growth, and will break through boundaries that shield them from their true essence. It is different for everyone, and no challenge is grander than another. How grand it is depends on its personal meaning for each individual.

How do you know what you need to overcome to remove your filters? Look at the areas of your life where you feel the most hurt or disappointed. Where do you constantly run into a blockage? What causes frustration and uncertainty? This will be different for everyone, and not necessarily what others think it should be for you. Someone may look at your life and think you need more friends, but for you this area causes no dissatisfaction at all. Things are not always as they appear. If you are feeling lonely, then you may want to seek out others. But, then again, you may need to learn to accept being with yourself. The answer can only be found within each soul. You will know you have hit the nail on the head when doing the opposite lights you up. If the lonely person finds a way to be happy within, and learns to gain satisfaction from their tasks, alone or not, then they have found their soul expression. If it turns out that an opportunity to share ideas with friends makes them soar, then they should seek more of that.

Challenges are our friends. Obstacles give us insight into how we can be better creators. In order for your soul to reach higher vibrations, it must face every challenge with exuberance at the possibility for further enlightenment. Some challenges force us to look at our attitudes and give us opportunities to shift our perception. This is ultimately what we each must do when encountering most hurdles. If a challenge appears to be negative, how can you transform it into something else? You can learn to be a transformer of frequency by gaining control of your perception.

Your perceptions are often rooted deeply in your programmed behaviors, from this life and others. So, digging up the roots may be necessary to change your perspective. Again, this is more opportunity for real change. Many of you will be tempted to put this book down about now. The thought of real work on oneself can be daunting. However, we know that you can do this, and it will get easier as you continue to try. Now is the time to gain invaluable growth as a soul, so do take advantage and give it a shot. The rewards will be astronomical.

Where do you begin to change? Look at an event that happened today in your life. Was there something that frustrated you? Take that situation and imagine that the next time it happens, you change your attitude about it. Is it easy for you to change your attitude? Can you think of ways to alter your view, or turn the situation around? The harder it is for you to change your reactions, the more deep rooted the personal filter is. The more that is covering your connection to light energy, the harder it will be to remove the layers. But, little by little, it can be done.

The areas of most frustration in your life will have more heavy material layers covering them. Imagine the change that is possible in you if you can take all the heavy layers off. You will be lighter and brighter, relative to the number of layers you take away. If one frustration was that you had to wait in a long line at the bank, and the next time you decide to bring a magazine and have a wonderful time enjoying an article, then you just added more light to the world and your soul. This was not too difficult for you. But, you made a change from anger to contentment, and it has an effect.

If, on the other hand, you just found out that your husband is sleeping with your best friend, then you may not be able to shift your reaction from anger, sadness and depression, as simply as reading an article. However, the opportunity to grow from this experience is profound. The hardest thing to realize in that situation is that you are the one that has the chance to change. You cannot change the other people involved. They also have a gift inherent in the challenge. Each person, in his or her own way, can become a brighter individual, depending on what they do with this prospect for transformation. All parties were equally involved in the creation of the event as it came about. All must take full responsibility for their part in its creation. Nothing was done to anyone. They each attracted the occurrence into their experience so that their soul can grow.

How else would you know what needs attention unless you present it in a way that it will be surely noticed?

If individuals are more observant of what they are creating along the way, and maintain their vibration at a higher level, they would need fewer "hammers over the head," so to speak, to wake themselves up. But, sometimes hammers are required, and offer a perfect chance for serious modification. An event like infidelity and betrayal can go in several directions, all of which will likely be life altering. Some reactions can take the individuals to a higher level of development while others can sink them. Such an event has high potential for good, if it is used as a chance to alter one's consciousness. Not an easy task, but it affords the potential for huge rewards. Drastic, emotionally draining situations, like this one, force people to take stock of what they have created, and how it was allowed into their existence. If the individuals can take responsibility, they can find ways to move on, and be stronger. They can open doors of awareness about themselves, and their relationships, as never before. If they do not take responsibility, however, they will inevitably create further disaster, and likely repeat the same or similar relationship issues again.

We would like to be able to tell you that meditating on pink lotus flowers is all that you need to do to raise your vibration. But, this is simply not the case. The vibrational shift in your consciousness will come from shifting your perception so that it resonates in the next octave. It means taking the worst situations and turning them into pink lotus flowers. When you can turn darkness into light in any circumstance, no matter how dismal, then you are changing your vibration. And, each time you do so, it becomes easier to match that higher frequency and do it again.

Your goal in this life should be to proactively seek situations that will help you grow, instead of attracting negative situations that force you to react in order to maybe grow, or not. You can learn to become a conscious creator for your own development, instead of a passive reactor to what seems to be happening to you. To live by this proactive means of growth requires consciousness and action. You can change your dynamic from waiting for life to happen to you so that you can dodge it, to one in which you purposely decide to make transformations. You, basically, must change from a passive existence to an active existence. But, the activity must be with awareness, and not come from a place of action as a reaction. Action as reaction comes from a passive life that was forced to move because of yet another hammer being slung on its head. Instead of waiting for disaster, you can become a conscious creator.

In order to transform yourself into a more vibrant being, you must be able to see what needs transforming. This requires that you be open to seeing what can be a painful side of yourself. It is often the aspects of oneself that one least wants to face that needs changing. Or, you may see the negative aspects that are damaging, but to change them appears to be too much effort. It is far easier to allow oneself the imperfections than to do what is required to alter them. You cannot change what you do not see, and you cannot improve what you are unwilling to. Many of you will have a million excuses as to why you cannot overcome the areas that you know are causing you to create negativity in your life. Many of you will believe that you do not have the power to do so. These are the sentiments that firstly need to be addressed in each individual's psyche.

Raise Your Level of Desire, Imagination, and Actions

There is nothing on your plate right now that you are not fully capable of addressing with the utmost success. If you have the desire to transform, then you have the power to do so. If you have lost any desire to raise yourself up, then obtaining that desire is where you must start. It does not matter how low to the ground you believe yourself to be, you can always pick yourself up. You have the power to elicit in your mind the desire to do, or be, whatever you believe is achievable. If you can fathom the possibility, and deeply believe that it could be true, then you can propagate your desire, and hence begin taking the steps up the ladder of change.

Desire is the spark that ignites our dreams on all levels of existence. The art of creating works something like this: You desire a sandwich. You think about going to the kitchen and making one, with some imagination as to what ingredients you can put into it. You can picture that sandwich all day, and become more and more desirous of it. But, until you get up and walk to the kitchen, open the fridge, and put that sandwich together, you will go hungry. All of these steps are necessary for creation to manifest in your physical world. All the pieces, for any type of sandwich, already exist in the fridge of the universe. In other words, anything you can imagine and believe in, exists for you to manifest. You must first desire it, second, think about it, and third, take an action toward materializing it.

You do not necessarily need to have thought through all of the steps precisely, in the sandwich making process. You can figure that out when you get to the fridge. But, you do need to get there. And, you do that through desire, thought, and taking steps. The rest is provided as you move. Your movement is causing a response that was initiated with your desires and thoughts. Hopefully this process appears obvious. Many of you, however, do not use this obvious manifestation process to its full advantage, mostly because you are so limited in your desires and imagination. Or, you have great desire and imagination, but fail to get off your living room chair.

To raise your vibration, you need to have the desire to transform yourself. You need to fall out of love with the restrictions caused by your egocentric view of yourself, and your life, and fall in love with the potential of your soul, and what it has come here to share, as an aspect of creation. How do you fall out of love with your ego? Look at what it causes in your life. Any thoughts of superiority or of self-pity come from the side of you that does not want to make the effort required to transform. Whether you are self-absorbed by thinking you are better, or already there, or self-absorbed by thinking you are unworthy, or a victim of circumstances, you are depriving your soul of its force as a creator. If you are already there, you will not have the desire to change. And, if you are not good enough, then you will not believe in yourself enough to have the desire to change. Either way, you are staying the same, and not connecting to the source of creation.

Your self-interested ego will always try to stop you from having the desire to reach your true potential, one way or the other. Your ego will also try to compare you to others. When desire comes from the need to satisfy the ego, as it is compared to another, it will ultimately leave your soul in the dark. Even if your ego gets you something you desire for a self-interested boost, it will fail to give you the fulfillment expected. Comparing yourself to others is futile. There are no two of you that are the same. Each is a unique reflection of the energy of creation.

We stress here the importance of where your desires are coming from. What aspect of you is driving your motives? Why do you want what you want? You should have this question in your mind when you begin to develop your desires every day. If you can develop the awareness of where your desires are coming from and where they lead, then you will be able to direct them to aid you in profound transformation of your soul. Compare the desire for a new car to impress the neighbors versus to get your children safely to school. Compare the desire to teach for status and recognition versus to impart knowledge to other souls. Think about the level of satisfaction from each, and if it will be truly lasting. Your level of desire will determine your consciousness.

The direction of your desire affects the frequency of consciousness that you attract to that desire. With the desire to impress your neighbor, and make your ego look big, you may get that object of desire, but you are attracting the frequency of competition and judgment along with it. When you desire the car for safety of your family, you are attracting the frequency of love and care. When you teach to share knowledge, you are attracting the energy of giving and enlightening. You can see that the energies of sharing are expansive and come from your soul, which is God, Light or Creation. When you desire gratification for your ego, it is restrictive and covers up your soul, keeping you from connection with your source.

There is something each one of you came here to do that is part of the larger picture of human evolution. This purpose, which is beyond any self-interested goals that you may have, is the desire at the core of your being. We wish to awaken this in you so that it becomes your primary motivation, instead of goals that are for your personal gain alone. The more layers you are able to dissolve from your energy field, the more able you will be to see the true flame in your soul that is burning to be released. Working through your personal karmic blockages and challenges set forth by your soul, will allow you to open up to your true nature as an individual of light and see your path more clearly.

Anyone alive in this era of change came here with an intention to assist. If you are reading this material, then you are likely on your way to discovering your truest path to aid in the coming shift, if you have not already found it. If you are completely confused as to your purpose at this moment, do not fret, as it will soon come if you are willing to spend time exploring your soul. Every thought and action you take toward raising your vibration will lead you closer to clarity of spirit. The more you observe and direct your desires toward the highest possible intentions for your soul and the souls of those around you, the more will be revealed to you. And, the red carpet will begin to unroll before your actions. Your desires with intention will lead you in your purpose.

Because all creation begins with desire, this is the crucial first step to guide your soul. You have control over your desires. You have the ability to refocus them. If your motivations and passions are presently on a lower level of consciousness, it is time to rethink that direction. If your motives are focused on ego fulfillment, you will be wasting your precious energy on something that will only bring you more lessons to overcome repeatedly. You have the possibility of bypassing much of the aches and pains of transformation by retuning your antenna of intention to a higher purpose. With this true desire will come true passion. With that will come the vibrational connections that spur imagination and movement. Remember, you are here to move mountains with your collective spirit. Each of you has your own molehill to add to the bigger picture. Even small steps with the correct intentions will increase the vibration of the Earth.

Heightened Desire and Purpose

Spend some time exploring your desires now, tomorrow, and every day. If you do not have any desires, start imagining that you have a special purpose and make your desires about finding it. Do you have desires for a better world? How strong are they? Are they strong enough to motivate you to make your own impact? What desires do you have that will make this world a better place? What desires fill you with positive feelings and a sense of knowing you are adding to the light in your world? Which desires will affect a few and which will impact many? Which desires give you a huge sense of fulfillment upon imagining them? What touches who you are and your special way of sharing? Again, the area you desire that will have the biggest impact may be one that appears to be an overwhelming challenge. However, as you embark in that direction, with consciousness and true passion, the way will be revealed and will be utterly fulfilling to your soul. You will know the correct desire by how the thought of accomplishing it makes you feel, and how you would feel about leaving that as a legacy when you depart from this plane.

If you all were to awaken to this higher purpose, you could move mountains. You can awaken your soul to its truest passion by exploring and focusing your desires on being the brightest source of creation possible for you in this existence. All of you have something in front of you that either you are already following, or you have entertained the thought of pursuing, which is related to your purpose for being here. Many of you have not pursued these goals because of your veils of ego that prevent you from risking the leap. Fear, laziness, procrastination, insecurity, and doubt are all culprits in preventing you from pushing forward. Seeking to overcome those interferences will remove the hindrances that keep you from succeeding in your higher venture. Begin with raising the bar on your desire by recognizing the higher level desire and walking in that direction. This will eventually squelch those personal demons that hold you back. The surpassing of negativity will raise your vibration so that you become a light that shines the way, and moves forward with ease.

What kind of beacon do you imagine yourself to be, at your best? Some of you have inventions on the burner, or minds to create in that way. Others can write words of inspiration that will affect millions. Still others can relay energy through art and music. Some are builders of innovative designs. Some of you can reorganize systems to benefit humanity and nature. There are healers among you of spirit, mind, and body. The avenues of approach for each spirit, and its contribution, are vast. And all are important.

Many of you are thinking that you feel so small, and too insignificant, to have such an impact. So, you do little, if anything, to impart your gifts. Some of you think you can do anything, but are not coming from the spirit of sharing from within. When you begin to walk on the path of self enlightenment, you begin to truly feel that everything you do to share of yourself is adding to a collective consciousness of movement. Even the smallest smile can have a far reaching effect. Remember that you each have butterfly wings. Spend every day, for at least a few minutes, imagining what you could do that day, and into the future, that would brighten your life and the life of another. Again, even imagining goodwill for others is adding to the collective creation. Add to that each physical step you take in that direction, and eventually miles will be traversed toward elevation.

Raising Your Frequency Will Elevate Others

There are millions of others that resonate with each of you individually, even though you may be unaware of them. When you make a small victory, those on your frequency are also given an opportunity to move forward. This is a great and wonderful law of the universe that is not understood in your present world. It can be evidenced when an invention is created, or a discovery unearthed, simultaneously from different sources around the world, without knowledge of one another. When animals of a particular species that live in different geographical areas suddenly alter their behaviors to match each other, it is because they have picked up the frequency of one another, and transmitted the opening across what appears to be a physical boundary. These frequency alignments cause alterations every day. Such power can be used to your species' advantage.

There is so much that you can do with an understanding of the effects of frequency alignment, and how to focus your vibration on opening

79

channels of light transference, so that you can impact others in a big way, with each wing beat. We will touch upon this later in more depth. For now, realize that the acts you think are small can be much farther reaching than you imagine.

The most amazing thing about this law is that the higher your vibration, the easier it is for the frequency to be tuned into by those on the same level. So, if you are thinking that you can do evil deeds with your mind, consider what frequency you are vibrating at before you plan for a successful attack on the White House. A low frequency of hatred, envy, or revenge will only attract more of the same to you, and will not touch those on a lighter vibrational octave. And, even those on the same low frequency will not get any clear connection from your transmittance. Remember, traveling through mud can be sticky.

If your vibration is elevated, however, your power to transmit is great. The higher the frequency, the faster and more accurately the message will be relayed. It is the difference between using a fiber optic cable to send a signal through space and banging on a pipe in the mud. By raising your vibration, you can have more influence, with less effort. And, as you raise your thoughts, you are allowing a connection to others of like mind, and therefore positively affect each other, even without knowing it. There is no geographical limitation to your impact. In fact, you may have no affect on the people in your immediate environment while having a large one on someone across the world that is vibrating in synchronicity with you. This may seem unreal because you cannot see it, but trust us, it is occurring in every second of your experience of time. By helping yourself, you are assisting others that you may not even know.

Let us recap the methods of raising your soul's vibration. First, make a connection with your personal protection. Second, look at yourself in the mirror and be prepared to conquer those aspects that stop your soul from shining. Third, do what you can to spark your desire to share your soul's light, and bit by bit, chip away at the layers of illusion that cover it. Fourth, always have certainty in the laws of the universe, knowing that they are on your side when you raise your consciousness. Finally, recognize that your intentions can take you everywhere, if you dare to follow them higher.

Every day affords an opportunity for another step, no matter how small, in transforming something in you that will pull the threads from your robe of deception. Look at what you do, and how you react to your environment, and ask yourself, "Is this really me? Or is this an illusion I have created out of self protection?" Let go of yourself, and you will find yourself. The self you think you are is the deception of your ego, and is not your spirit. Your true soul has none of the insecurities that you hide behind. Your soul is completely free and utterly certain in its place in the universe. It knows why it is here and where it may go. It is waiting for you to listen. When you hear the music of your soul, you will raise your vibration and affect others in each action you take. We invite you to open the door to self-enlightenment and be who you are meant to be, a vibrant self-aware soul.

Chapter 5

Your New Self-Aware Soul

As you shed your illusions, your soul becomes increasingly aware of its place in the universe and hence becomes an intentional participant in its creation. This is the goal of your species. Your soul's enhanced awareness is part of your evolution in revealing more of the source of your very existence. The closer you are to the source, the more satisfaction and reward you experience as a creative expression. Your new self-aware soul has the potential to flow with ebbs of light beyond your present comprehension. You will see the ebbs more clearly as you unveil yourself of the limitations of your illusory ego that hides true vision. We urge you to continually seek self-awareness in all your thoughts and actions, as it will lead you to further evolution on a grand scale.

You Are More Than the Role You Play in This Life

In order to be self-aware you must be willing to delve into the core of what you perceive yourself to be, what others perceive you to be, and finally to acknowledge what your real source is. All can be quite different realities and the process of discovery may feel overwhelming at first. The self that you have created through past lives and by your development in this life, together with the imprint of the universal energies surrounding you, which includes mass consciousness and astrological or astronomical influences, is self-designed to express a certain aspect of your true soul essence. This present experience is a portion of your true self, as might be the case for an actor playing a role. The role the actor is playing is not the person playing it, but much of the energy of the role comes from within the heart and essence of the actor's life experience, and is therefore a part of him. The role, then, is played with energy from the core of the actor, but he is not the role. Your present experience in this lifetime is much the same. You are not the self you are playing, but you come to the role with the essence of who you really are. As you begin to see the character you are playing, and to see that your nuances are an act that you can learn from and mold, you awaken the essence of soul that is really running the show, the real you.

You are all actors that have forgotten you are acting and have become consumed by your roles. Naturally, your evolution thus far has only allowed for this limited awareness. But, you are now ready to see your character and learn to take a birds-eye perspective on the stage of your life, so that you can bypass the illusions and envision more of creation. By simply practicing the perception of yourself as an actor playing this role of your life, you can take yourself out of yourself long enough to begin to have a different awareness of the meaning of it all. Looking from the outside, you can see the patterns in your life and how you keep playing the same dramas over and over again. It is time to open your awareness to these repetitions and to understand that you intended to play these dramas for a reason. It is time to look at how you can break the patterns and become more than this stage will allow.

There are core issues that your egocentric self view uses to keep your ego self in the play, and your real self behind the curtain. When the curtain opens and you realize that even the audience is another aspect of yourself, you begin to understand how overcoming the illusory perceptions of your character can release you from the stage. Only then can you walk off and build a new stage that is a better expression of your true soul source.

This exercise of envisioning your character as outside of your consciousness can be quite powerful in separating your ego self from your soul, and can reveal much about why you are playing this game. We urge you to use this technique regularly and to contemplate what you see, and how that fits into a bigger picture of your life. Then, imagine how your soul may have intended for you to grow and become greater from these experiences. The more you do this the more you will start to see the connections between events in your life and your reactions to them. You may also start to notice how you prevent yourself from being the free-spirited being that you can be, by allowing your role to govern your every move.

Continued Soul Discovery Spurs Evolution

As your soul becomes enlightened to its importance as an expression of creation, it has the opportunity to draw more energy from this life force and to share it with others. As more energy of creation is filtered through each individual soul, outward to other souls, all become increasingly connected and aware of the web of light they are dancing within. This dance of energy transference becomes the true expression of creativity, which is the essence of the universe and the creation of all that exists. Personal soul awareness allows each aspect of creation to be a creator on a level closer to the pure spark that ignites life. The feeling associated with being connected to that spark is difficult to describe. But, when it is felt at the core level, it is empowering beyond any exterior physical fulfillment. The ignition pushes the desire for more of the same, and propels the soul into forward movement. This is how the universe continually expands and evolves.

Through continued self-discovery of one's true soul, the sparks are awakened and the desire spurs a greater expansion, and so on and so on. Your soul is then expanded beyond its perceived limits again and again, and becomes filled with sparks that fill space and time. This requires an every day, every month, and every year effort towards further connection. There is no such thing as a final end result. You are not simply enlightened one day. We are all continually being enlightened as long as we are seeking. When we stop progressing our consciousness, we are adding to the diminishment of our soul, and hence of the creative flow of the universe. We are either moving creation forward, or we are allowing it to consume itself. We are never there! We will never have made it! There is no such thing as completion. There will always be more, and further to go. And, it will always be a satisfying road to traverse when there is a knowing that the road is the very process of being God.

When you stop going down the road, you are merely thwarting your addition to creation. When you allow your consciousness to limit its perspective then you are disconnecting from the source of creation. Again, the source is within you, not outside of you. You can expand it, add to it, and reveal more of it, or you can simply keep it small and continually cover it with blankets of illusion. This is your choice, as a unit of creation.

Awareness of How You Fit Into the Bigger Picture

A self-aware soul is one that understands and appreciates its place in the evolutionary process of the whole. It sees the bigger perspective and revels in the dance of life at whatever level it is presently experiencing. Even small efforts make for a huge impact in the long run. A self-aware soul sees this in every thought, imagination, and action it takes. This soul sees how all these moments add to the greater benefit of the one soul that unites all. Eventually, there is less and less separation experienced, and the self-aware soul becomes increasingly aware of its connection to all the souls in the universe.

As you become one of these connected souls, you know that each step you take on that ladder of evolution adds strength to that rung for your fellow traveler. Ultimately, the more togetherness you feel, the more power you elicit for your progress as a species. It is your natural state to want more of this connection. When you feel the lack of it, this is an indication from your soul that you need to increase your desire, and push your imagination and actions in that direction. You so often see lack, or challenge, as something negative instead of seeing it as the push your soul needs. You allow the lack to stop you, and this keeps you from attaining the motivation that propels your evolution.

You already have the privilege of conscious awareness. Now you can take it to the next level, into a dimension of increased fluidity. This is not being given to you. It is a challenge you are all faced with. Do you intend to stop here, or will you wake up your senses and see beyond your limited dimensional awareness and into the next. You must practice your self-awareness every day to push it onward. Be aware of your imaginations and make a decision to take them to a higher level. Do not limit yourself. Go all the way. Enjoy it! Do not allow your mind to feel guilty about your desires to be more. And do not feel badly about where you are now. Appreciate that you are in exactly the right place to allow you to paint your canvas anew. You have already created this canvas so that you can continually repaint your creative masterpiece. When you are self-aware, you will enjoy stretching your canvas to encompass an expanding scene with lively colors, deeper peace, and ever changing joy.

When your canvas expands it will be able to envelop the scenes of other souls and encourage them to expand their visions. In other words, you can pull others into a vision that allows them to see beyond their limits. This is true sharing of source energy and is what increases the expansion of the whole, like a wave flowing across an ocean. As the wave moves, it carries molecules of water along with it giving momentum to the whole body of water. The momentum is powerful and has a profound effect. You each have the potential to create waves. When you join together within a higher level of consciousness, you make tidal waves that move massive amounts of source energy in a particular direction. With your new self-aware soul, you will each decide what that direction will be.

Benefiting from the Energy Portals in Time

We are excited about the changes that your world is going through now as it impacts us as well. We see the potential and are thrilled to be a part of the cycle. There are many beings nudging you in various directions, encouraging and discouraging certain potential outcomes. Remember that there are many levels of energy and dimensional aware-ness that are involved in your development due to their own interest in expansion. There are distinct times, in your awareness of time, that are portals that allow other dimensional energies to filter into your level with increased fluidity. Those of you that are aware can use these portals to gain further connections and wisdom. The month of April for example, in which this chapter was written, is influenced by a particular energy you call Aries that is an opening for vast rejuvenating vibrations.

As your soul becomes increasingly aware of energy patterns it will feel the fluctuations in the days, months, and years. Some moments offer deeper or easier passages into higher dimensional existences. These pathways have been created through the collective consciousness that makes up the grid to your reality and others of a similar nature. These energy portals allow your consciousness to move from level to level and progress into a multidimensional understanding.

In a sense, time is also vibration. Hence, your experience of time in each moment, day, month, and year, has a vibration associated with it that gives it its own life. Each particular time vibration affects all within it. Dusk and Dawn for example arouse a certain vibration that causes all life to be stirred, and each year has a particular pattern of energy.

Astrology is the closest understanding on your planet to these subtle nuances and how they influence the frequencies of all life within your time dimension. Part of being self-aware is to sense and use these changing influences to your deeper advantage. As each of you was born during a particular time signature, you are likewise printed with the vibrations associated with that time and will be affected each year by the times that resonate on that frequency. You can allow this to govern you haphazardly, or you can have an awareness that allows you to use it for advancement and transcend or transform the energy as needed.

The portals in time offer an exceptional opportunity to gain a boost that propels you forward. There is much help from other dimensions available to you during these portal periods. These times are like windows that allow passage. There are also openings to lower level energy at certain times of each year, so all should be sensed and attended to with the appropriate consciousness. Many religions, astrologers, and scientists have tapped into this knowledge of cycles and vibrational planetary pulls. For example, the moon's influence has been known by humans since before they could speak words. This knowledge was used to great effect in their evolution from hunters to farmers and for mating rituals that promoted the strongest offspring. More important than having a physical understanding of such dynamics, is having a sensibility to the influence that the physical cycles and movements have on the whole.

Planets are merely vibrational bodies that affect the signature vibrations of time. What that impact is must be measured by an awareness of the frequency itself. We have already suggested that planets are life forms that have the same source energy as you, and we do. They are evolving forms of creation that have their own personalities and evolutionary path just as all life does. They are influenced by your collective energy, just as you are moved by theirs. A healthy respect for the power of both can lead to an improved path for all.

Mars has a huge influence during your month of Aries and can burn away extraneous negativity that you have collected in your field of energy on the planet and individually. If you tap into this cosmic force, you can leave the month feeling like a new you, lighter and more able to tackle the year with greater courage and efficiency. You can, in essence, shed a lot of excess weight from your soul. You can get rid of baggage that you have been carrying around and were unable to shake. The energy of Mars and its accompanying entities is bold and forceful. It takes action and has no room for the weight of the past. Having an awareness of the potential of this month, allows you to tap into the instigating, charging energy that pushes the first burst of life from the seed. There is potential for new sprouts to come forth with the vigor that motivates life to continue. The old is burnt away so that the new can be born. It takes a great surge of life force for that to occur and it is available from all dimensional levels during the month that is Aries.

As higher frequency beings, we can feel the surge of these signature vibrations and are able to give extra light charge to your world along these lines. The more open your soul is to the frequencies available, the more positive touch we can make. The more you can get out of your ego self and be into your soul, and its connection to the vibrations of the universe, the more likely you are to feel and connect to the higher aspects of whatever time realm you are presently within. Always remember that you are not alone and that there is a great deal of energy in the universe for you to tap into and add to. We are here in complete support as requested.

Strengthen Awareness to Work in Unison

It is entirely up to each of you, as to how much awareness you wish to take on. There will be degrees of development among you. The more aware you are of your vibrational levels and of those around you, the more you will be able to manipulate what is in your program. When you can rise above the status of those around you and also impel them to raise their vibration, then you will gain the satisfaction you crave as a creator. Those that are pulled around without awareness are easily swayed by the mass consciousness and fall prey to negative motives. If you are allowing yourselves to be pulled around in this manner, you have no power and will succumb to the will of the stronger mass movement.

As self-aware souls, you are able to govern your own path and transcend any vibration that does not suit your soul. Since you are also able to recognize lower frequencies, you can avoid them or use your strength of mind to transform those influences. This takes a leader, not a follower mentality. In order to be strong against such forces, you must be aware of the power of your soul and your connection to others within this super conductive level of vibration.

As you grow in strength of soul character, you will be guided to those of a similar nature. Together you are forming a bond of light transference that can in fact change the world. The more you are able to flow with the ebbs of light, the more you will see synchronism and advancements in the moves that you make every day. On the days when the pathways are open, you can then make giant leaps and aid in the propelling of all on the grid with you. Again, practice being this way using the power of your imagination. Imagine that you are in tune with the universe and the flow of creation in your every action. Then allow that flow to take you to the perfect place. Trust that you are becoming a truly self-aware soul, as you are. The more you are able to let go of what you think is the right path, the more you allow your soul to actually flow with the path of light. In essence, you would be tuning into a vibrational track, so to speak, and would follow the conductive flow to another bright link in your evolution as a soul in harmony with the One Soul of creation.

Continuing to break away the barriers that bind you to your present position and block you from seeing the light track, is essential. The more you chip away at the limited thinking and views of yourself and others, the more possibilities you will encounter. When you can see the potential in yourself and others, you will connect in ways you have not dreamed possible in your limited thoughts. There is so much more for you than you can see with all the blinders on. As you take them off, the doors fly open and a world of connections will be revealed before your eyes.

You can see with your soul rather than your physical eyes. The colors and dynamics visible in your soul mind's eye are vast. Your physical vision only sees a tiny percentage of what your soul vision is capable of. Each of you has a special piece of the puzzle of the whole. For example, one will have soul vision in the realm of music, while another in the realm of prophecy. The higher the vibration, the more defined and polished the transference of this vision can be. The less that is blocking the soul view, the more brilliantly the puzzle piece will shine. Hence, more of the big picture is revealed and more of the One Soul is unified.

In this same way, each of you has pieces of the puzzle to give one another on a global, national, and individual level. If you are able to flow with a higher frequency, you will find and reveal secrets and wisdom from each other that leads to your evolution as a species. Your separation is an illusion. It is time for you to find all your parts again and become one universal force in creation. Ultimately, you should be working like a healthy body. All the parts have a job to do and each does it well so that the whole may walk and talk and create. All aspects of the body should be aware of the purpose and movement of the whole. If all parts are on the same wave length, the body will be strong, purposeful and fully engaged in living. If and when any part decides it would like to steal or deny energy to other parts and stop working in unison with the other parts, a breakdown occurs and the whole body eventually falls apart in a cruel and punishing way for all concerned.

In your world today, you are a body torn apart. Parts are scattered about aimlessly and the whole is suffering a cancerous disease as a result. Your individual awareness and unification is the only way that will bring you together so that you may evolve. Basically, if you do not unify your consciousness, the cancerous energy caused by the separation will consume you. This takes form in diseases in all aspects of your world.... biological, political, social, mental, environmental, etcetera. All will break down and eventually completely fail to sustain the whole. Only self-awareness leading to connection to each other will remedy this disease. As you unveil your soul of its personal bondage, the boundaries between your fellow souls will dissipate and you will naturally see each other as aspects of one soul. You will then work together to nourish all elements of your One Soul.

The Magnetic Force of Unity

Your collective consciousness has the power to change your world. As you wake up to this collective consciousness individually, you will one by one, join the whole and begin to alter your creations with focus and intention. The power inherent in this level of connection will only allow for intentions of a finer vibration as we have discussed. Only when you join at this level will you be able to create what you desire at the deepest levels of your soul. When you know that every action you make affects another aspect of yourself in the soul beside you, you will awaken the truest part of your abilities and become a force to make lasting change for the better.

The challenges you face as a species are getting ever more demanding and are important in your transformation. Those who change their awareness and join souls will be able to overcome the barrage of difficulties your species will and does face. Those that resist the pull of the connected souls will not make it through these opportunities and will have lost out on the potential for unity with creation. They will dissolve into another phase of creation and be a loss of energy for the unified soul that survives and flourishes. Those lost souls will have to reinitiate a connection through even deeper challenges to regain the hope of ever joining again. In other words, you do not want to miss this chance to elevate.

The absolute best outcome is that there are enough of you evolving to create a potent gravitational pull causing all to unify. However, we regret to inform you that if there are not enough with a strong enough pull, many will be left behind. As you unite you become a magnet pulling those of a compatible metal, so to speak, along. As you grab more souls the magnet gets larger and more forceful reaching ever more distant souls.

There may, however, be some that are too far from the magnetic attraction, or that are so covered in other materials, as in their own garbage, that they are not affected by the force. In particular, those that have done nothing to increase their awareness and shed their veil of muck, will be immune to the draw of the increasing higher frequency vibrations. In any possible probable outcome, the Earth will evolve at some point or another, the timing of which is dependent to a significant degree upon the energy amassed by humanity.

Only You can Play Your Part

It is in all your best interests to assist one another so that you become the most powerful unified soul possible. Any loss of energy will affect the collective. It is each individual's responsibility to transform their own soul to increase their awareness of and connection to one another and the natural world so that all will evolve together. In reality, you are already united. However, you have created boundaries that give you the illusion that you are separate. Everything is interconnected and dependent on another. You can either continue to kill those other aspects of yourself with judgment, or you can nurture those elements with acceptance. Much depends on how you decide to treat your fellow human souls and all life.

It is time to accept your role in the bigger picture and step up to the plate. Others are waiting for you to join and/or lead them or both. Each of you has other souls that only you can touch in a way that will truly reach them. You are each vital. We encourage you to recognize and accept that only you can do what you have to do. You cannot sit back and let another do it, for there are things that only you have the essence to add and affect. As we have said, there are souls on your frequency that need a boost. Every action of forward movement you make will influence others remotely, and will afford you an opportunity to meet and inspire them first-hand. Our challenge to you is to find the courage in yourselves to be crusaders for heightened awareness toward the goal of unified soul evolution.

On that note, we hope you are encouraged to take up the challenge of digging into your figurative dirt to uproot your weeds and replant your soil with seeds of enlightenment. There are many useful methods of self-discovery available to you that can aid you in uncovering your darkness. Find the right methods for your soul. Again, you are each so different that you will want to find what resonates with you. Join the group that has a similar quality and rhythm as your personality will allow. However, at the same time, we suggest you do not take the easy way out, as it likely does not work. There is no quick fix. It takes concerted effort and deep reflection to truly transform that which you have spent a lifetime, and then some, building in defense of your identity.

You will know you are on the right path when you begin to care less about your personal identity and more about the feeling tone of your inner self. When you feel more regard for the vibrational advantage of others than you do about your own losses, then you are going in the right direction. When you can make a simple shift of consciousness outside of your proclaimed identity to an understanding of your place in the big picture, then you are elevating. When masses of you are able to transcend in this manner, an evolutionary collective consciousness will arise and new revolutionary systems of belief will begin to change your world.

Chapter 6

New Systems of Belief and How They Will Affect Your New Era

*T*he key impetus to your species, and planetary evolution, will be the new systems of belief that will cause revolutionary changes in your perceptions of reality. The new beliefs will launch understanding and advancements in all areas of study that will literally push your planet into the new dimension. Starting with each individual, and spreading like a wildfire through the collective consciousness, the new perceptions of reality will cause doors to swing open that have been locked by limited thinking. You have been like elephants tied to a string that you did not realize you could easily break free of merely by using your entire weight. Once you break free of the misleading illusions you have collectively created, a whole new era of discovery will occur. This is not just a move toward innovations; it is a fundamental shift in your collective perception of your universe, and the dynamics that govern its advancement.

Mass Belief in the Power of Consciousness Will Alter Reality

In order for any innovation to take place in your present system, a belief or idea must be reworked, or seen from another point of view. The shift in ideas that is coming of age has the ability to make a major shift in the energy patterns that have held your system back for millennia. The consciousness change will be so dramatic that molecular structures will be altered with thoughts, and the world will be entirely transformed into a higher dimensional realm.

Most of you are seeing how a simple change in belief can alter your perception, and hence change your experience. As you begin to do this on a global level, with awareness, the beliefs you promote will have the collective power to completely revamp humanity and its environmental impact. The power of your mass beliefs is being unleashed, and amplified, so that the causes and effects are understood with deeper appreciation, and hence more profound manipulation is achieved. Once again, we emphasize that this is only possible within a state of elevated vibration. As you alter your fundamental beliefs about energy, thoughts, and matter, and enhance your ability to elevate these vibrations, then you are increasing your inherent capabilities to manipulate energy at the consciousness level. This is the core level of creation, and where dimensional reality is altered. The phrase "What you believe, you can achieve" will take on real meaning as you shift your core awareness.

Your beliefs in the energy of consciousness will be at the root of your shift and evolution. This is the force for your forward momentum. The eventual mass certainty in the power of consciousness to drive energy systems will propel dimensional shifts that will be revealed in ever increasing personal, and mass awareness of what was previously unknown and unseen. There will be new relationships established with beings, and energy forms, in other dimensions. The boundaries between worlds will be less distinct. This, in and of itself, will lead to further understanding of life energy, and will promote further development. As you stretch the limits of your conscious awareness, more is revealed and pulled into the next dimensional octave.

The belief, and more importantly the deep understanding, that consciousness is the root of all creation and all matter as you perceive it, will alter your entire world. Firstly, there will be an acceptance of this reality. Then, there will be a movement to use this understanding to change existence. Until you collectively reach a level of vibration that can change the atomic structures, there will be no considerable progress in the reformation of matter. But, as you develop the importance of intention within conscious thought at the seed level, you will be able to collectively reshape molecular structures and change your world from the atomic level up. This may seem farfetched, but it is a closer reality than you fathom. Again, you already change your world on the consciousness level haphazardly. You will begin to do so with awareness, and globally allow universal alterations.

It is simply a matter of raising the vibration of enough aware individuals to begin to affect a larger group with focus. A focused group of consciously aware souls will be able to change matter. Systems will be completely reformed, seemingly overnight. Of course, it will have taken time, in your understanding, for the thought seed to develop and then be accentuated by the focused group consciousness. Once that has formed, then materialization of the focused thought will happen rapidly. Fortunately, this type of manipulation cannot occur with thoughts of a lower, or destructive vibration. It cannot occur if any individual in the chain has self-centered intentions. There must be cohesion of conscious focus for the bond of creation to be effective on a molecular level. This is the spectacular fail-safe of creation. If the bond of unity is broken, then the result is fizzled down to an ineffectual mishmash of undirected consciousness. In other words, the goal will not be reached without a collective higher intention to form a unified result for the benefit of all concerned.

Focused Collective Consciousness Affects Matter

Many of you are still at a stage of experimenting with the use of conscious thought to create for selfish reasons. However, you will eventually learn that this method ultimately is a dead-end road that leads to further dissatisfaction. This is simply because the energy signature is weak when the focus is on individual material, or emotional, gain. As we discussed earlier, the intention of consciousness is key. Placing the intention outside of oneself, and joining with the collective good, is the only way to create lasting change.

Let us give an example. With collective human consciousness you can purify the waters on your entire planet. This is a vast example. But, nonetheless, it is as doable as any smaller feat. If you were to collectively communicate on a consciousness level within a higher vibrational octave, with the intentions of purifying the Earth's water, you would change the molecular level of all the water. Furthermore, if you collectively wished the water to remain pure, you are capable of creating systems that maintain that purity perpetually. The clear focus of consciousness would need to be significant. But, we are here to inform you that this is where you can exist if you continue down the path of awareness.

If you understand that you are one with all consciousness on your planet, then you will appreciate that all consciousness is influenced by the state of vibrancy of the whole. As your beliefs about consciousness advance, so will your effectiveness as creators. You will learn to infuse your physical creations with the seeds of the final result, and allow the structures and systems to be built within a completely synchronistic flow. In other words, all the elements will fall into place when your collective intentions are focused on the ultimate result for a higher good. The energy of the intention will feed the atomic creation, and materialization will take place at an alarming speed.

The sooner you each are able to shed your self-absorption, and realize that you are a part of a much bigger picture that is also an aspect of you, the sooner you can get on with some exciting creative progress. You are on the verge of fulfilling your potential. We urge you to imagine what it would be like to be unified in your intentions to make a better world. Imagine what it would be like to use your consciousness to feed the world on a physical and spiritual level. What do you think unity of consciousness might feel like? The more you can fathom your connection to the souls around you, the more you build a bridge of light between you, and strengthen your collective power.

The world will change as your beliefs about it change. Fundamentally, your world is your beliefs about it, because your world is determined by consciousness. All seeking, all desire, and the action that follows, is the act of consciousness creating the world you experience. As your science physically and mathematically perceives the inherent power of consciousness, the doorways of understanding will spring wide open. It only takes a small leap for much to become clear. You are on the threshold of an evolution in beliefs that will skyrocket your ability as creators. Science may see, but your species will only be able to use the knowing when your consciousness is elevated to the frequencies that allow consciousness to be altered at the core. The seed of creation is in unity of consciousness.

Rising Above Self Interest Will Lead to Enhanced Fulfillment

Unity will occur when boundaries are dissolved within each individual consciousness. The impact will, in turn, be global and you will find yourselves walking through doorways of inter-dimensional existence. This shift in awareness will allow deeper knowing, clairvoyance, remote viewing, and extrasensory perceptions otherwise thought impossible. Communications will occur on a telepathic level from soul to soul, and synchronicities will be the norm. Your group paths will be clearer as you interact on a deeper level with the souls around you for common aims. There will be less preventing encounters that need to occur in order to fulfill the purpose of your souls.

You will each be tested to the degree that you need to be to obtain the level of consciousness required to make the shift for your species. Many of you will be given large burdens to overcome physically and mentally. These are opportunities for you to test your metal. If you can raise your state of mind beyond that of self-interested greed or self-pity, and are able to shift your thinking to the bigger picture, then you will be ready to join the collective realm of forward evolution. If enough of you rise above your normal reactions, you will be on the way to using your consciousness to collectively leap ahead.

Your newfound belief in the ability of your collective consciousness to create solutions to problems, and continually better your world for yourselves and all the life forms that exist within it, will revolutionize all systems on your planet. This is your challenge, and it is a worthy one. There is nothing more important and desired by your individual souls, and by all those energy forms that are assisting.

When you reach that mode of creating, then all that you do will be joyous, freeing, and fulfilling. It will be as if your lives are filled with light. You each will know the significance of your individual spark in the creative process, as opposed to being in a state of competition or jealousy that causes emptiness and pain. Imagine everyone being happy for you, and you being happy for everyone else, as you make life happen for all. This is not just fluff. That is the way you were meant to express your aspect of God or The Source. You are in the process of learning that, as it should be. You are much like children learning how to be independent, and how to use your talents to their utmost. Firstly, children think they need to get it all for themselves. Through much trial, they learn to share begrudgingly. And then, they learn that they will get something back if they share. If they advance enough, they will learn the true pleasures of sharing for the sake of sharing to enlighten another. Of course, most humans get stuck along the way, and many even stay at the first stage of being completely out for themselves. This is a dead-end street that never leaves them with enough to satisfy.

As your belief in consciousness changes, so will everything you are conscious about as a species. What and how you use that consciousness will be completely up to you. That is the fun part. What you can envision, you can create. More minds are always better than one, and together you will be able to fly.

Stretching the Limits of Belief Systems

There is actually no limit to what kind of world you create, and what you can do within it. We urge you to consider what belief systems you wish to promote. If you continue your belief that technology is the only way to fly, then you will remain dependent on this mode of creation. Physical technologies as tools are quite limited when there are more pliable and poetic modes of making things happen. Though you feel dependent on your technology now, as your awareness awakens, you will be able to fathom other ways to influence and move. The world of consciousness reaches beyond the limitations of what you perceive presently as physical, with your five senses. Your consciousness can reach beyond your presently limited perspective of space and time. Keep this in mind as you begin to envision a world among evolved souls. Why stop at something as mundane as a robot field tiller, when you can communicate with biological life forms that prepare your soil, in a way that is beneficial to them, and you, as a unified consciousness, for example.

As evolving conscious beings, you will be creating systems of belief that in turn create your reality. You have the opportunity in your advanced awareness to do this with intention. Therefore, you may want to stretch your thinking. Have fun with it. It may seem childish to envision a world with connections to fairies, rocks, and planets, but this is the place of joy that will make it real. Many of you are so bored with life because you stopped believing that there is anything beyond the routine dependency on technology. Wake up and dream a little. The dreams can help get you into a state of hope and desire for something better for your planet. Collectively you are starved for this.

Practice expanding your beliefs now. Allow your consciousness to go beyond everything you think you know about the world, and yourself. What abilities would you desire to have in a limitless, yes limitless, world? Begin imagining yourself having such abilities. The only way you will get closer to expansion is to let the possibilities arise in your mind and emotions. How will your new abilities assist the collective soul? Perhaps you will be part of a group of individuals that have a similar talent, and together you will be a great force. What you start creating at the consciousness level now, will add to what becomes possible in the coming era. Get out of the box and push the limits. The more you all do this, the more expansive the belief systems will be and hence the greater the effect. If you start radical, the lowest denominator will at least be beyond the limitations projected by the least imaginative among you.

Go into the world and start pretending everyone cares for one another, and that you can sense each other's needs without using words. Pretend that you can see someone's sadness from afar and can send them encouragement to bring them out of that mood. Imagine your spark as all-knowing, connected, and able to reach around the world. It can do this. You can do this. You can sense angel forces in a room, and around others. Imagine that you can push negative energies away from your friends with your thoughts. Imagine that you can see energy forms and help others to redirect their intentions. What if you could be in two places at once? Go on, think about it. It is all possible.

We are astounded by the limitations humankind puts upon itself. We can see how much you are capable of, if you reach beyond your limited ways of thinking and stretch yourselves. Each stretch expands the possibilities. Your minds are set on the material realm, which is such a small part of what you are, and what the world is, that you exist within. You are so much more than that. Yet, you set your highest ambitions on obtaining advances that are limited by past beliefs about your environment, and how you can move about within it. The answers are in the unseen. The truths are in the world beyond your physical senses. Truth exists in the dimensions of thought, imagination, and blissful exaltations. It is everything between and beyond the physical that contains all the power and all the joy. The physical is a mere image of what is created in the higher reality of pure consciousness.

Each Small Change in Beliefs has an Exponential Impact

If you get out of your limited, self-interested physical obsessions, and look beyond at the bigger picture of conscious awareness, you can embark upon a journey of conscious mastery of all the energy that surrounds you. You each see your small world of everyday existence as evidence of your insignificance in the big picture. We advise you that it is not small. You can have the same mastery in your seemingly small sphere of reality as you could in a larger sphere, and it can have an equally exponential effect, if it engenders a transformative consciousness. We see how you each have an issue with smallness. You think you are one lost soul in a vast soup. Just as one atom can change a whole molecular structure and completely alter the physical object, so can each unit of conscious thought alter surrounding thought dynamics. We urge you with all sincerity to consider that you are each a hugely important part of the development of your species right now. You cannot afford to be concerned with how little you are. You must appreciate that your mind and imagination is key in changing the beliefs of your world. Every small effort has serious meaning for all humanity, and for the universe.

As you are now at the threshold of your potential, you have the option to forge ahead with vigor and enlightenment. Contrastly, you can plunge yourselves into a pit of darkness that you will be forced to scrape and crawl agonizingly through, with much pain and travail, in order to finally see what we and other elevated souls are revealing to you now. You have this choice, and each one of you is a significant part of that choice. What will it be? The moment that will tip your scales in one direction or another is upon you. You do not have to experience suffering to know a higher consciousness. You can reveal the light within you and brighten the world now. The moment of potential transition is coming and the time to prepare is now. There is nothing to wait for but you. You each must act now, not tomorrow.

It is each soul's responsibility to add to the new system of beliefs with its own expansion, so that you are each adding to the final potential, and not diminishing it. The power of each individual makes the whole. If you can each take five minutes a day to envision a reformed race of humanity, it would have an enormous effect. If it is conceived, it can be achieved. And furthermore, if you can each change your beliefs about your individual potential a little each day, you will be raising the possibilities for yourself, and all those on your wavelength. Every step moves you along the super-conductive highway of existence in the direction of your evolution. But, the question remains, will you be prepared for the moment of transition?

The answer to this query is entirely up to the lot of you. In the next chapter we will discuss the moment of transition, and what it means to be prepared for a dimensional shift. Again, you collectively create the details of how, but the planet will be making her move regardless. So, it is largely a matter of asking yourself, "Are you in? Or are you out?"

Chapter 7

The Moment of Transition and Preparedness

*T*he big moment is inevitably coming. Make no mistake about that. What on Earth this moment brings will depend on all the energy factors involved? There will be a culmination point when the planet will either be forced to flush the wasted energy for recycling in order to push herself from the ashes, or there will be a powerful surge of energy that literally slings her into a new dimension of reality.

The Transition: Painful Versus Refreshing

One culmination option will be painful and drastic on a physical and spiritual level. That option is the unprepared version. That version is the easier one, in that it does not require much work in terms of preparedness. It is the hardest route to endure, but the easiest to bring about. Simply act as you have been, remaining unconscious and unaware of the need to change, and you will be right in place for a rocky, long, and hard transition that will take perhaps a few more lifetimes of endurance.

The second option, clearly the preferred in the long run, requires extensive preparation now, but will make the transition smooth and quite refreshing. Both may be happening at the same time and within the same space. Some will transit smoothly while others will suffer. There are and will be various levels of awareness coexisting. However, as we have discussed, if there is a momentum created with strong elevated souls, a magnetic reaction can pull the lot of humanity into the slingshot version, instead of the tumultuous agonizing crawl. The energy of human souls can drag Mother Earth into a slow grueling transition, or spin her around full force. You are here to make this decision individually, and as a collective.

There is a side to each of you that wants to take the lazy way out. You are familiar with suffering, and satisfied with a quick fix for your agonies that only lasts a few seconds or hours. You do not know anything other than emptiness most of the time. You all desire growth and connection, but many have lost the desire to make the effort to find it. Unless you choose to prepare yourselves for the moment of transition, you will fall, and fall hard, in your own den of self-created iniquity. You all knew what you were in for this time around, and you thought you were ready for the challenge. If you still think you are ready, then let us discuss some practical methods of preparedness.

Minimum Level of Awareness For a Smooth Transition

We have given you much to ponder in terms of your place in the universe and the importance of transforming your soul. We have urged you to dig deep into your natures to find what needs attention. Provided you continue to do this, and revise your limited visions, there are some qualities that will prove most useful for a beautiful transition into the next dimension of awareness. We are not suggesting that you will be able to become the ideal overnight. But, every push will be exponential in its impact, so all efforts will go a long way towards your preparedness. Here are a few guidelines to keep in mind, or better yet, goals to aspire to.

- Think of others. Get out of yourself and feel the souls that surround you. They are you.

- Love those souls unconditionally. Look for the spark of creation within them, as it is the same spark that is within you.

- Appreciate the inter-connectedness of everything in the universe and hence the importance of every thought and action.

- See the light of creation in every moment and situation, no matter how it appears superficially. Change challenging events into light filled opportunities.

- Use your powerful imaginations to alter your world, starting with your own perceptions. In one second you can change everything. Keep adding those up.

This is the minimum level of consciousness that can exist in the next dimension of awareness. Only with the same frequency of conscious thought can one reside there. If you are prepared with this level of being, then the transition will come naturally. You can obtain this same level of consciousness through personal and mass hardship, eventually, but there is absolutely no need to continue in this way. There is extensive assistance available to you now that will make your growth possible.

As we have relayed, in order to achieve those goals, you will have to dig up your roots and clean out the cobwebs that stop you from perceiving with this level of awareness. Remember, you have a cloud of self-centered, animalistic survival motivations that block your clarity and connection. In this period of increased energy, however, you can shed a lifetime of veils in minutes. You can also experience a lifetime of agony in minutes, if you choose that route. Your will is free.

Amplification of Densities During the Transition

Although the transition to the next dimension appears to be happening gradually, there will be a moment when the ultimate push occurs, and perception will be completely altered. Leading up to this moment, those who are preparing will experience glimpses into a new domain, and likely have been for some time. These moments of stepping into another realm of reality will increase in frequency and amplification until the new awareness becomes more the norm than the exception. Then, it will be your very life experience. You will transit into a world of inner knowing and flow. Navigation in this new world will be a new learning experience that we will discuss in more detail later. The more prepared you are, the easier the process will be.

Your connection to one another, and general group consciousness, will be acute at the time of transition, and will aid in the natural movement. The feeling will be light, buoyant, and freeing. Your body will flow with your mind in a delicate dance of creation, as you exist in a vibration that is bright with illumination of source energy. As always, there will still be lower and higher levels within this new dimension, and most will enter at the last rung and be working their way up, just as in this present world. There will always be frequencies that are denser than others, but in this next octave, the muddy level will not have the density that it does in your present realm. As we have said, the highest thought at this level is akin to the lower levels of the next octave of awareness.

When the energy culminates and the moment of transition is upon you, the acceleration will be obvious, especially to those most prepared, and to a lesser degree to those on the edge of awareness. For those that are unprepared, the energy increase will amplify whatever they have in their consciousness, and it may not be so pretty. It may be drawn out over time as well. Those that are transiting will still have a chance to pull others into the shift as they coexist between two octaves. However, there will be a point when it will be too late and the planet will make her final move with those that are aligned. Those souls that do not make the transition will continue their journey in realms that match their frequency until they are able to join the new octave. Of course, this is provided that enough of you are able to push a general evolutionary shift when the moment of transition is possible in this era. Those that evolve now will make it possible for the next group to evolve in their own timing, instead of all enduring the hundreds of years of trials and tribulations. The critical mass of evolved souls will play a new role of encouraging those left behind in a slower mode of travel.

Take Advantage of This Opportunity to Evolve

The opportunity upon you is so great and will be so rewarding that we encourage, with all our being, that you take up the challenge and prepare yourselves for the transition. In preparing yourselves, you are creating the chance for the evolution of your souls. The seeking will be gaining in strength as well, so each of you will have the opportunity to inspire the searching souls around you. Simply being there and making connections with others will assist them. You each have pieces of the puzzle for one another. The more open you are to each other and the more willingness you have to listen to the messages within every situation you are in, the more you will see of the higher realms.

Remember, you are already there, and simply must unveil the curtains that you are hiding behind to see another dimension of reality. Practice shifting your perception so that you see more in every person, thing, and event. Seek the real meaning, message or hidden truth behind your limited perceptions. Look for what is trying to be revealed to you. So much of what is occurring around you are messages from guardian energy forces, or are situations attracted by your inner self to wake you up. Seek the messages actively and you will begin to see and feel beyond your five senses and will open gateways to a lighter viewpoint of the universe.

Continue to seek also the true you beneath the layers of social and emotional garbage you have built around you. See also the inner poetry of your soul. The light within you is bright and true, and is ready to be shared with the world. Be your true self and allow others to be who they are as well. When you are being your true essence, there is nothing to be afraid of because you will be in complete synchronicity with the vibration of your source. That source is pure and unconditional love. When you come from this place in every thought and action, then your every move will be a creative expression of pure light. Any darkness you experience, or see around you, is the result of the light of creation being hidden from view. See the light in you and your surroundings, and you will be encouraging the same in others. When you all have that vision, you are evolving.

Assisting to Reveal the True Light in All

Everything, and we mean everything, has a path of vibration that led it to be what it is. The source of everything is the light of creation. How much was revealed of the source along the way in each thing or event depends on the consciousness involved. For example, the cup of tea sitting beside you had a journey to get to where it is in your present reality. Every step of its journey involved consciousness, from the seed of the tea plant, to the picker of the leaves, to the packaging company, and the person boxing it. Everything that touched it, such as machines, which were created with a consciousness, to the shipping and placement of it on a shelf at the store, right up to the advertisements, and action of you purchasing the tea, involved consciousness in one form or another. This is only a summary of the story of the tea, as it would take a long time to go through every bit of thought energy that touched that tea up to your body digesting it.

The interconnectedness of every single element in your reality is astronomical to ponder, but when your species recognizes the importance of all the bits of energy that are put into everything around you, you will begin to appreciate how your thoughts and actions influence the whole organism that is your planet and universe.

Within each step of the tea's production there was either more light revealed of the source energy of the tea, or its source energy was covered along the way and veiled in darkness. Each bit of consciousness that focused in any way on that tea getting to your bedside, affected the revelation of its true light. However, and here is the gem, your present consciousness has the power to assist the tea in revealing its true nature, to be free of the burdens it has gathered along the way. When you are able to see the source of creation in your tea, you allow the tea to reveal itself. The same is true of everything, and everyone, in your world.

When you see the light within each other and the circumstances in your lives, you make it possible for more light to be revealed. The more difficult it is to see the brightness of a given situation or within a person, the more potential that situation or person has to make an impact. In other words, the more darkness that shrouds the event or soul, the more source energy will come bursting forth into your world when it is unveiled.

This is way beyond mere positive thinking; this is how the universe works. Remember, it is all about vibration. The vibration of your true essence is hidden from perception in your world. It is your job to unveil the masterpiece. Many of your artists recognize this element of creation as they understand that the piece of work was already there and they simply revealed it to the world. They unveiled an essence into the physical dimension. Yet it can only be appreciated to the level of the consciousness of those viewing or listening. And there, the cycle of interdependence goes on.

Find the Inner Spark Behind Your Darkness

It is completely natural and is the very nature of creation that you should be constantly evolving. This coming transition is a part of an evolutionary pattern that has been occurring since the beginning of your universe. It cannot be stopped. It can only be delayed. If you prepare yourselves, it can be delightful and exhilarating. The very act of preparing can be a joy if you set your minds to making it so. There really is a whole world to discover, and individual talents to awaken.

As you uncover you inner light, abilities will begin to appear that you will want to pursue. Often, your best ability is hiding under your worst quality or behavior. The universe is designed this way. When you are forced to confront areas of difficulty, you have a chance to reveal the gem within. It is the very process of chipping at the stone, and finding what was hidden, that makes the diamond shine. Therefore, a big hint in helping you prepare is to look at what gives you pain. What causes you aggravation or struggle in your life? It is different for everyone, but you each will find that you have repetitive events or relationship issues.

Within the agony of your failures and sadness, there is something that is keeping you in darkness. Under that darkness is your gem. Within these struggles there is usually a huge hidden desire. There are answers in your desires. If the darkness is removed, then the desires can spawn the spark of light. Finding your inner spark is important in your preparation, and will allow you to see the world as we described earlier. When you are shining your light, you will see the world around you much differently. It will no longer be seen as a place of darkness, but rather a place of possibility.

We suggest you take some time to look at all the pain you have had in your life. Look at all the circumstances that make you unhappy or dissatisfied. Then, see if you can identify the desires beneath the pain. Within these desires are your talents. Where you wish you were more, or feel you are lacking, under your fear, shame or disbelief, you actually have hidden light. The more you can uncover of your natural ability, the more prepared you will be to see the world with a new sensibility.

You each have a place within the whole, and it can be discovered and followed with certainty. There need not be such indecision and despair about your future. You can all walk within a path of light and certainty in the inner spark that is connected to the eternal blessings of creation. When your light shines, you can see the way. It is not easy to seriously look into the dark places of your life. But, ironically, it is where your light is being blocked. Or maybe it is not so ironic. Your tendency is to avoid those zones because it hurts too much, or is just too much work. Again, you want the easy way out…the quick fix, or obvious answer. Sometimes the obvious is not the answer. Sometimes it is the very thing you least expect, and never thought you could do, that holds your inner spark. It can be the garbage that smells the worst that holds the special treasure. You may not want to look there because you do not want to get dirty, but if you dare to, you will be forever rewarded.

Become Your Ultimate Expression

What we are asking you to do is to become the best and brightest that your soul can be in its present incarnation. This is how you prepare for the benefits of the new era of enlightenment. We are also aware that this is much easier said than done, given the baggage you all carry. If you are willing to face your demons, however, you can find your truth. Welcoming and searching past and present challenges for your core reactions, and the essence of what made them difficult for you in particular, will lead you to monumental self discovery. Within each obstacle, from everyday puny annoyances, to big life changing dramas, there is a fiber of knowledge that is woven into the larger garment that covers your hidden gifts. Mind you, this does not mean that you do not have talents that are already easy and apparent that should be encouraged. You all have these as well, and you should continue to cultivate them. Those are the gifts that you have already revealed in past lives, or earlier in this life. Those will come most easily to you. Although, it is the hidden gifts that will most expand your potential in all areas of this existence, and the next. Revealing the hidden sparks will allow the already developed self to flourish.

For example, if you have a real challenge with self-discipline in this life, but have a natural ability to play music, you may not have allowed your talent to blossom because of your lack in the former area. You may have a brilliant philosophical mind, but be unable to share your thoughts, because you are hiding behind a fear that you are socially inept. The examples are endless, and you each have a few to contend with. As you can surmise, your abilities cannot reach their full potential unless you deal with the trouble spots in your nature. Even a simple awareness of how you are stopping yourself will aid in your transition. Once you know what you are up against, then you can ask for the tremendous assistance available to guide you to your next level. If you do not know what to ask for, you will not get any answers.

When you become aware of how your shortcomings are stopping you, the guidance is possible, and a direction can be seen. If the door is opened, you can see at least a few steps ahead. And, more is revealed as you go. If your door is closed, or even locked, there is not much hope in seeing where you can go from there. Denial is a tragic enemy. As long as you deny yourself the truth, you can go nowhere. The flip side of that is that, as soon as you let go of the denial and face the reality, you can go everywhere. It can be a hard switch to flip, but once you do it, the whole room is illuminated, giving you an opportunity to navigate from there.

When you allow yourself to be in your own darkness, you are deciding not to see your potential, out of fear of the unknown. You become comfortable in the darkness, like a caterpillar in a cocoon. This is what you know, and you think it is what you are, completely. Little do you know that if you break out of your self-created cocoon, you will become a butterfly, which is what you are meant to be. Your origin and ending is that of a butterfly. Everything in the middle is the delight of becoming what you already are. This is where it can become complex to understand in a world of time and space. But, creation is the very act of continually creating and expanding what you are. Being the ultimate expression of you is being the ultimate expression of God, The Light, or The Source Energy of existence.

Everything is exactly as it is right now in your life for the purpose of allowing you to see more of who you are. You attract to you the vibration of what you are, and hence are able to confront yourself within what you create around you. Therefore, take a good look at what you have created your whole life and in this very moment. Really look at every detail, the good the bad and the ugly. The areas of delight are your accomplishments, and are the areas where you can have more, provided you contend with the areas that are not so joyous. Every single physical and emotional element in your surroundings is a poetic creation by attraction. As you learn to seek the meaning in your environment, you are becoming aware of the poet's intentions. The poet is you, and you are a perfect expression of The Source of life.

Your preparation for the moment of transition is an ongoing discovery of your inner essence and truth that will allow you to see the essence and truth of the souls, and world, around you. When you live within this awareness of true essence, you will flow into the next dimension like a butterfly from its cocoon.

Finding Assistance on Your Journey of Transformation

There are many tools and methods of connection and understanding that can assist you in your journey of transformation, as we have mentioned. As long as you are seeking, you are on your way. Remember that real change will be felt in a profound way. If you do not have regular epiphanies about yourself, then you are not really moving anywhere.

One of the more useful tools we recommend that you explore is your astrological influences. You are each born with a map of energy influences from the planets and time signatures that make up your universe. Knowing these patterns can guide you in discovering where your soul intended to progress, and where it has already done so. Find out all you can from the knowledge base available. You will also find much in Astrology to assist you in understanding those that surround you. Astrology is a tool that takes into account past life experiences, and can reveal much that is in your blueprint for this life.

We again urge you to surround yourself with others on the journey to discovery. You have strength in numbers and can teach each other about each other. Then you will have more to give those that have yet to embark on a path. As long as the intentions of those you learn with are for the benefit of personal growth, and you feel that you are being assisted in true discovery, then it is useful. If you feel your acquaintances are bringing you down, or are simply placating your ego, step away and find a more challenging and fulfilling environment in which to associate. The support of others taking the same journey can make all the difference in your success, and you can add to theirs. The strength you develop by working together can have far-reaching consequences and enhance anything you manage to do on your own. Make sure you join others that have integrity, and a genuine sense of purpose for the betterment of your collective well-being. Such unity is also excellent preparation for developing your collective consciousness, and for developing your ability to maintain your individuality while enhancing the whole. Thus, those that you join should welcome the spirit of the individual soul, while strengthening its, and the group's, connection to the source of creation. If your associations give you a chance to shine, encourage your self-discovery, and value your addition of energy to the larger dynamic, then you are in a good place.

One must determine the environment that best suits his or her particular style of expression. Often, what feels right will be a group of souls that you already have a deeper connection with. You will feel it when you come across them. Again, we warn you to be aware of the trappings of over-emotional, ego gratifying, or fear-based belief systems. Fear is a sign of disconnection. If you feel emotionally stimulated in a sappy way, then it is likely not genuine. If you feel elation on a deeper consciousness level, then soak it up. If you are around the right people for you to grow with, you will get the sensation of coming home or feel as if you have known the people, or their methods, before. There will be a knowing within your soul. If you have not yet found such a support system, keep searching. They are out there, and can use your assistance.

While there are many outwardly diverse expressions of connection, the actual vibration is the same internally. While you may wear different clothing, your soul has the same source of life. Languages and words may be strangely unique, but those that are truly making a connection to the light of the universe are, internally, no different from one another. The source is one and the same, and will feel the same for those that are sensitive to vibration. If you are able to connect to the higher realms, you will see beyond the physical differences and styles, and will accept the light as it is, no matter the exterior display. However, that does not mean that all methods have the same ability to connect, and much depends on the consciousness of all those associated with the group, now, and through time.

Your associations with others on a spiritually evolving path will greatly assist in your preparedness for the transition. You need each other to evolve. You need each other's strength and diversity. Just as each soul in each collective is unique, but strengthened by the whole, the same is true of each group's connection to each other on a global level. The more acceptance there is among diverse spiritual paths, the stronger all will become. Those that are most connected will positively influence the others by their acceptance, and all will benefit. The core knowledge that is truth resonates as such. The ways and means may be diverse, but the truth behind the methods will shine through the physical differences in appearance.

There are many loners out there still who are reading this message and are resisting. We encourage you to find your group of souls to grow with. Going it alone is a difficult, and possibly perilous journey. Find those that you can gain from, and that will gain from you. "Seek and ye shall find." The vibrations of those on the evolutionary path are strong now, and they are beckoning those of like mind. When you set out to find your soul-mates, you will succeed, and feel as though a portion of your emptiness has been filled.

Ways You Will Feel the Amplified Energy

As you get closer to the culmination of accelerated energy, you will begin to feel the shift more deeply. Those that have been preparing will be sensitive to new sensations and alterations in perception. If you have not prepared, the world and your life may appear increasingly chaotic and out of control. If you have prepared, and are in tune with at least the minimal required frequency, then your life and the world around you will have the sensation of rising above or flowing in, around, and among what was previously perceived as normal life in the physical plane. You will have a sensation of being there, but in a capacity you previously did not comprehend or feel. Your awareness will increase to encompass another level related to everything and one you encounter. Events that appear to be bringing some down will be uplifting those that can see the larger picture. As the acuteness of perceptions increases, it will be easier for those with the visions to convince those that cannot yet see, and potentially pull them along.

Your perceptions of each other will amplify and you will increasingly be able to intuit, or actually see the inner nature of individual souls, and groups of souls. Some of you will even reach into realms of angels, spirits, and beings in parallel dimensions. You may slowly develop the capacity to see colors, holes, or darkness in human auras, and many will be able to sense disease in mind and body. Many of you will be able to perceive alternative probabilities for yourselves and others. The ability to travel through time and space with the mind will become possible for some. Gifts will be accentuated in all areas of expression, as they are infused with deeper meaning.

The process will be gradual and then, at some point, those that are there will be in a new dimensional awareness, while others will exist in parallel, but be unaware of the dynamics that exist for those who have crossed over. For a while it will be as if two worlds are coexisting in unison. This is the transitional period. This is the time when transformation of all is actually possible, as the energy of vibration for those moving on can still affect the others.

For a majority of you, there will simply be a feeling of floating through life. You may feel as though you are disconnected from what is happening around you and have no emotional attachment to the events. If you have this feeling, we suggest you take that to a deeper level by seeking the meaning, and allowing yourself to delve into a higher awareness of the occurrences, instead of simply existing above or around them. Your efforts to seek more meaning without the emotional reactions will assist you in finding your heightened awareness. Instead of merely being outside of your emotions, look into the situation or person. Seek the clarity of vision. Use your imagination to carry you at first, and follow the lines of thought that you perceive. It does take practice. After all, you are increasing your perception beyond what you previously thought was possible, so it takes some stretching of your mental and spiritual muscles.

As you develop your enhanced perceptions, you will eventually become more adept at manipulating your environment in the higher dimension. This will occur over time and with collective efforts, which we will delve into in later chapters. Firstly, you must work diligently at clearing away your cobwebs to allow your butterfly to fly. As the butterfly emerges, its perceptions will be altered so that it can see the interconnectedness of its wing beats with the universe in which it flaps them. As the butterfly recognizes itself as a beautiful creature of light, it will see itself and others as coming from, and being supported by, the same ray of light. The separation will be replaced by the recognition of the expression of uniqueness within a unified whole. This enlightenment is the awareness of what is already there, which in turn frees your souls from the bondage of non–clarity, where it has suffered for so long.

The time of transition will be a lifting of the last fibers of the veil, or the clearing of the last layers of smoke, that have held you in a world of limitations. The more you clear away now, the more beautiful the culminating moments will be for your individual and collective soul. It will be worth every minute of effort and imagination you put into it. So continue to look and love deeply, and think big. Remember to ask for guidance, and keep seeking and sharing your spark. You will get there, and we will be with you.

As you continue to have glimpses of the transition, you will see that it is possible, and quite real. It will happen slowly for most as you get used to new perceptions and sensations around you. The feeling of being disconnected from the physical world can be disconcerting at first, so easing into the transition is necessary. As you begin to feel the sensation more often, you will be able to explore the nature of it. At first you will feel separated from the world around you in a surreal way, like you are not really there. It may even feel as though others cannot even see you. Your physical body will seem unimportant and you will be able to focus more on thoughts and sensations. As you learn to do this, you will soon be able to feel your connection to everything around you, despite the physical separation. You will be able to feel the dichotomy of separation and connection simultaneously. The more you can let go of your self-involvement under these conditions, the more you can feel the energy flow of your environment.

When you are open to the flow of inter-connectedness, you will then learn to relate with others and objects on a consciousness level that begins at the core molecular structure. This learning is a process that will be part of your new era. It will not happen overnight. We will be discussing some tools to assist you in moving and creating at the source consciousness level, but for now, understand that the process and preparation for the transition is leading you to that stage of development. It will be a wondrous journey, once you get through the hurdles of overcoming your self-imposed limitations.

Increasing Frequency to Connect to Higher Beings

As you get closer to your transition phase, you will be able to connect with your spiritual guides and beings of a higher frequency. You will feel us, or even see us. We will be able to guide you more directly as you begin to hear our voices within, and learn to distinguish the higher voices from anything of a lower nature. In fact, the more evolved your consciousness becomes, the less you will be influenced by denser frequencies, until eventually you will not even hear those levels. You will only be connected and flowing with beings of a brighter vibration in dimensions less shrouded in darkness.

We encourage you to ask and seek our attention. We can guide you if you want this. You have free will, and therefore, we will not interfere when you have not invited us. And, we cannot connect with you if your vibration is buzzing at a low level. We cannot get through the dark energy that you cover yourselves with. When you free yourselves of your personal demons, we can be with you, and you can feel our presence. If you are not vibrating within a degree of our vibration, then you will not be able to handle our energy. You would experience a sensory overload and your brain chemistry would be affected. This is why you must build up your frequency slowly to handle more of our light.

We can affect your physical reality, but, if you are not ready, it can be damaging to your evolutionary cycle. The misuse of drugs can have this effect as well. Your brains operate with electrical impulses that have a certain frequency. Some psychotropic drugs can change these frequencies artificially and open pathways to perceptions that you are not ready to handle. In this way, you can short circuit your ability to create these pathways in an organic manner. You can quite literally fry your electrical pathways to higher dimensions by connecting to too much voltage for your wiring to contain. This is why it is a process of evolution and cannot happen in one swoop of movement. This is why it is so important that you prepare yourselves a little at a time. Each tiny step allows new circuitry to be created at your molecular level. You are making a new circuit board as you open more doors of perception and learn to work within new light paths. With this in mind, you should be patient with yourselves. Work hard to push away your darkness, but be patient with your process of higher frequency connection while you build your bridges a rail at a time. The links will be made as you stretch your perception and seek higher realms of association.

In many ways, facing your darkness can be an easier process than connecting with new realms of reality, as you are very familiar with your frequencies of despair and hardship, whereas the areas of light are fleeting and seem out of reach. But, once the black spots are finally dissipated, you will have nowhere to go but into the light. Soon you will seek nothing in the lower frequencies and will be longing to make the connection with higher vibrations. Such desire will make the transition possible for you. So, while you may not be able to see what we are describing as likely within your world of darkness, it will become more visible over time. And, soon you will see only the world of possibility and will push forward into that realm. For now, keep plugging away at your personal transformation, and trust that your inner soul knows what is coming and will be able to make the transition to be what it truly is. The time will come when you will know exactly where to be and when.

Chapter 8

Where to Be and When

A las, the much awaited where to be and when is upon us. Before we delve into this thrilling topic, please ask yourself where you want to be and when do you want to be there? Much of the outcome will depend on the consciousness of your answer. You all want this question to be answered for you with concrete latitudes and longitudes, and precise dates and times. This attitude is certainly an aspect of your limited thinking in space and time, which we encourage you to break out of as much as possible. But, we do understand that you exist within this framework and at present only comprehend the world within such parameters. Given your insatiable desire to know when the world will change, and if there is a particular place you should be when it does, we will oblige you to the extent that you need to know, and that we can know, given the probabilities based on global consciousness. Furthermore, we will aid you in finding your own answers regarding where to be and when on a personal level.

The Larger Context of Probable Outcomes

On a global and universal level, there are ten major probable outcomes possible as a result of the coming shift. Within those ten dimensional realities, there are multitudes of smaller alternate outcomes, all beautifully dependent on your collective consciousness. We are able to follow the trends, and see where the energy of those trends leads in a generally timeless way. All of the various dimensional options already exist in our view. We are able to pop in and view the energy signatures of the various outcomes. An aspect of your soul lives within each of the probable realities and they affect one another. This concept of everything happening in a timeless world is almost impossible for you to truly grasp, as you can only see one point at a time, consecutively.

It is hard for you to see how there can be such a thing as evolution, without it building over time and within space. However, you are in fact evolving in a timeless, infinite space constantly. Do not let your head explode trying to think of this. You were not meant to. You are meant to experience the luxury of being in a direct, cause and effect space where you can view, and live, the choices that you make with the grace of the unknown. Remember that you are already a perfect expression of creation. You are simply discovering what you already are and know. In a sense you are expressing an aspect of the endless light of creation by living in a world of preset limitations. You are, in essence, the creator creating an aspect of itself. Your head is no doubt already bursting at the seams, and you still want to know where and when to be. However, in order to know this you must step out of where and when. Hence, you will be challenging your sense of space and time.

You can learn to see the alternate probabilities, and flow with those that benefit you, and the whole, as a result. When you transcend the limitations of space and time, you see the events from a larger perspective and can move accordingly. This takes quite a bit of practice and enhanced awareness to do effectively. You can start by pretending that you can see various probable outcomes, and eventually you will actually start keying in on the astral light signatures for the realities.

In order to know where to be and when, you must fathom the multidimensional nature of the universe. Where to be moment to moment will change as the probabilities fluctuate as well. The more supporting energy an action or event has, the more likely it will occur in multiple realities simultaneously. If you think the same thoughts and do the same thing every Tuesday evening, then your probabilities increase for that action. This is basic odds, mind you, but it does work much like this. The energy of collective consciousness then increases or decreases the odds for events occurring. If most of your thoughts are of how unsuccessful you are at something, then you increase the chances that you will fail. We have already gone over the importance of your thoughts and feelings in creating your reality, but it is highly significant if you want to flow with the best probable place and time to be in as well.

Your Intentions and Frequency of Attraction

As we have said, the most important consideration is where do you want to be and when. Without consciousness behind this question, you will go nowhere but where you have already been, and may likely get swept up in the collective trends that exist in your energy field. If your intention is to be somewhere beyond where you were before, in a spiritual sense, then this should be a focus as you decide, or intuit, where you should be on a physical level to best support your highest intentions. Your intentions are obviously the key to getting you to the where and when that is appropriate.

If you want to have random, meaningless sex with a stranger, then you may end up at bars every night in populated areas. However, if your intention is to meet your soul mate, and develop a divine spiritual connection that changes the world, then you will have to fine tune your intuition as to where to be and when. It may be in a bar, or it may be on a mountain top in Hawaii. Clearly, the level of the desire will affect the level of awareness required as well. But, even a search for random sex will benefit from sensitivity to the flow of energy around you. Not that we are recommending this as the best use of your time and connection.

As your sensitivity does increase, it will be even more important for you to be aware of where your consciousness resides when you get impulses, or sense where to be. You will be attracted to what is on the level of your projected frequency. If your thoughts are on the best place to be for financial success, you may end up in the right place at the right time to make money, but you may lose everything that you forgot to think about, like love and creative fulfillment. When you rethink with the bigger picture in mind, your sense of where to be may completely change. Consciousness is everything, and awareness of this is vital for being in the place and time that is most conducive to your healthy transition.

We can see that there are physical places in your world that you likely do not want to be when the energy increases during the transition phase. The energy fields surrounding these areas are already wrought with pain and suffering and have high probability of amplifying this in most dimensions. There are also areas that will have much stronger energy than others, and also have a stronger magnetic pull. Some of these areas have the possibility of going very low or very high, depending on the consciousness that develops over the next several years. We can feel the options wavering in these areas, and see the drastically different alternate outcomes.

As you can imagine, then, your sensitivity to the energy of an area will be important for your movement as well. If your thoughts are in a destructive place, you will be attracted to the physical places that are increasing in destruction. This may be what your soul needs to grow. You may not have been able to make soul changes on a conscious level, and may need to be drawn into a particular drama. This drama may be exactly what you require to make the leap in the next era. However, it may also bring you down into further agony and darkness.

We would love to tell you places to avoid, but this would be completely irresponsible of us, and could unduly influence your outcomes. You must discover for yourselves what energy is appropriate for your individual, and group, growth. The process of sensing this is a part of your evolution. If we were to tell you all the answers, you would not be developing the skills needed to navigate in a world of higher vibration. Mind you, within all geographies of the world there exist varying degrees and layers of darkness, and potential for brightness. The nature and quality of the energy is different in each area, depending on the history contained in its astral field.

Each of you must decide, with awareness, what type and quality of energy you wish to be connected to when the dynamics accelerate. In any given location, there are particular signatures of lower and higher vibrations. If you allow yourselves, you can feel and see the degrees, and how they relate or do not. There may be completely opposing sides to a particular dynamic, or the place may have only produced a negative, denser frequency, related to an event or judgment. Then again, there may exist another high frequency, but only for a particular quality.

For example, a place could have a strong karma of prejudice, yet have an amazing ability to produce tranquility. Each quality developed separately, and possibly the opposite frequency for those separate natures was never promoted in the population. Then again, another location could have both sides of a value, such as the ability to be extremely prejudiced and completely accepting of differences, within the same energy field. Then, individuals within this community have more opportunity to connect to the higher view, and draw energy away from the denser view.

Listening to Your Soul Guidance

There are those of you who have been preparing for this transitional time throughout human history so that you can assist others in certain places. And so, you will be drawn to locations for the purpose of elevating souls around you. Careful soul listening skills will be helpful in your assessment of where to be and when, not only for yourself, but for those that need your assistance. You may feel inexplicably drawn to a particular geography, often without warning or any previously conceived notions or interest in the area. Opportunities may come out of the blue, that your soul has been attracting, to force you to think of something entirely out of your usual box. Often these are important leads in discovering your direction as time accelerates. Remember, your intentions will determine the nature of the lures that come your way. If you keep your attention focused on the advancement of your soul and soul-mates, then you will attract the invitations that coincide with what is most appropriate for your connection.

Meditate on your highest motivation and ask for guidance from higher vibrational beings as to where you will benefit the world the most, and then be open to the signs. Feel the vibration of the signs that come to you. If you feel lit up when you contemplate the move, then it will likely be a good one. Some of you will be moving often, to affect many people and places around the globe, while others will have the greatest impact by concentrating their energy on one particular place, and group of souls.

When you feel unsettled, pay attention. Firstly, take a look at what you may be avoiding in the place where you are currently. If you are getting a sensation to flee out of fear or some other egocentric desire, then you may want to stay put and confront that issue before you jump into a repeat of the same personal difficulty with different scenery. In other words, make sure you are not running away from yourself, which

134

of course does not work.

If your feeling of restlessness is an aching in your soul for fulfillment of your purpose, then listen. Often the urges appear contrary to what you rationally think is best for you, or is most comfortable. Intuitively, you may know that the hard way will reap the most reward. In that case, you should be able to glimpse the light filled outcome that is possible if you take up the challenge. If the thought makes you feel dismal, then you are not ready for the challenge. Your soul does know. You must learn to listen.

Learning to weed out the self-centered thoughts that are temporarily gratifying or self-deprecating is an art form that you must develop. The more you have prepared by removing the garbled garbage of your mind, the more you can hear your soul, and messages from higher frequency beings that can assist you. When you can recognize the difference between thoughts of personal gain or destruction, and confront them as such, they will begin to significantly lose their power to govern your movements. Suddenly, you will not need to listen to those controlling thoughts as you will be aware of their design of confusion. That is how you develop your soul listening skills. This sensitivity will allow you to make decisions that are best for your evolution. The art of getting outside of yourself will allow you to see where you should be and when.

No matter what happens on your planet, and what you attract to yourself, you always have free will, and will need to choose alternatives. Even if you seemingly do nothing, you are making a choice. The more tuned in you are to the desires of your soul, the more likely that you will make a choice with profound and lasting impact. It may not be trumpets sounding in your head that demand your attention. In many cases it will be the subtle signal that pops in from left field and literally feels like a spark. If you are open to the warmth and light of that spark, you can follow the path down the well lit road. If you dismiss the message, your soul may keep trying, or push you into a more direct or drastic route. We suggest you expand your awareness to the small moments and quiet hints that lead to the more enlightened path. Miracles will begin to happen for those that prepare and are able to be where they are most needed.

Lower E-Motions as Signals to Reassess

If you find that you are riddled with doubt and uncertainty, this is a powerful message to slow down and reassess where you are mentally and physically. If you find yourself being tremendously indecisive, fretting with a sense of despair, or lacking motivation to do what is in front of you, then this is a sign to stop and look at where your consciousness is within your daily life. Such feelings are a wake up call from your soul, telling you to reboot. That means you must turn off the computer completely and restart. If your programs are freezing and failing, there may be a bug in the system. You need to find the bug and annihilate it before your computer will function at its best capacity again. You may even need to entirely reformat your drive and start from a clean slate. Or, you may have to purchase new antivirus software, or updated programs, to make your computer efficient again. Rebooting yourself is a similar undertaking. And, if you feel stuck and unsure in your life, then you may need a change of various layers.

If you have been preparing for some while, you will already be ridding yourself of viruses and trying new programs. If you are still confused, then you have not found the culprit, or your system is too overloaded. Again, time to reboot. Spend some time cleaning your hard drive. Get rid of the old files and prepare some space for something new. Listen to what makes your system hum quietly, making best use of its RAM. Be patient with your programs, and wait for a response before charging ahead to open up another page before the system is ready. When the drives are clear and clean, and the best programs are in place, then your system will run smoothly, and the jobs you give it will be done well. It is up to you to pay attention to your machine. If you can get to the core and reprogram the source code, your soul will be running the show, and not the tangle of superficial impulses that run by you daily.

In a very real way, you are much like your computer. You have been programmed, and you get jammed and freeze. Rebooting your life may not be as easy as pushing a button, but if you are open and aware that you need it, you will eventually find the buttons to push, and will be on your way to recovery. When you shut down the chatter, you can finally hear your soul. You need to listen so that you know what button to turn on. It may be a new you, in a new place, with new people that supports a drastic change. Not running away, but reforming. You must pause in the shut down mode to find out where to go. If you rush into turning on the old computer, it may end up exhibiting the same exact problems as before, and the same goes for your soul. Slow yourself down and take time to assess where you are, and where your soul wants and needs to be to take itself to the next stage of development.

The approach you need to take may end up being something that is right in front of you that you have been avoiding out of fear, laziness, or from some other self-centered emotion. Believe it or not, your soul does know where to be and when. When you shut down the constant barrage of noise, you can hear what you are trying to tell yourself within whatever situation you have put yourself in. When you allow your soul to be heard, you will make choices that can change the world. And again, sometimes it is the very small choices that change frequencies beyond what you thought possible, and can have exponential impact. Sometimes changing one small piece of code in your human system can alter the quality and productivity of your life program. The one-liner change may be exactly what you needed to transform yourself and help others.

When the time is right, you will know where to be if you are preparing yourself for your transition. You will be guided by your soul and higher vibrational beings. Look for the light within and around you, and trust it to show you the path. If you cannot feel or see the light, continue to reboot until you are cleansed of interferences. Even though the world may appear to be falling apart around you, there is light force to be seen if you can bring yourself to rise above the pain, and feel the greater forces at work. If you are suffering, gather your strength to rise above the ego that has you captivated. Every moment that you switch from being the victim of your tragedy to having an understanding of the meaning exhibited within it, you have gained a measure of connection. In those moments, you can seek the clarity to envision your future, and your place, here and now.

Ask for Assistance, Listen, and Note Synchronicities

Keep your intentions on making your evolutionary leap and assisting your planet, and meditate in quiet on this whenever you can. Take even a few minutes a day to allow your soul to speak, or show you where to be and when. Trust any images that come to you repeatedly when you are in the right consciousness and asking for assistance. Follow these images and allow your imagination to take you some place. See and hear where it takes you. If you practice this technique of visualization, it can lead you to revelations. Then, look for reinforcements of your visions in your daily life. Take note of the synchronicities. They will be telling you whether you are on the right path or not.

Recognize that you are in a fight for your soul now. The forces that take you down will gain strength as well. If you let yourself fall into the trap, then you can be pulled down into an awful spiral to a place you will not want to be. It will become increasingly important for you to rise above any interference that alters your best intentions. If you are having any trouble, simply ask for help from the source within and around you. All efforts are answered. All questions will be answered if you are patient, and learn to allow your inner vision to be revealed. If you are not willing to listen, then your soul and higher beings will not bother to speak to you.

We recommend you take some time every day for a vision quest of sorts. Allow your mind to be quiet, and use whatever visualization technique works for you to go to a place where you will be able to get answers to your questions. Keep a journal of your experiences and ask for signals that affirm your answers in your daily life. This is a way to practice listening. Eventually, you may begin to see results and will develop a trust in your inner truth. Remember to make a note of the feelings that come up in association with your visions, voices, and synchronicities. Sooner or later, your soul will have a rapport with your brain, body, and emotions. When this occurs, you will become adept at being guided to the best where and when for your intentions.

Maintain Courage and Determination

We are aware that many of you are still confused and uncertain about where you are going and what is happening in the world. It appears to be hopeless at times, and hardship surrounds you. Even if your life is fine and you have what you need to survive, you may still feel a pit in your gut that feels as though it will not ever be filled. But, it will be filled if you keep on trudging ahead, despite what the world appears to be and what you feel in your aching belly. It is your willingness to keep going when the going gets tough that will get you to where you need to be.

You must not give up because you are down one day and up the next. If you give up because the people around you do not seem to get it, they will not ever get it. They may not see it the way you do. But, if you keep moving, eventually the energy of all those like you, who also keep moving, will be powerful. The change will come and you will see and hear where to be and when. Now may not be the moment. But, the moment is near and you will see it if you push ahead, no matter what occurs in your mind and environment, and within your governments. Keep forging ahead as if it is all up to you, because it is all up to each of you that has the ache in your belly for a better world and an evolved human consciousness. This is important, because there will be times when you are tested. Such are the moments when you cannot stop.

Do not ever give up on trying to see where you should be. You can develop this clairvoyance if you continue to believe and push yourself. Remember that others who are pushing are adding to your energy, and vice versa. You are not alone. If this was easy you would already be there. You are about to make a leap as significant as the discovery of fire, and your use of tools and language. Yes, it happened a little at a time, but never without the constant pushing of the envelope by those that believed it possible for humans to be more than they are.

Being in the right place at the right time means you are following the ebbs of light, and are tuning into energy fields. This skill is at the heart of your new experience as a self-aware soul. And, while you may feel as though you are in the dark about where to be right now, that will change if you continue to look for the glimmers in the little moments of your life.

Recognizing Who to Be With and When

When you do finally walk down the path of purpose and see the way lit ahead of you, your life will be filled with a sense of fulfillment and meaning. You will know that you are moving as you should be, and encountering those that you can assist, and that will further your aims.

Your goal is to shine your inner light upon the world and help others do the same.

The well lit path is filled with the joy of discovery, and of sharing the true essence of your soul. There is nothing more rewarding than that. Once you are in this place of consciousness, you can see where to go and when, with a delightful clarity. When you get on the wave length, you will be drawn to others on the path and they will be drawn to you, even from afar. As you shed your dark robes, those on the path can see the real you. You may find that you must leave behind those that are still covered in their own robes of deceit. You will no longer gain from their company. And, unless they are driven to remove their boundaries, they will barely see you, because your light will almost literally blind them.

It is okay to disassociate with those that are not seeking. You cannot help them until they wish to be helped, and they may need a very different frequency than you can offer. When they are ready, they will find the path that will inspire them. It is not for you to be everyone's savior nor is there one answer as to how to develop your consciousness. Again, the fundamental laws of the universe apply to all, but the way to comprehend them can vary tremendously, which does not make one way more right than another. Also, it may be in your best interest to be with those souls that can move you to your next level, which may mean giving up on what and who is holding you back from new associations. An important part of knowing where to be and when is knowing who to be with and when. There will always be individuals on a slower plane of development in your sphere of being. But, it can be hard to find those that are farther along and can guide you to be closer to your God Source.

Furthermore, there are likely people in your life that are holding you back, and keeping you from being your best self. Open your eyes and observe your surroundings. Who are you allowing in your sphere of reality and why? Are they benefiting you or vice versa? What is the level of growth inherent in your dealings? If you sense a karmic debt, then seek to resolve it and either move on to the next tier with this person, or let them go. Knowing when to let go of relationships that are bringing you down, or keeping you stagnant, is as important as sensing where to be in terms of a physical location. Where to be is also a matter of who to be with.

The souls around you are a significant aspect of your environment. You can actually change your entire "where" within the same geographic location by changing the "who" that is in it. Seek those that challenge you out of love, and who see your spark. Believe that you deserve to be with others that recognize your soul's truth. Look for the truth in others, as they will appreciate it as well. Be among those that bring out the light force within each other and are not afraid to do what it takes to get to the core of life's purpose.

So, the big question of where to be and when is a matter of who and what you want to be and when, and how much conscious awareness you intend to put into being in the right place at the right time, with the right souls. Contemplate these considerations as you move through your days and nights, as each insight and action will lead you to your intentions. Keep your intentions strong and unwavering. When you are down, remember to be clear and certain, and keep your vision even within those moments of doubt. Have the doubt, observe it, but come back to your true intention and seek it always. Eventually, the doubts will subside and the path will become clearer and clearer.

Soon you will want only to go, and be where and when, you were meant to be. As you do this, you will be seeing with new eyes, the eyes of your soul. When you glimpse the path and desire to follow only the light, you will be ready to create with your soul mind's eye, which is an exciting way to create, and is at a level closer to the source of creation itself.

Chapter 9

Creation With Your Soul Mind's Eye

*T*he delight of your transition to the next dimensional octave will be your discovery of your ability to create your reality with your soul mind's eye. Instead of creating haphazardly with your self-interested ego, you will be focusing your manifestations on the deep desires of your soul. Your soul will advance to see everything in your environment with an increased depth and meaning. Soul vision is like having an additional mind with enhanced sensory perceptions. In other words, everything you encounter will be seen with more depth, layers, and mental acumen, and therefore your resulting creations will contain greater richness and spirit. This is where you are headed with your soul evolution and is something to look fondly forward to. We wish to offer you a glimpse of what this creativity entails, and prepare you for what to expect as you become more adept in soul level creation.

A Leap in Your Ability as a Creator

Once you have cleared away the cobwebs of your current mode of thinking and have opened the doors to conscious awareness, you can begin creating with spirit. Presuming you are at the level of seeing through the limitations of your physical realm, are going beyond preconceived notions of who you are, and are following synchronistic paths of light, then you are ready to begin playing in your new world view. If you are at this level, then you will indeed be lighthearted enough to realize the playfulness of creation.

As you develop, your soul will feel like a kid in a candy shop, entranced by all the colors, sweet smells, and mouth watering possibilities. When you can see light filled options and make decisions that are truly fulfilling for your soul, then you will want to play. And much like a child, you will be learning in every moment. You will make mistakes, learn from them, and be better next time. You will not be an expert at soul mind's eye play over night. It should be a joyful learning experience even when you fail, as you will quickly see that at this level of consciousness you can switch directions rapidly. This is why you are being so well tested where you are now, or were, as the case may be. Learning to change your consciousness is more important when your thoughts are super-conductive.

If you are truly in touch with your soul, which you will be if you are making the transition, you have an internal guidance system and insight that is not limited by your physical reality. Your body and brain, and the physical objects around you, are no longer a limitation in the same way they once were. With your soul mind's eye, you can learn to manipulate matter on an elemental level. By tuning in with the sameness of the underlying consciousness and at the same time appreciating the uniqueness of such, you will be able to move in a synchronistic ballet with the elements in your sphere of existence. As profound as this may seem, it is the destiny of your soul to create on this level. We did say you are taking a giant leap.

Collective Creation at a Molecular Level

Your soul mind's eye can communicate with the consciousness of everything in its environment, and collectively create with it. This is connection creation. This is connection on a deep molecular level of consciousness communication and interdependence. A give and take balance is formed that causes a dance of creation with the interest of the whole in mind. When your soul barriers are removed, you can see the universe with this perspective. If you can see with this enhanced vision, then you can create with it.

Your sciences are delving into an understanding of the power in the manipulation of the molecular level, but are still missing the important factor that consciousness plays in this dynamic. Science can learn to force changes on a physical level, but consciousness will always play a part, whether the scientist is aware of it or not. Becoming aware of that fact is evolution. Using consciousness to move consciousness is creation with the soul mind's eye. Such consciousness can only be seen with the soul. Otherwise, the level of molecular consciousness is covered in darkness and is invisible, or appears as the illusion that the underlying consciousness created. The world without soul vision is an illusion. Or rather, we should say, is a world that is unaware that it is an illusion.

With your soul mind's eye vision you will learn to create with precision, collectively with the elements of consciousness inherent in every atom. As you become aware of the consciousness in every bit of energy that makes up your universe, you will learn to become attuned to underlying frequencies and vibrate in tune with them so that your creations are effective cooperatively. In other words, you will learn to create a vision in cooperation with the units of consciousness that make up all matter in your universe. This can be done on an individual level, but more significantly on a group and global level.

As you are able to dissolve the seeming separation that exists between souls, you will be able to work in groups of consciousness that are of a similar vibration and interest to you. Just as you already do today when you join minds to create, you will be able to do so with a deeper level of cooperation and power. Instead of arguing or stealing energy from one another for recognition or attention in a group, you will complement each other with increased energy. When you are each in tune with your soul, you are in tune with the source of molecular energy. You, therefore, have an unlimited supply to draw from and have no need to be competing for energy. Instead, you will desire to share and invigorate each other's connection with fresh and enlightened perspectives that increase the entire group's productivity.

Seven Soul Perceptions to Acknowledge

The ability to sense with your soul perceptions will evolve with practice and at first involves a great deal of trust in senses that you previously would not have paid attention to, and therefore did not develop for the most part. We would like to outline some of the sensations so you may recognize them. We encourage you to take note of when you sense in these ways, no matter what level of development you are at presently. For some of you these may already be developed, while others may be merely on the verge of trusting, or just noticing such sensations. When you feel or notice the following, acknowledge it. If you can, allow yourself to flow with the sensation to see where it may lead. Any or all such perceptions may be your soul speaking to you. Of course, you may think you are going crazy. But, you will feel and be quite sane.

1. **Visual anomalies**, such as colors or clouds in your vision, brightness around people or objects, shapes appearing in your line of sight, and blurry or tunnel vision. These can be signs of connection with another dimensional perception or indicate a path or topic to be pursued.

2. **Out of the ordinary sounds**, such as ringing or voices in your

146

head, especially sudden and unexpected messages that seem illogical and random. Sounds in your ears can be a way of getting your attention. Take heed of what is happening when you experience this, as well as any peculiar messages that seem as if completely out of the blue. Your soul and guides will purposely catch you off guard so that a message stands out from the usual noise of your brain.

3. **Buoyant sensations** that draw you to a place or situation inexplicably. This would be a light feeling, not heavy and burdensome, but free and floating. If there is a heavy sensation, stay away, but if it is buoyant go with it.

4. **Repeated visions and imaginations** of people and situations. Allow yourself to follow a vision mentally to see where it takes you. Often images that repeat have some special meaning for you, or are trying to tell you something important.

5. **Unpleasant feelings in your gut.** These sensations can be warnings of lower energy interference and call for mental and spiritual protection. Feelings of nausea or headache or other unexplained physical sensation in a place, or around certain people, can be warnings that negative frequencies are intruding, or that you are overloading your circuitry and need to step away.

6. **Tingly surge of energy** in your body, often in the hands or top of the head, is an indication of connection to source light. Take note at these times of what you are thinking, doing, or associating with. It will always mean you are on a connected frequency.

7. **Intuitions about people, places, or events.** Trust the odd and seemingly unknowable. At least listen and observe. You will never give your soul a chance if you do not listen to what you know that appears to be unknowable.

We assure you that if you begin to give some attention to these out of the ordinary perceptions, you will be encouraging your soul to communicate on another level. And, the sensations will increase and become a valuable guide by which to navigate. The more aware you become of your soul and its connection to various frequencies, the more likely you will create with power and intention. When your soul is placed in charge, you will be in the flow of light transference. This energetic flow is where creativity can flourish. When you put your soul in the driver's seat, you will be able to create without the preconceived limits that you previously had blocking your way.

When you follow the sensations described above, you will be on your way to allowing your soul to take charge. You can then fly through blockades on a personal, and global, level. As you imagine the boundaries dissolving between you and objects in space and time, your soul is set free to create something new. Imagine your present life without all the blocks you have placed upon it. What would you create? Before you can be or create anything new, you must be able to imagine and feel the new reality. And, you must trust the sensations that lead you to become more than you are. Nothing was ever created without first being imagined and tested. Allow yourself the freedom to embark on a journey of soul discovery as you never thought possible before. Stretch beyond your fears, insecurities, and doubts, and follow the signs of your soul. Use your new connections and ultra sensory perceptions to assist you in creating a new soul mind's eye vision for your future, starting now.

The Lightness and Flow of Soul Creation

Take your visions a step at a time. You will not be able to break all the collective limitations with your individual thoughts. It starts with each person's small steps towards stretching their views and builds one upon the other. What do you suppose your next step toward soul creation would be?

You can go from being a self-aware soul, to one that follows the flow of creative light, to ultimately being a soul that creates reality from the heart of source energy. Again, without the desire to evolve, you cannot move forward. Raise your desire to be a self-aware soul that creates with your soul mind's eye for the sake of evolving your consciousness, and that of your collective planetary soul. Accept your chosen destiny to play a part in this amazing challenge to take a huge leap for universal light. The opportunity exists now, and depends on each of you.

If you are truly fed up with the horrors and lack of forward movement exhibited by humanity, then you have a chance to be a part of real change in human consciousness today. We recognize that the leap can seem daunting, given that you have lived for millennia with such limited perceptions and have a very hard time imagining a world beyond this one. But, those of you alive today have chosen to assist with raising the bar on your future potential, which requires thinking outside of everything you previously thought possible.

We are here to reassure you that what you can imagine is possible, and to assist those that try to create with their soul's intentions in being successful. Every effort, again, will be given a boost of energy from our dimension. Take time every day, even if just a few seconds, to imagine what your best soul governed life would look and feel like. Allow your imagination to soar a little. Where might you be and who might you be with? What will you act like and how will your soul follow its light? What will you be able to do if you are flowing from your source energy connection? What would life feel and look like in a world that was created in collaboration with like-minded souls? What boundaries would be dissolved in this new world?

When you are creating with your soul, you will be able to flow easily from imagination to creation in your physical world. You will be less fettered by what you now perceive as limitations of matter and time. Materialization will happen more quickly and effortlessly when you are creating from your soul. You will recognize easily that the path is beneficial when you, and those around you, are feeling the positive sensations as described previously. The sensations will become more acute as you flow in a given direction of light.

Eventually, you will find yourself moving so freely that it hardly feels like you are making an effort. Creation becomes like a flowing stream when you are able to follow a higher vibrational path. What used to seem difficult will come with focused intention and little physical effort. You will find that your frequency becomes aligned with others, and your mutual intentions amplify and accelerate materialization as well. The world you are in will, in essence, feel less material. Hence the physicality of your world will feel much less dense, as you will be connecting to the cause consciousness of the material world, instead of the effects that it produces. You will be working with the vibration of creation, instead of the picture or result created by the vibration. When you sense and create with your soul you are able to see, be, and move more freely through vibrations, with an understanding and acceptance of the illusory nature of the universe you exist within. In other words, objects and events become much more malleable and fluid.

Living in a world driven by soul consciousness will feel elevated from what you experienced in a denser reality. When you are on a soul creation level, the negativity you experienced in your everyday life and thoughts will no longer haunt your mind. Therefore, you will feel lighter and brighter. The weight of your thoughts will not be so heavy. Your emotional being will rise above the once draining state that ruled your life. When such burdens of your ego consciousness are dissolved, you will be able to connect with the inner essence of your soul, and follow its conceptions in your creation of life in every moment.

Your soul has the capacity to see and feel much more than it does when it is constantly bombarded with your negativity and insecurities, and the low vibrational beings that are attracted to you as a result of them. When your soul is uncovered from that darkness, you will be able to feel and intuit what and how to create with deeper intention and connection. Enjoy the fleeting moments of weightlessness you feel as you shed yourself of your inner demons. This feeling will increase as you continue to connect with your soul, and begin creating a new you.

Creating a New Self That Reflects Your Inner Light

Your first creation with your soul mind's eye will be a new you that is unfettered by previous layers of muck. When your self-aware soul realizes that it is in a whole new realm of possibility and understanding, it will want to create an outward reality that reflects its newly found inner essence. The moments when this realization occurs, and they will increase as the layers come off, will be revolutionary and truly liberating for your soul. Even more exciting will be the sensation that the creation of a new image that is a true reflection of your light, is inevitable.

It is one step to take off the coat of armor you donned, and another to replace it with a cloak of many colors and sparks that radiate your inner core. This time it is not a cover up, but rather a continued revealing or accentuation of what is uncovered. It is as if you are now given the chance to polish your diamond and share its beauty with the world. You will be recreating the you that is at your core, and continually discovering its many facets, and how they relate with and assist the facets of others.

The process of revealing the new you will be wonderfully creative and much more fulfilling than the struggles of letting go that you have dealt with to get here. The challenges will not disappear, but the way in which you approach them will be so markedly different that they will seem as mere bumps in the road and will often be seen as stimulators instead of hurdles. What was once agonizing could actually become exciting. When you see the situation through your soul lens it will take an entirely different shape, as it is seen without the filters that previously destroyed the poetry of the event.

Your soul will be able to delight in the challenges, and create something interesting and amusing from what was once seen as awful. You will, instead, be filled with awe as you see each event. As your soul shines, it will see and appreciate the fine nuances and incredible beauty in creation that were previously overlooked among the shadows of darkness. Indeed, there is so much you are missing in your creative endeavors that, once revealed, will give you the inspiration to be and do more.

If you are still in a state of mind where you feel the weight of life and emotions on your shoulders, and feel as if you are completely stuck in the mud of a dreary existence, take heart in knowing that this is a sign that you are ready to shed that baggage. If you are feeling particularly heavy hearted and confused, understand that this is your soul telling you it is time to let go of the rest of your armor, and free your true self from bondage.

If you are already letting go, you will start to have more of the sensations of weightlessness. You are poking holes in your shield and letting light shine forth, which is allowing you to see your next level of opportunity. Still others are working on polishing and revealing abilities, and qualities of their spirit. Wherever you are now, upon reading this, know that you are on your way to revealing your true soul, and creating a new experience of life. Once you break free, creation becomes an elevated challenge in a completely new and exciting reality.

With your soul mind's eye you will be discovering your new abilities and recreating yourself to match those talents as you go. Your enhanced perception will inspire a different motivation for your new self that you had previously based on your material desires and needs. Desires will be elevated to greater consciousness, yet your needs will be simpler in regard to self interest. In other words, you may find yourself more content with appreciating the petals of a flower over a new car stereo. Although, even the mundane modern world will take on a new flavor as experienced by the new self you are actively creating. Generally, you will find that environments that do not suit your frequency will not be tolerable with your new sensitivity, and you will therefore seek situations that help you to flourish. As you create yourself, you will be creating your environment alongside others of like vibration.

Synchronizing and Recharging with Source Energy

No matter where you are in your development and self discovery, you can be formulating yourself in preparation for when you will be doing so with increasing ease. At first, you will feel as though you are forcing yourself to imagine or do actions that are difficult or seem unreal. As you overcome your burdens and free your mind, your soul will take more control and the process will get easier. You will basically be flexing your soul's muscles and building them up to handle more activity, but on a spiritual plane, which is less dependent on direct physical manipulations. Or rather, the manipulation will be done largely on an energy level so that the physical will go smoothly.

Whereas you may be in a place now where you do not see how you can be all that you might imagine your ideal self to be, there will be a time when you will more easily become exactly what you imagine. Your soul is able to create in sync with the universal energy that it is a part of, and so all the forces in tune with its frequency will work in unison with its creation, as opposed to the manner in which your ego tries to push against forces.

Your soul is able to literally tune itself to surrounding energy. By sharing its light with other aspects of creation, it can move easily. There becomes a sharing of energy so that all elements in a given environment or situation are fueling one another, and all can flow with ease to a mutually beneficial aim. As you discover your soul's potential, you will also see its ability to create in synchronicity with the rest of the universe. In that case, the energy in your atmosphere goes from one characterized by the grabbing of limited energy resources for the self, to that of a balanced receiving and sharing of unlimited source energy.

When there is balance and frequency synchronizing on a fundamental molecular level, the source of never ending fuel is tapped. It continues to flow, as long as the balance and frequency match exists. Your body and soul run out of energy when you are in the mentality of stealing from the limited resources of others. When in this frequency of consciousness, the connection to the unlimited source is cut off and a world of fighting for resources is created. A balanced state of consciousness will end all need for greed and lack.

Your soul knows that its source of energy is everlasting, and that its consciousness does not die in the way your physical body does. Your soul is aware that there is no need to steal energy from others, and that if it lets go of that need, it will find it has unlimited energy to share. Once you are able to tune into what your soul knows, and let go of the fears that there will not be enough to keep you sustained if you do not grab your share of the loot, then you will begin to find your battery continually recharged. When you continually recharge, you will find you can follow your bliss and truly become, and share, who you were meant to be. You will find yourself sharing what you were meant to share in this world, and be forever enriched as a result.

We are aware that it sounds neatly simplistic, and that letting go of what you have been holding onto for many lifetimes is a process that takes time. You have been working on letting go for millennia and are nearing the end of that long, arduous process, as viewed from a perspective of time. The era you live in is offering an opportunity to let go of everything that came before, and that would, in the future, stop you from evolving to a soul level creator.

If you wish to jump octaves, then a leap is required. You must be willing to jump into what appears as an abyss of the unknown. If you are willing to turn on your own light, you will be able to see that there is an endlessly creative world to discover in that abyss. It only appears dark and unfamiliar because you are hiding in your own shadows, and are afraid of your own self-created demons. When you realize that the demons do not even exist, you can turn on your lights and one by one see a brighter future. With your soul turned on, you will see that you can create the road ahead with your soul mind's eye. You will see that the abyss is actually a canvas of color that you can draw upon with your creative brush of consciousness.

Revealing your soul, and creating a new self, based on its multi-faceted nature, is the first step in the creation of a new world for your species and planet. Each newly revealed and developed soul adds to the next, and to the creation of a vastly expanded existence. As each soul evolves, and creates from core energy, so does the environment in which it wanders. The elevation of your soul shines light on the whole picture. Soon you will all be seeing the bigger dimensional experience, and creating in unison will become amazing. If you are still hiding, then you may see others as though they are out to get what is yours. You may also think that what the other is doing is not important, unless it affects you personally. The world is perceived this way only when the soul vision is covered. All such interpretations that are based on the coat of delusion will disappear once the soul creates a new material version of itself. When you are all seeing beyond the cloaks and take the disguises off, everything and everyone will be seen and felt anew. You will then be able to elevate each other instead of stealing from one another energetically. It is important that you each focus on elevating your own soul perception, as global elevation will follow.

Following the Soul's Path of Least Resistance

In summary, in order to create with your soul mind's eye, you must become a self-aware soul by shedding your egocentric blockages to reveal the true light of your essence, and then follow its messages and perceptions. In doing so, you will be able to recreate a self that reflects your source energy and adds to creation with inner purpose. The art of listening to your soul's guidance will aid you in creating a new self in a new world. Tapping into this inner power requires you to let go of all the fears and beliefs that prevent you from envisioning a new self with enhanced perceptions. Once your soul follows the enlightened path, its ability to create with conscious intention will continue to develop in connection with a universal consciousness. Matter will be manipulated on an atomic level by connecting to the elemental consciousness that is the fundamental building material of All That Is. Knowledge and advancements will be possible by connecting on an energy level with the building blocks of creation, through the use of conscious awareness.

Within your soul's chosen sphere of specialty, you will be able to impact your world in ways you never thought possible. Flowing through creation at the soul consciousness level allows for accelerated manifestations. Thus, a considerable amount of focus will be necessary to have the desired results. If individual desires are out of sync, and go astray from the intentions of the whole, then adjustments will need to be made rapidly, by shifting or fine tuning the vision. Again, the more connected the intentions are to a finer vibration that benefits the whole, the faster they will materialize. Generally, the higher the vibrational frequency, the more unified the soul group will be, and consequently the more rapid the results.

The less resistance you feel in your consciousness, the easier will be the flow of your creation. When resistance is felt, it is usually lower frequency interference. When you feel resistance in your personal life, then you are fighting an aspect of your ego. In order to fight it, you need to resist its inclinations, and find the path where your soul knows to go. There, it will have no need for resistance, as it will be flowing in a synchronized wave. There is an irony in the fact that you must resist when you feel resistance, so that you have no resistance to resist. Only your soul can find the path of least resistance that will not create a resistance that ultimately blocks the intended creation. Your ego will sometimes follow a path that it thinks is the one of least resistance, only to find that you have actually created more resistance in the long run. Again, your soul will come from an intention for connection to your source, whereas your ego will come from a desire for personal gain that is superficial and temporary.

When we speak of resistance, we mean emotional and mental obstacles and hindrances that affect our decisions and actions. The soul will be able to remove any such hindrances and see a clear path. Whereas the self you have created based on lower frequency desires, will fight against obstacles and go nowhere. The tools that the ego uses are dense emotions such as fear, envy, self pity, doubt and despair. All of these densities of energy create resistance in obtaining any higher intentions, and must be resisted. When they are resisted, the resistance on your path disappears and your soul can freely create. Therefore, removing such self-absorbed behaviors is the only way your soul can gain control. As long as you are governed by lower emotions and selfish desires, your soul cannot flourish. If you sense these frequencies in your imaginations or intentions, you are not creating with your soul mind's eye.

Whenever you feel friction in your life, you are not connected to your soul's light. All lower emotions that cause tensions are of an egocentric frequency. They cover your light, and do not allow you to see the truth. Your soul will have a different consciousness about the same event, and therefore will not experience the same emotional reaction. Instead, it will have the awareness to go beyond the illusion and find the gem to be extracted. The gem will not be found by seeking what is in a situation to satisfy oneself, but will be found by searching for what connects one to light, and how that can be expanded. Clearly, without developing soul awareness and sensitivity, creation with the soul mind's eye could not exist. One must be able to shed the darkness to be able to see and create from the motivation for connection to a higher vibration, and the expansion thereof.

Replace Your Draining Ego View With Abundant Soul Vision

Seeing through the soul's lens will be unfamiliar at first, and will therefore be challenging for you to trust, until the new knowing is tested and accepted. Expect this to be the case. Your ego mind will not let go all at once. It is a process, and rightly so. If you were to lose the ego self that you have built through your life, and before, all at once, you would go insane. You must lose it slowly, and replace it with the vision your soul creates. One way of seeing must replace another. If you have not attempted to develop your soul mind's eye and suddenly lose your ego, you would not understand your true self, and what you are capable of, and you would feel lost.

Your developed soul vision allows you to see more of your universe, and gives you the opportunity to recreate your life and surroundings according to a much expanded perspective. Give yourself time for this transition from one type of awareness to another. Your ego self has served you on many levels in dealing with your evolution as a species to this point. It has allowed you to be self-aware on a particular level. Now it is time to expound upon that awareness and create an image that reflects the heart of your existence, synchronized with the life force itself.

It will benefit you to continually challenge yourself to look beyond your fears and insecurities, as much of your ego comes from those concepts, and free your soul to take a fresh view of everything that you are and do. Check with your soul, in every decision you make, for wisdom that your outer shell may be hiding from you. What is the outer picture you are afraid to let go of? What does the inner you really cherish and desire? Recreating your life around your soul's innermost desire for evolution will be a rewarding and invigorating experience, when you are on a connected track. If you are off the track, you will feel confused and fearful.

When you let go, you will feel complete freedom of expression, without limitation. However, you may still be haunted by that rational side which wants to talk you out of doing or being, based on what it still believes may cause you harm. The rational aspect will tell you that you will end up starving, homeless, and unloved if you follow your heart. What a strong deterrent that can be. However, your soul has the ability to completely let go of these fears, and have utter certainty that it will be taken care of and will shine brightly if it follows that path of light which leads you to inner joy. And it will be correct. Your life will be far richer when your soul is in charge of creating on a level that is deeply rewarding beyond what you have been programmed to think. It is the very act of letting go, despite the fears, that can set you free of them. Again, it is a matter of taking the plunge without yet having fully comprehended the outcome.

As you build on trusting your soul, the leaps will be easier. As you take steps in the direction of the unknown, and have glimpses of what is there, you will become stronger in your desire and ability to let go of your old self. Each leap will give you more stamina to build on the strength of your soul, and to trust its insight. When you realize that not only will you not die if you take the jump, but you will actually feel brighter, you are more likely to risk the next action of your soul. It is a trial and error process to be aware, follow, and discover the results of your soul vision and creation. Actions taken from your soul will make you feel full, while those taken from your ego will make you feel empty. The latter will give you a momentary sense of satisfaction, but inevitably will leave you depleted. When your soul is fulfilled, all those around you will also be filled. If you are acting from your ego, those in your company will feel that you are draining them.

Your soul actions create endless light, while your ego believes it must steal and fight for it. The soul energy is in complete balance of drawing and transmitting energy from the universe, whereas your old self is constantly out of balance, and tries to find its energy from superficial means of which it cannot keep a consistent supply. Your soul can connect to the abundance of the universe, whereas your unconscious ego self must constantly find outside sources of energy to get bits of abundance that are fleeting. It is your whole mission in this life to find your personal connection to the source of universal abundance by shedding all that stops you from knowing what you really are. It is your challenge to find, and become, what you truly are. When you tap into the real you, then you can create with the soul mind's eye and open doors of possibility endlessly.

Once you are on your way to soul creation, your sense of time will be greatly altered, and your world will begin to expand into a multidimensional experience. Your soul is capable of comprehending the multifaceted nature of time and space, and will be able to see beyond the one plane of reality and sequential frame work of time that your consciousness is presently locked into. Your soul mind's eye reaches backward and forward in time and space at will, and can affect the outcomes and experiences of your now. If you feel that you are ready to embark on a journey through the consciousness of time, follow your soul's vision to the next chapter.

Chapter 10

As Today, So Yesterday and Tomorrow

*T*he experience of chronological time is an illusion, based on the limits of perception you experience within your dimension, and is designed to allow you the appreciation of the causes and effects of your creations. Time affords you the opportunity to learn how you influence yourself, and your environment, by what your consciousness dwells and acts upon. As you become more aware of your soul connection with the source of creation, you will gain a new appreciation of the gift and meaning of your experience of time.

Time is Illusory and Malleable

When you realize the illusory nature of time expression, you will be able to manipulate cause and effect by traveling through seemingly chronological time within your present moment. You can alter yesterday and tomorrow by your consciousness today. Your entire personal reality can be changed by traveling in time with your conscious awareness. Your past, future, and now is not set in stone. Something occurring in your consciousness in a future probable reality is influencing your present consciousness, just as your present energy is affecting the expression of your past, and vice versa.

When you hold onto events from your past as if they were real, you are holding yourself in a limited image for today. By re-envisioning your past memories, you can quite literally alter the past event's effect on who you are today and tomorrow.

Generally, your consciousness is always slightly revising your past unconsciously, as you change in the present. However, you can make such revisions with focus and intention. Think of when you have held an emotional grudge against someone from a past pain they caused you. The more you contemplate that event, the more you relive, and worsen, its impact on your present personality. Think of a time when, or imagine that, you forgave a past hurtful act, and were able to send goodwill to the culprit. By forgiving, you infuse positive energy into the past, and rewrite its influence in the present. Imagine taking responsibility for creating the event. By recognizing the lessons in the event, you can take the past situation to an even higher level of impact. The past occurrence can be completely reformulated, from a damaging low vibration, to one that offers life affirming growth.

You may say this is merely changing your perception of the past. But, we are here to inform you that, in fact, you are transforming the actual reality of the past. Firstly, as we have discussed, you must understand that there really was no definitive past in the first place. It did not really exist as you perceive that it did. It is always an alterable illusion created by your present state of consciousness. Since you have a memory of a past, and can ponder a potential future, it appears that you are what you are, based on what you were. You have chosen this type of perception so that you can learn heightened awareness of how one thing influences another. What better way to acknowledge this than to see it unfold in a sequential fashion. However, you should be learning by now that every experience you have is defined by how you perceive it as you attune to the vibration of your senses. Your consciousness creates your experience, now and in the so called past.

Why do you suppose that siblings and parents in the same family can have a completely different memory of an event that they all presumably shared? Some family members may not recall the event at all, while others have vivid memories, or vague ones, that do not match each other. They shared a collective event and then each has continually edited the occurrence as their awareness developed. The event has actually been changed, according to each individual present.

Detectives and psychologists will tell you how easily the human mind can edit a memory, and how varied the individual witness's accounts can be. This is why pinpointing details of past events can be so difficult, and will be fuzzier as your consciousness moves on to other things. Then, of course, those that are peering into the past occurrence will also influence the energy of the so-called history. The very act of trying to determine the details of the past affects the present perception, and rewrites the events. Historians are in fact playing a huge role in creating the events they are studying. The act of observing is an act of creation. One's consciousness will inevitably alter the illusion of whatever reality it pays attention to in the past, present, or future.

One can see how powerful an understanding of this knowledge of the illusory expression of time can be. With such awareness, your current existence and future can be completely reformed with your consciousness right now. Of course, since you are not the only conscious being on the planet, you must contend with the influence of multiple lives in the history of events. The more souls that were involved, the more energy the illusion has in shaping the present consciousness. As the memories fade, and souls move on from your world, the events have less influence. Unless, the consciousness behind the event is reinvigorated with present observations of history. In this way, you can surmise how the recording of, or probing into, the historical past, or a news event, by historians or reporters, etcetera, can have a considerable impact on recreating events, and how they impact your collective consciousness today. In other words, your history is constantly being rewritten, and the present and future is affected by the editing.

Manipulating Past Causes and Effects

The present moment is also constantly editing the probable future, and the probable future is continually editing the past. All this creation is occurring on the level of consciousness, individually and en masse. The most important, and the only real moment for you is now. The rest is affected by your consciousness in every passing moment. You can alter the future by changing your thinking about what you did a few minutes ago. In the future, you may have already changed it and created a different consciousness in your now. It probably appears rather complex and incomprehensible. But, as you become more open to perceiving the malleability of the chronology of cause and effect, you will be more accepting of these notions, and able to navigate accordingly.

If you are already delving into creating a new self, based on your soul mind's eye motives, then you will want to take full advantage of the manipulation of effects in time. You can start recreating a past that is more conducive to your soul's growth now. Firstly, letting go of blame, grudges, and painful memories by forgiving others and yourself is a powerful start. Just as you may replay and rewrite a negative action you did today, you can rewrite events of your childhood by reliving them, accepting the pain they caused, forgiving, taking responsibility for the creation of them, and then envisioning what a better reaction or occurrence would have looked and felt like. You must feel and let go of the pain that has you attached to the past before you can accept an alternative. When you release the pain, and see the lessons in the event, then you can change the past and become a new you in the present moment. The easiest situations to change are those that were largely a result of your perceptions or emotions. Basically, you may be who you are, not because of a physical action, but as a result of the emotions tied to a behavior. The guilt about something you did can affect you more than the action itself.

When your actions have had an impact on other souls, then changing your past is more complicated. You can alter your perception of the actions, which will affect you today, but the negative or positive energy that you transmitted to another may still be alive in other individuals. Therefore, you must include a spiritual amends to those damaged. Just as you alter your consciousness in the past, you can smooth the past of those you hurt by sending them positive energy. You can spend time in your thoughts rewriting their past with a positive frequency of love and forgiveness, that they will feel then and now. Your consciousness regarding the event, and their place in it, will influence their energy through time. The frequency you transmit from your intention about any given event transcends time and place. So what is done is not, in fact, totally done.

When you put your soul in charge, you can alter your history and recreate yourself in time. Collectively, you can recreate events that involved several individuals, or whole nations and cultures. No matter how drastic and permanent you feel that your actions were, they have the potential to be recast in the energy fields of time, so that what you experience in your present moment is forever changed. With your consciousness right now, you can change the reason why you are where you are, allowing an entirely new direction to be initiated, even if your present position depends on other people. It is possible for you to infuse a higher vibrational energy into everything that has happened, and will happen in your life span, and in the lives of those who touch you in some way.

You will probably argue that there are some actions that cannot be changed. For example, if you are responsible for the physical death of another person. You think it is done and cannot be changed. On one level you are correct. The action of physical death has impacted that soul, and those that knew the person, profoundly. Even though in one probability they did not die by your hand, in your path of probable existence they are gone. However, every aspect that surrounds the death of the person can be altered.

What you do with your consciousness about this event can have a major affect on the soul of the deceased, all the loved ones left behind, and your own soul's progress. In fact, by confronting your behavior and emotions, you have the opportunity to reveal an even more profound result than the physical death. The vibration surrounding the death can become enriching for all the souls involved, instead of dark and draining. Mind you, the challenge is greater after the fact. And, it would have been more beneficial to have resisted and repaired the root cause of your motive to kill the person in the first place. However, there still exists a potential to reach into the past and influence the vibration, and how it imprints the souls at play.

An individual can change the energy of an event's inception in time, to the point that he or she is found not guilty in the future, and is completely absolved of a crime, or negative action, that he or she committed and was convicted of, in a previous frame of consciousness. Basically, the vibration of history can be heightened. And, parties linked to its frequency can shift the situation, and actually change the events through altered consciousness.

While it may sound preposterous to you now, as your soul gains clarity, you will feel the shifts in vibrations in the fabric of time, in the past and future, as well as the present. You will sense the illusiveness of the reality that time implies, and will learn to use the ebb of light waves that transcend time. Your soul knows the events that it must repair to gain freedom to be its best version, and to widen its impact.

Observing the past images that lurk in your mind is a place to begin exploring and repairing your soul wounds, and assisting those you have affected. Reviving your soul means revitalizing yourself through time, and rewriting the cause and effect dynamics that keep you in the dark. As you see results from your soul's attempts to re-guide your history, you will understand the power your thoughts and actions have through time. You will see that you can be in the flow in your present moment, so that you do not have to go backwards and forward trying to repair your damages. Instead, you will be traveling in time to continually invigorate your life and the lives of others.

Altering Future Probabilities and Encouraging Outcomes

We have spoken mostly of travel into the past, but you can just as easily explore the future. All the probabilities for the future of humanity, and each individual, can be visited with the soul's vision. And, the odds for future event fruition can be impacted by the type of consciousness you inject into the possibilities. With your soul mind's eye you can envision, and sense, the emotional elements of all events related to your existence and influence their occurrence. The events are actually happening now, from a multi-dimensional perspective. You can tap into the vibration of the event and make an impression on it. You can decide what events you will create, from where you are now, on a personal level. Globally, you can give energy to encourage certain planet wide outcomes. Using your soul consciousness in a directed way to impact the future, is a powerful tool. We are not speaking of merely pondering the future, but rather connecting with the frequency signatures of probable realities, and using your consciousness to change particular outcomes.

This skill of manipulating events through time will be vital as you shift into the next level of density. Your practice of this skill now will influence if and how your kind will make that transition. You can quite literally change your course as a species by changing your past, and infusing your future with light vibration. The more of you there are focusing now on altering your outcome, the more likely that your transition will be smooth and rich.

When you travel in your mind's eye to the probable futures of your planet, you will see various outcomes, some disastrous, some hopeful, and some invigorating. You can infuse added energy to the latter, and diminish the power of the former, by offering forgiveness, comfort, and a higher perspective for the path of most resistance. However, we suggest you spend less time on the path of hardship, and give greater attention to that of your highest potential. You may not create the highest outcome overnight, but you will help to lead the way for the potential in that direction. This can be said for your global probable futures and your personal potential.

Influences of Other Worldly and Future Beings

You are in a tug of war consciousness debate on your planet, not only among your own kind, but also among those that are involved in various capacities with your planet from other worlds and times. There are multiple levels and meanings to this current Earth game that impact many beings beyond those residing there at present. Only a few are given the ability or permission to meddle with your ensuing drama. In some respect, you can rest assured that you will not be tampered with beyond what you can handle, and are given tremendous leeway to make your own impact now, and through the time signatures of your planet. You must make the shift by your own efforts, largely, with a little help from your friends. Some of your friends are influencing you from your evolutionary future, and this has been allowed to some extent. But again, you decide whether or not to accept this assistance. You have complete control, whether you are aware of it or not. Never allow yourselves to be swayed into any reality other than one that ensures your spiritual progress. As you become soul-aware beings, you will be able to discern those that are causing you harm, and those that are guiding your best interest.

When you begin to travel into the future with your conscious soul, you will see associations with other beings on a physical and spiritual level. Only as you advance your awareness will you be able to understand and communicate with these beings, and influence their impression on you through time. You can attract or dispel the appearance of beings in your future. There are probable realities where you interact readily with many beings on a multi-dimensional level, just as there are probable outcomes where you are left completely alone to fend for yourselves. The choice is still yours, although you are headed for the former choice, given the strength of your frequency upon the writing of these words. Your current signature is leading to a deeper interaction with fourth dimensional beings, and with some that reside at higher vibrations. The level to which you do so, and how much control you allow them, is still up in the air.

We strongly suggest that you keep your consciousness firm, yet open and willing. There is much you can learn from off planetary beings and higher vibrational life forms. If you keep your frequency of thought and awareness at your higher end, you will be able to tap into the best of those beings, and avoid entanglements that would bring your species into a submissive role. Remember that, despite the seemingly higher intelligence and technological or spiritual development of these beings, they cannot tamper with your consciousness as long as you do not let them. You have more power in this dynamic than you may be tempted to think. Use your time travel journeys to elevate your associations and envision the best possible relationships for all concerned. Keep your mind in a place of communion, not one of fear and control. What you feel is what you will get. Also, be aware that as long as you can keep your consciousness in resonance with light beings, such as us, that are here to assist your highest potential, you will have a great deal of power behind you each step of the way.

Multi-Dimensional Evolution

By no means is your past and future already set. Even though time and space do not exist the way that you perceive, and instead, everything is happening at once, with all outcomes occurring at the same point, there is still evolution of the whole occurring. This is a difficult concept for you to grasp, as you only see one thing leading to another in order, whereas we see evolution occurring in many time frames at once. There is still evolution in this multi-verse. There is still a progression. However, the progress happens multi-dimensionally and spans millennia all at once.

As you change your past and future, as individuals and en masse, you change the larger dynamic probabilities, and hence evolve inside and outside of time. In other words, if you have ten large probable paths as a species now, you can alter and raise those ten paths by affecting the past and future simultaneously. Hence, what was your lowest among the ten options can become less and less probable until you dissolve the option entirely and create a new, greater option for your world that goes beyond the previous ten. So, you evolve your potentials through the annals of what you perceive as time and space.

All the other beings, and light entities of the universe, are just as motivated to improve as your race is. Since we are all of one universe, or one verse, ultimately, we all affect one another. As we have said, many beings are interested in your evolution because it impacts theirs, in turn. When you raise your bar of advancement, many others will also be raised. Future humans, and beings involved in the creation of your Earth, and the species upon it, are also interested in the advancement of your world. They come back through time to influence your now, in the hopes of infusing your consciousness with seeds of development. There are those that come from a future where this influence can take place purely at a soul energy level, and there are those that are still dependent on a technological means of relating. Both persuasions are occurring on your planet as you allow them to. You have the opportunity, as a species, to tap into these alternate futures and move toward particular outcomes. So, as you can see, you can visit the future and the future is visiting you, right now.

When you focus on one type of visitation, that reality gains power and influence, and the probability is strengthened. This assists the future beings in giving more energy to their particular time line to ensure a result. They may also be trying to alter their own reality by changing your focus in the present. All of this is happening intensely now because you are existing in one of the major pivotal time signature periods, when large evolutionary changes occur throughout the time space continuum in multiple dimensions.

There are also lower frequency beings, and future humans, that still exist in a state of fear and have an interest in keeping your planet at a lower level. Mostly, however, these energies exist in your present and past, as the survival rate of the denser frequencies has moved off your planet in most future time lines. Therefore, you have a great advantage for forward evolution as long as you are able to transcend the limits of your perceived views of time and power, and give your conscious focus to all those that have a universal interest in your next step and theirs in unison. We all realize that this is harder than it sounds. It requires a leap of consciousness into a world less physical. This is not so easy when your history has been built on the limits of a perceived matter-based consciousness.

Probable Future Human Developments

You are dependent on the notion that you need to make machines to create on your behalf, or must physically alter life to make changes. In many future time lines, you will progress in this way with technical advancements. Other probabilities allow you to influence matter with your consciousness which allows you to be less dependent on making a physical thing do the work. Instead of making a machine to move a boulder, for example, you could use your mind to alter the molecules in space and time to move the same boulder. The latter has repercussions that are far more beneficial to your planet in the long run. Which direction would you like to emphasize for your future world? You have a huge chance to influence that direction in the coming years, as the energy supporting change increases on your planet.

Many of you already are, or will have the opportunity, to be working with off world beings to assist with human and Earth evolution. The more you are able to shift your focus out of the limited dynamic of linear time, the more able you will be at associating with, and taking advantage of, what the lighter vibration entities can offer in altering your probable realities. When you are able to stay in a pure focus on your purpose for a greater soul evolution, then it will be easier and easier to alter your viewpoint into a timeless understanding of your actions and thoughts. When you focus on the bigger picture, and allow your purpose to flow within that higher view, then you will be able to envision the past and future as your higher collective consciousness wishes it to be, and hence flow appropriately in your now to elicit the desired result in all time frames. In other words, you can be in a place of knowing and certainty in each present moment, without concern for the details of how it will unfold. You will know where and when to be in the present, in order that the appropriate future is created according to your vision. You will be assisted by the entities that vibrate on the same frequency of soul evolution.

It will be increasingly important that you are able to have a moment to moment flexibility encased in the certainty of your vibration. When you fall out of the higher vision, you fall prey to lesser influences, and can be led astray. This is why keeping vigilance to a future ideal in your mind, altering your past to accommodate the needs of that future, and acting accordingly in the present, will be vital. You cannot force the present based on what you analytically think should be. You must remain open to the light path as you tune into the highest probable energy signatures. There will be subtle fluctuations in the path. We cannot tell you the way to go right now, as it changes per second, based on shifts in global consciousness. What we can say is that you can shape those global aims and be in a perpetual place of allowing the greatest potential in every moment.

Using Mental Time Travel to Strengthen Potential

In order to be in the state of mind to create the greatest positive change, you must become the best potential you. Each of you has this responsibility first and foremost. You can envision a better future. But, without a better you, there cannot be a better future world. Each of you makes up that whole vision. The power of the future lies within the individual consciousness added to the larger group. You should start envisioning an advanced human race, and then determine how you need to develop to meet that vision. What past experiences have you exhibited that you could have followed to greater development, but did not? You can go and change those experiences in time. What skills or interests did you seemingly fail to develop to their fullest? You can go back and accentuate these abilities and bring them to the forefront. Rewrite your past and strengthen the qualities you will need for the future.

You each have abilities that you started to pursue and left behind because of cultural pressures, which will be beneficial to your race. Use your mental time travel to change the events that diminished these talents or interests. See those events in a way that accentuates those gifts, and imagine that you did cultivate that side of yourself. Imagine yourself through time, building upon those latent abilities. By doing this, you are allowing these gifts to be strengthened now, and in your future world, for yourself and others.

There is not one among you that has yet lived up to your highest potential within your physical body and mind. Some have awakened faster than others, but all have time left to reach for the sky. This is the beauty of time. You can see a shift in your reality within minutes, days, hours. What took someone a lifetime previously can occur in moments these days, because of the work that your fellow pathfinders have done for you in preparation for the energy portals that are opening all over your planet. A few have earned much for the many, and continue to do so. Just as one person's invention will change the lives of multitudes, one person's shift in consciousness can, and has, changed the potential for all. Each of you is continuing to change each other's potential through time by stretching yourself today.

We wish you to also note that there is a strong chance that many of your physical bodies will not make it into the next era. Of course, you will all die at some point anyway, but there may be a large die off of human beings in a short period of time. This does not mean that those who die were not of a developed consciousness. Many will pass on physically, and join the fragmented aspects of their souls in unity, upon reincarnation on your planet in the next dimensional Earth. Those that have raised their consciousness will move on in their evolution, whether or not they survive physically. In fact, those that do survive physically will often find themselves joined by the other parts of their souls that were scattered about the Earth. In some cases, all the bodies that were inhabited by a single fragmented soul may die and be reborn together in one new child of the future world. We tell you this because you may not be in the same form as you are now in your visions of the new world, and this should not concern you.

Your consciousness should be focused on the larger picture of a unified human consciousness, where all your fragmented sparks are unified in a common evolutionary goal. Also, there should be no sorrow for your death or the deaths of others, as they will be moving in the direction of unity, or will continue on a planet that supports their further growth. Remember that your personal development affects all aspects of your presently divided soul.

When you travel with your consciousness into potential futures, you may, in fact, see yourself and loved ones as different people than you are now. This may be a potential "after the shift" existence. You may see a future many lifetimes after your present life. Allow yourself to explore these possibilities. They may even teach you something about your present path. Clearly, by allowing your soul to venture into visionary futures and altered pasts, you will be developing your psychic, or enhanced sensory perceptions. These abilities are the soul's natural sensory modes and will be the norm in a less dense dimensional reality. While you may feel that you are making up your envisioned future when you play with these notions now, in time, it will be the way you create knowingly. It is okay that you do not think it is necessarily real. The point is to practice using your soul vision to see and create multi-dimensionally. Eventually, you will see results, and a much larger view of reality will open up to you, and lead you to personal discovery and advancement previously thought impossible.

We can just as easily say, as tomorrow, so yesterday and today, or as yesterday, so tomorrow and today. All are continually shaping one another, with your point of power being what you know as your present moment, as fleeting as it is. You have the choice and power in each moment to recreate your yesterday, today, and tomorrow. We encourage you to use this power to its fullest as you move into your density shift. Trust the knowing that comes from the records of time, and use your consciousness to focus and enhance the energy desired. As you walk into the coming era of transcendence, this skill will allow you to glimpse and travel along the paths of light that can lead you in any direction that your consciousness is ready to experience. When you are able to see the winks of light transference that exist inter-dimensionally, you are welcomed into a bright world of discovery and creativity that sparks the core of your soul and accelerates your evolution. You can create this reality now.

Chapter 11

The Winks of
Light Transference

Our collective consciousness communicates by means of light transference. We share sparks of light with one another, with a larger collective soul, and with various aspects of creation, such as you. All of our connections are based on the transference of source sparks, or bits of consciousness in the form of energy rays or bursts of light. We travel and communicate over the lines of light to which we are all connected on an atomic level. Thoughts then move over the lines, as sparks of intent, to particular targets. We are communicating with the channel for this writing in this way. There is a thread of light that connects us, and we share sparks of consciousness from our collective, to the soul of the channel. This connection exists in multiple dimensions, outside and inside of time and space as you perceive them.

Everything in our universe is made up of energy, and takes on shape based on its frequency. Connections exist between every unit of energy, as it is actually all one. Communication and attraction allows energy units to combine and create a flow with a particular frequency signature. That signature attracts more of the same, and strengthens the creation. All consciousness creates our universe; that includes you, us, and every particle. We are all dynamically involved in the creation of the vibrations that make up our experiences. Hence, the art of creation is found in the understanding of the winks of light transference.

The Inter-Connected Web of Light

When you are able to see all your transactions with yourself, others, and everything in your environment as an exchange of energy, you will be on your way to navigating and creating inter-dimensionally. Once your soul is able to see its interconnection to its surroundings, now and through time and space, then movement through the threads of light will be second nature. Presently, you may think this is far from your sphere of knowing. But, you are closer than you realize, and need to be prepared for relating in this way.

We have already explained that by nature the universe is super-conductive, and that by shedding your baggage or barriers to your inner light, you are more able to play in this field of conductivity. This world of light is what you are, and exist within already. You merely must open your awareness to it within yourself and then around you. As you do this, you are becoming a member of the greater universe that surrounds you, but was previously unseen. This is what your transition is all about. It is you becoming a being in further awareness of its ability to contribute to the waves of light transference that invigorate worlds. In doing so, your creation experience becomes richer and in turn so does all that touches you, which includes all that exists in this universe and beyond.

Knowing that the universe works by transference of energy from one unit to another, and that we all affect that transfer, is key to effective creation. You, and the objects and life you experience, are an assemblage of units of consciousness in agreement to express together. You are in agreement to appear separate so that you can discover your own creativity. You are expressing your creative flair as part of creation by living your particular lives. You are learning how your energy manipulates your surroundings. Hopefully, you are learning that you are all moving each other on an energetic level. The more aware you are of this fact, the more control you can have over the effects of your energy. Also, you are presumably learning that you can tap into the never ending source of energy that the universe is made of. Seeing the light transfer and replenishment will allow you to understand how to alter your surroundings with ease.

Your physical reality, and many beyond, is held together by strands of light. If you were to see these strands from an outside viewpoint, it would appear that your entire world is a grid system of vibrant strands of energy connecting all components therein. You would see a web of light. As connections are made between seemingly separate objects, the light threads between them brighten. New threads are made when one object's vibration matches another. This happens between what you classify as inanimate and animate forms. These light threads connect cells and atomic particles, as well as animals and mountains. There are, then, many layers to this web of light. From our view, we can see the sparks of light traveling between objects in this dance of light. Stronger connections are made between units of the same vibration.

When the consciousness is self-absorbed, it tends to fight for the sparks and is constantly trying to steal light from the objects around it. When the unit of consciousness is in a state of sharing energy with that which exists in its sphere, then its pathways are replenished. This state of being perpetually lit is unconditional giving. However, sometimes sharing energy takes the form of restriction rather than charity, as often withdrawing is actually giving.

Humanity has predominantly been in a place of fighting for light for many millennia, and therefore much strife has been manufactured. Sparks cannot be kept lit when they are stolen. They fizzle out and are not replenished. The consciousness unit then looks to grab more with whatever connection threads it has established. If you can begin to perceive your world and its interactions in this way, you will see why it is so important to change your way of thinking. By giving your sparks away, you are creating more of that which is fulfilling. We can see your brightness, through your haze of ego, when you share your sparks in this way.

Sustainable Balancing of Energy Transference

Even animals, that you deem beneath you in spiritual development, are aware of their connection with objects in their world. They make fewer connections because of their limits in frequency, but they have an innate knowing of how they fit into the matrix of light, and are in tune with their environment on that level. They have an instinct of the balance of give and take in the world that they occupy. As humans evolved to being self-aware and technologically advanced, they inadvertently lost their sensitivity to the balance of energy transference. It is your goal now to maintain self-understanding, and simultaneously reawaken the internal knowing of balance that gives endless life to creation. Your species has so badly upset this balance of light transference on your mother Earth that she has no choice but to equalize. When, however, you are able to balance with all the units of consciousness in her sphere, you bring her elevation because you reach into depths of light that other forms of matter cannot.

Degradation in your world is the result of the war for light energy. From the atomic level to the human political and social level, energy is fought for on your planet. If your species were able to connect with the source energy that exists in you and in everything around you, there would be no need for war over resources, and the degradation of physical matter in your world would be slowed, or stalled. When you can each replenish your source energy, you will live longer, as you will be constantly replenishing your cells. This is done by means of vibration.

There is no need to take a magic pill to replenish your system. When your consciousness resonates with the vibration of sharing light, then it will stay healthy. When the bulk of your society is sharing light and refilling from the cosmic field, then resources will be plentiful. When you are able to transfer light from your soul to the plants and animals that you eat, they will offer the best possible nutritional value to you and at the same time will be elevating their consciousness. Your current systems for food production are failing miserably because the energy put into them is dismal. The vibration is that of greed, not sharing. Plants and animals are being used and abused with no regard to their consciousness. This can easily change with the conscious infusion of life force by means of light transference.

When you understand the importance and power of your ability to communicate with and regenerate all material forms by the conscious projection of eternal sparks of light, then you can transform your world into one that is truly sustainable on a molecular level. You can, in fact, power your house from energy that is in the atmosphere by tapping into the energy field of creation. This can actually be done organically, with no need for complex machines. You may be some years away from grasping this notion, but it is doable. If you gain an appreciation for the power of your consciousness in affecting all matter, then you will be on your way to finding such solutions. You would, then, also be able to move objects by tuning your mind to the atoms in the object, and sharing source energy between it and you through the threads of light that connect you. Remember that you and the object already contain energy.

In sharing your source light with an object, you infuse it with your ability to move. You are made of the same atomic particles as the objects around you. Therefore, just as you can move parts of your body as thoughts trigger electrical impulses in your brain neurons, you can use that same electrical dynamic to move objects outside of yourself by transferring your winks of charge.

Light as Electrically Charged Information

The light you transfer contains information and an electrical charge. When you send this charge along the filaments of light, you are sending electrical and information signals. When humans communicate there is an electrical charge with a frequency that is exchanged through written and spoken words. The thought that preceded those words contained the energy that was transmitted. Where do you suppose that thought energy came from? This is still a big mystery to your sciences, and a very interesting question to ponder. It is known that your brains fire electrical impulses, aided by certain brain chemicals that allow or disallow pathways and connections among neurons. But, why do you have particular thoughts? There are theories by your sciences, but no real answers. It was only recently that you began to accept that there is such a thing as a collective unconscious that connects your group thoughts. This is on the right track to understanding the interconnected nature of thought energy transfer.

It would be a good practice for you all to begin imagining the energy that accompanies your words. Emotions are an indicator of the nature of the energy you are transmitting. Begin to imagine the light filaments that connect you to others when you communicate. Every thought has a charge that is being emanated. Be aware whether you are using words to steal energy from others, or to give to them. Practice giving energy through threads of light to others when you speak, and when you listen to them. By doing this, you are developing your awareness of light transference, and are becoming an energy invigorator instead of an energy drainer. This practice alone can transform your being. By doing this, you can become a conduit of force from the universe. The surrounding source field will re-supply you and hence you become a generator for light.

By imagining a silver thread connection to other aspects of the universe, you can also establish information links that can heighten your awareness. Remember that thoughts are energy and information. You can connect with other life forms and obtain energy information from them. And, thoughts will form in your consciousness about those lives. In a way, you will be telepathically communicating. You are extremely limited, presently, by your means of thought transference. There are so few new thoughts in your system because the majority of you are simply recycling the thoughts of others. There are more ways to obtain thought energy than from television and books. You each have the capacity to connect with the astral knowledge of your planet, and with the knowledge stored in inanimate and animate forms. You can also take this energy transference to another level and connect with other worldly beings and distant star systems.

Communicating and Replenishing Through Light Filaments

Not only can you build your connection and your transmissions through the larger universe, but you can also develop a stronger link with the world of the seemingly small. For example, you can develop a deeper connection with the cells in your body. Imagine all the strands of light connecting all your cells to one another in an intricate web. Now visualize those strands becoming brighter and more vibrant. Visualize sparks of light being shared along those lines of light, and all the individual cells being illuminated as a result. You can invigorate the consciousness of your cells by sharing your light vibration in this way. Where is the energy coming from? You are tapping into the God frequency of creation as you formulate thoughts of sharing energy. The thoughts of light are coming from the frequency of the creation process, which is your link to the renewable force of the universe. In this way, you can manifest a healthy physical system.

You can, likewise, assist others in manifesting their own healthy bodies and minds. Each of you has the ability to uplift one another by invigorating cells with renewable light. The cells are excited by your input. You can help them to renew each other by adding your level of awareness, just as higher beings can do for the human race. Not that we envision you as cells, per se; however, in a way, we are all cells in a cosmic field of creation. You could say that all matter and energy forms are cells of God, with an understanding that God is the whole of us all.

By infusing the cells of your system with higher thought energy, you are raising the vibrational experience and evolution of God. Yes, All That Is, is evolving. The natural state of everything is to evolve as a creator and revealer of the endless light. By envisioning the world as light energy interaction, you can be a productive player in evolution, as opposed to an unproductive destroyer of the process. Your free will allows you to make this decision in every second of your existence. You can be rejuvenating, by infusing high frequency light into your life and the lives of others, or you can be struggling against one another for the light to produce a world of lack. By strengthening your ability to become a conduit of light transference, you are choosing a world of health and abundance.

Becoming Orchestrators of the Underlying Light Forms

As you approach your transition into the next dimensional reality, your sensitivity to your light bodies, the strands that connect them within the web of light, and the sparks of thought that travel between forms, will amplify. When you finally cross over, you will be able to see the dance of light all around you. You will have the capacity to turn on this light vision as needed, giving you a tool of discernment and communication. The frequencies in the next octave allow the energy forms of matter to be seen and felt. In the 4D realm you will be spending time developing your skills and traversing the highways of light. At first you will evolve in mental prowess, communication, healing, and advancing unified concepts. Eventually, you will be traveling through space and time.

As seventh dimension entities, we are intimately involved with the highways of light that make up the energy signatures, and hence structures, of this universe and others beyond. We are orchestrators of light forms. We are builders with light energy. We have evolved to grow and mold the atomic particles of consciousness that are integral to creation. By infusing, and communing with these particles in a symbiotic balance, we encourage consciousness building. In this way, we are assisting in the evolutionary creation process of worlds. Groups of us focus on uplifting particular light structures, as needed. We are foundation builders and enhancers of all forms of life within the multi-verse. All beings are involved in this process per the level of awareness and frequency control they have obtained.

You will be learning to use the light signatures that we have enhanced to eventually create your own, in unison with us, and other life forms. All of creation is cooperative in this way. Again, if you cooperate with the energy force of all, then you will flow with creativity. If you fight against the source in disunity, you diminish your abilities as creators. Learning to flow down these paths of interconnection will lead you to many amazing discoveries and abilities. The means by which you use the connections will vary, depending on your inclinations as individuals and groups. You will begin to develop expertise in the field of light transfer and travel that suits your internal nature. Since your soul will be recreating itself to match something closer to its true being, and will also likely be joined by aspects of itself that were residing in other bodies, your enhanced insight will be tremendous.

In your developed 4D condition, you will see through objects that once appeared solid. You will be able to see the structures of light that make up the appearance of each separate object. It will be much like seeing the grid that makes up a holographic image. Within the particles, atoms, molecules, cells, organs, and other parts that make up a life form, for example, you will see the light that radiates and connects those parts, and forms a structure that creates the physical manifestation of that form. You will then be able to see any part of that form that is out of balance, or is dim. You will be able to inject it with source light generated by your thoughts. You will learn to detect the frequency at which the life form or object vibrates, so that you will be able to tune your thoughts to that particular level, for the greatest result. In this way, you will be assisting the life form with its own regeneration. In fact, you could help in regenerating any aspect of your world in this way. Imagine the implications. This is the essence of true co-creation and evolution.

With this energy transference and regeneration knowledge, you could one day forfeit your dependency on technology. However, it will take some time for you to develop your aptitude in this area. So, you will transition with some level of attachment to your physical tools. But, as you can imagine, the ability to see the energy that makes up the tools will soon give them less control over your lives. In the seventh dimensional realm, for example, we use no tools other than our consciousness. However, we also have no physical form. We live in a pure light form. Whereas even in the fourth dimension you will have a physical form and live among objects that you can interact with, and learn to create with. The lightening of the density, however, will be mentally and spiritually freeing and at the same time will offer new challenges in creating.

As you embark upon your 4D journey, your advancing light vision will make it possible for you to be increasingly creative within your world. For those that make it this far, it will be quite exciting. In seeing how your energy interplays, you will find new ways of interacting with your world, and each other, as you observe the way you are connected and how your thoughts and emotions each transmit a force. This is when you will truly begin to realize that you can, in fact, really move mountains. Together with planet Earth, the beings of 4D will work to recreate a sustainable system that enlightens all. Since the first prerogative will be to do so, it can be so. When you see how your winks of light transference impact everything they touch, you will want nothing less than to beam the highest intentions within any thing, or system, you interact with. There will be a sense of deep satisfaction in being able to alter the vibration of your existence, and you will experiment with ways to enrich your environment and cohabitants.

Harmonizing With Mother Earth's Vibration

There will inevitably be much stumbling as you work together to understand your new sight, and explore how to best use the skills. With focus and high intentions, you will succeed at forming new systems and ways of being over time. The planet will also be working at revitalizing and envisioning herself anew. She will be undergoing a significant transition, just as you will be. Human beings have the potential to give her much additional creative influx and invigoration during her development. By sending your light vibration to her during the tough years of motion, you will assist her and yourselves in a smoother journey. It is to her benefit to see you progress. You are quite connected with her, so always remember to have reverence for her as an inherent source of beauty and light.

It may be strange for you to imagine that the planet is a sentient being, but she has intelligence with a consciousness, just as you do. She has many cells and parts that make up her being as well. Just as there are life forms that live in symbiosis, and some as parasites, within your form, the same occurs for Mother Earth. When you envision the light fibers joining everything, remember to include the heart and soul of the amazing planet on which you reside. She needs support, just as you do. She would much prefer that you come along with her to the next octave.

All life forms that are in support of the Earth will follow the paths of light that she will illuminate for them to see their way into the new world. From single-celled organisms to octopuses, coral, and orangutans, her doors will open for those that serve her. Those that no longer vibrate in harmony with her will not see the winks of light, and will miss their transfer signal. They will not be on the highway of light and will instead find themselves in a pit of darkness. So the Earth will take with her all that is in synchronization with her form.

Humans are not the only ones with the potential to rise. All beings have this opportunity to shift. The awareness level is pointedly different for human beings than it is for other life on the planet, but all have the potential to exist in the next degree of density. The awareness requirement for humans is one particular level, while for other creatures there are quite different factors that determine their progression. Each is a special creative force of the God energy and has its own unique path of expression. All should be respected as a part of the whole. All forms of life on your planet are important aspects of your creation, and the Earth's consciousness. As she cleanses herself, she will invite many to help her revise herself anew. If you can begin to appreciate the Earth, and all her parts, with a deeper reverence, by recognizing the beams of light that connect you, there is a chance you can play an important role in creating a whole new world.

Your planet is a spectacular example of a consciousness that is full of creative life force. She is constantly invigorating all aspects of herself with her source energy. She is a beautiful being with a true zest for existence. She is an example for you to model. Unfortunately, your species has done the opposite for hundreds, if not thousands, of years. You have tried to conquer her, instead of learning from her and working with her to create. Your species has escalated its selfish destruction to the point of absurdity. What would you do if you had such a parasite eating away at your life? There comes a time when we all must shed our darkness and come up from the ashes. Earth is intending to shed her veils as well. You can transform with her by shedding your own darkness, learning to share energy with her, and creating a symphony of light transference. Or you can continue to generate discord and wreak havoc. You already know, by now, where these choices lead.

If your species chooses to alter its attitude and meet Earth on the other side, you can rest assured that a whole new world of discovery will await you. Within this new world, you will have a wonderful opportunity to shine once again, and be partners with the evolving Mother Earth. With your new found light vision and ability to transfer sparks of creation, you can be part of building an advanced humanity in symbiotic harmony with all life on the planet. Imagine that now, for as you feel the possibilities, a whole new world is being created.

Chapter 12

A Whole New World
Is Created

*I*f you only truly recognized the power you have as creators, you would think only of your highest potential outcome. If only you were aware of how your thoughts are currently amplified in their ability to materialize intentions, you would be taking full advantage. A whole new world will soon be created, and you each are responsible for a large part of its design. The time is ripe for your new visions to be real. The impact of your collective creation will determine what will be at play, and what directions your new world will take.

You are at the engineering stage of the creation of a new era of your civilization that can go beyond anything that existed on the planet yet. As the transition occurs, you will be in the execution stages of the new world plan. Therefore, the groundwork you set in motion now will make a significant impression on what your new world will look like, and how it will be governed. This is why each and every one of you must be in the mix, as your construction will benefit from a well-rounded perspective. The unification of ideas, spanning disciplines and styles of expression, must come together in a meeting place of like frequency. This way, your new world will be a balanced and harmonious creation that takes full advantage of the power of individual creativity.

Targeting Positive Outcomes With Higher Intentions

There are waves of possibilities flowing among you that have set in motion various probabilities. As this is being read, and in any given moment, the waves are swelling or dispelling dependent on the direction of push you collectively exert with the vibration of your consciousness. We remind you quite happily that the higher the vibrational tone to which you resonate, the easier the manifestation and more power there is behind those waves. So, when you look around you and say that the world is in a shambles, remember two things; one, it is all about to change, and two, those with thought energy on the higher end of the scale have exponentially more influence over the outcome.

A change is occurring, and it may appear at times that you are headed for a world of chaos and destruction, and that the majority is complacent or feeding selfish interests. However, we assure you that it takes much less of you resonating at a high frequency to create your new world than it does for those on lower frequencies to create anything. If you recall, in a previous chapter, we discussed how lower vibrational thoughts have a difficult time hitting their intended targets, while faster, lighter vibrations fly through to their destination without friction. This is why the seemingly large population of people bent on destruction, or living with a dog-eat-dog mentality, will have the least effect. This is especially true given that they will not be able to process the amplified finer energies that will increase on your planet.

Not only will those with lighter thoughts have better mastery of targeted creation, they will also have the added advantage of being in resonance with new incoming vibrational bandwidths that will offer a further boost to every connection made. Thus it is important that you each maintain your consciousness in the direction of your greatest possible outcome, for yourselves individually, and for the whole civilization.

You are the holders of the light frequency and you are not small. Each of you is worth thousands and thousands of those who do not yet know what they are capable of. And so, we hope that it is clearly understood that you have the power to create a world filled with light, promise, and blossoming creativity. Knowing that it only takes a few among you to collectively alter the design of the new world, is key now, and will be after the transition. You must always appreciate the strength of this driving force as you forge ahead.

Now that you know it is possible that a whole new world can be created, what do you want it to look like? Every thought you have sends a signal into creation. If those thoughts are met with the force of other, similarly resonating thoughts, you begin to manifest a probability. Imagine those multiple sparks of thought energy creating a ball of light with increasing amperage. Since these sparks are traveling along light wires and not through mud, they combine quickly and effortlessly, and grow exponentially into a force to contend with. Those balls of light have a frequency that has the potential to create material forms. The largest collective thought forms drive the direction of your world's manifestations.

The more thought energy, and the higher its vibration, the more likely you will be to experience the material forms to match. It takes hundreds of times more low frequency thoughts to create a form that becomes a reality, than high frequency ones. Emotions of hate and anger will create complete chaos and appear completely random. On the other hand, thoughts of unity, joy, appreciation, and peace, can change your world in minutes. You are at the stage in your development where enough of you have this understanding to actually push your species into the new world of your imagination.

The Manifestation of Endless Abundance

We are here to assure you that there are probabilities in the works among you that have splendid outcomes that you will be quite pleased with. The brightness of the collective energy forms attached to these probabilities can grow for your reality, if enough of you desire and give attention to these options. For example, you can create a new world that is richly abundant for all humanity and all creatures of Earth, if you are able to focus your consciousness on this frequency. The universe is endlessly abundant with life force. You can have a world in which you tap into this resource in every aspect of your lives. Meditate every day on the idea that the more everyone and everything receives, the more all can share, and the more abundant are all. You can create this new world of freedom, prosperity, and joy, by focusing your minds and hearts on this end.

Giving attention to lack, and fear of the diminishment of your resources, will only produce more of the same. Be aware that you are living in a world of lack presently. But, know that it is because you have created it by your collective thoughts of lack, and always wanting something that you feel you do not have. You already have everything your soul desires, yet you are hiding behind the illusion that you lack everything.

You can each wake up now to the abundance that is already within and among you. To tap into this, all you need do is know that it is there, and to have complete certainty that all the energy needed is available by conscious connection to the field of light that joins everything. Whenever you find yourself feeling thoughts of doubt and lack in any aspect of your life, be it love, friendship, wealth, health, time or freedom, stop and remind yourself that the universe is eternally abundant and that the more you give of your heart, the more will be revived. This is the kind of world you can create; one in which all beings are sharing abundantly, and creating endless abundance throughout the kingdom.

You can have this fulfilling world to the degree that you all desire it, and have certainty that it is the true way for each of you to flourish in your development. Your new world will not be without challenges. The obstacles will simply be seen as opportunities. Remember, it is your level of awareness that will be leaping forward. And, in its doing so, your ability to transcend and transform situations that block your progress will be determined by your spiritual link, and understanding of energy transference.

In the newly created world view, hurdles will be welcomed with vigor and enthusiasm, and you will be able to envision solutions that follow ebbs of light with ease. Creativity and invention can take off with such awareness. Expression will take on new heights and depth, and relationships will have enhanced meaning. We hope that you will add all your vibrancy to thoughts of such a world and make it so.

The minute details of how this world will operate, and how you may get there, will be ironed out as you go. There is no need to worry or obsess on how such a transition will occur from where you are today. It is much more important for you to focus on the end result, and feel the state of being in that world. The how of it will be made known as you maintain the frequency of the world you envision. Doorways and paths of light will open to you, with the help of the Earth, all her companions, and those from outside your planet that also benefit from your evolution.

You will all be shown the way, if you remain open, intent, and certain of your highest potential, no matter what happens around you. There may be many tests to strengthen your conviction and desire for something better. If you can hold your vibration amidst the seeming jambalaya of frequency, you will create lasting and rewarding changes right in the middle of the stew.

Waves of Probability: Worst and Best Case Scenarios

Surely you are aware that, at this point, we cannot make exact predictions as to what world you will create following the shift to a fourth dimensional density. We can, however, give you glimpses into the probabilities that we see arising out of your present global consciousness. You, as of yet, have not set any avenues in stone. And for that matter, nothing is ever completely set. Tides can fluctuate in any given second, and a new direction can be forged. So, while we can see waves of light plowing over your collective consciousness, and can foresee where they will lead in a general sense, much can and will be altered. You are the makers of your own destinies, individually and globally. One person can rise up unpredictably and push one person, who pushes five, who push a nation to divert a wave of energy that feeds an alternate outcome. It is a volatile endeavor, especially in the state of uncertainty within which most of your species is living.

The major factor to consider in the creation of the new world is how you manage the transition period. The aftermath will depend on what you create as a changeover period. There are several levels of intensity possible, and many options for how they will occur and affect the populace. We have already suggested that there is a likely scenario that millions of you will not make it, physically, through the shift. There is another likelihood that smaller numbers would need to be sacrificed during the shift. Presuming that many will not make it, the matter becomes how they will pass over, and how dramatic the cultural, social, and geological changes need to be before you are transformed? This is a topic for you to consider as you are projecting your future. The more of you there are maintaining a lighter frequency, the less painful the movement, and the less drastic the aftermath.

Let us put it this way, you can still globally create a nuclear war that decimates and maims millions, resulting in a particularly challenging clean up job. It will not be as though you leave behind the resulting mess. What that scenario would mean is more drastic cleansing on behalf of the planet. And, it may even mean that humanity does not survive at all. So that case, added to all the other natural disasters, is one of the worst probabilities. It is a potential no-win option for humanity. However, given the vibration detected among the light bearers, this is an unlikely event.

A better scenario would be that the majority of your species is able to reach a state of vibration that at least minimally matches the planet, and she is able to shift with your assistance. In this probability, she makes a polar shift as quickly and smoothly as possible, with short-lived physical upheavals that will cause difficulty, but be dealt with effectively, given your global consciousness to share. As she shifts, every life form that makes it will find it is in a world less dense. All life forms will begin to gather together with a new vision. Firstly, they will pick themselves up in small communities. Over time, they will create a world that is sustainably united with Earth. These probabilities, and everything in between, are possible.

Basically, the more you can assist the Earth, the easier her transition and yours will be. And, the easier you will find your new world will be to create anew. Also, consider how much you want to bring with you to this new world. There are scenarios where you are able to salvage much of your inventions, and other probabilities where you must depend more on your mental resources to start up again. This is yet another undetermined outcome that you can help shape now. Even supposing you manifest the smoothest polar shift, with the least amount of natural disasters and Earth changes, what is left and what you do with it, will depend on the level of development you obtained leading up to the shift. The level of fourth dimensional skills you already cultivated will affect your readiness to venture into a new realm of discovery in the lighter frequency, and how much you will be able to benefit from the other 4D beings that may greet you.

Clarifying Purpose to Maximize Contribution

Let us presume that those that make the transition into the fourth dimension, along with the planet, without leaving physical form are prepared to some degree for the strangeness of being in a less dense reality. If they have, in fact, gradually glimpsed the sensations of being multi-dimensional, they will have a magical experience as they come into their new plane of existence. All the skills that they were touching upon in their final days of 3D will begin to truly awaken, and new visions will be the norm.

In this new state of awareness you each will be able to find others that resonate most closely with you, or that have a piece of your puzzle. Gatherings are already occurring, but they will be intensified as you make the final shift, because it will be important to join minds to recreate a new type of civilization. If you have not already gravitated to a particular physical location, then you may be drawn somewhere by a well-lit road or intuitive guidance. Others may need to be travelers, as they will be messengers or bringers of goods and services. The important point here is that your cultivated abilities will begin to blossom, and you will find your way most easily, if you have prepared.

Many of you are finding that your purpose is becoming clearer and you are more driven to give up all that held you back, and consequently are pursuing dreams with passion. This is what happens when you let go of your shields and become governed by your spirit. These feelings and drives will only accelerate as the shift occurs, and desires will be in tune with your soul's natural inclinations. The more you allow yourself to follow such soul urges now, the more prepared you will be to move right into your best role in the new world. Being open and flexible will always be assets. Your new world can, and most likely will, be focused around the natural inclinations and joys that each citizen brings to bear on the bigger picture. Learning to tune into your specialty, and having the gift of seeing the talents of others, will help in creating a synchronistic and harmonious lifestyle.

There is concern among many of you that you must be physically prepared for natural disasters and therefore must build shelters and store food for hard times. We encourage you always to do what your soul feels compelled to do, but never if it is out of fear of lack. If your heart is coming from a place of purpose and benefit to your species, then share your knowledge with kindness, but be open to changing your views or plans in a moment's notice. Be aware that your ability to be sensitive and tuned in to the frequency of the planet will serve you better than any amount of food storage.

The Earth will provide for those that are in tune with her energy field. She will not leave her children to starve if they are benefiting her growth. If you feel the need to connect to the Earth by farming and finding ways to live sustainably, then by all means pursue your dreams. They are a calling from the Earth and should not be ignored. If you are being called to sing songs about overcoming struggle and being reborn, then sing. There is not one way, or place, to bring energy to the Earth and your fellow humans. There are as many paths to the new world as there are souls upon it, and all will be integral in the new communities.

It is not everyone's job to create a community location, but those that do must be open to sharing with others whose job it is to bring particular energy patterns of life to those communities. Many individuals will be looking for the place that welcomes their resonance, while others among you will have already prepared a place for cultural growth. If the singer, for example, focused on farming, out of fear of not having food, when her role was to bring the magic of music, everyone will have lost her special energy. So you see, you must each follow the vision of your soul, so that when the transformation comes you are able to contribute in the best way for all. That is what the essence of community is. You will find that you are much more when you collaborate in this way. And, your new world will be a considerably richer place as a result.

Greater Astronomical Sentient Influences

It is important for you to also be aware that there are influences from other planets and dimensions that will have an affect on the transition period, and the following era. Firstly, the other heavenly bodies within your solar system each have an impact on your planet, as they too are sentient beings in the process of evolution. They can exert pressures that can make the shift easier or more challenging, depending on what electromagnetic force they exert. The sun, in particular, can radiate cosmic rays that assist in a speedy polar shift.

There are also planets in your system, as yet unknown by your sciences that can force great unexpected change. Being in the central plane of the Milky Way, as we have said, allows for a force that will make an impression on the Earth. But the details of the Earth's exact position, in relation to the other celestial bodies, will make a difference as to how strong this force impacts the shift. So, while human consciousness is significant in this process, and of course has the largest impact on its own evolution, there are other factors that are involved on an even greater consciousness level. There will be many more findings in your fields of astronomy and astrophysics that will expand the perspective of your planet's place in the galaxy and universe in the coming years, and will open doors of understanding.

On an energetic level, you can each tune into vibrations from particular heavenly bodies by thinking of the astral frequencies. Ancient civilizations on your planet have passed on many secrets of the cycles and influences of star systems and planets. There is much for you to learn from the ancients, and from connecting with the universal forces emanating from outer space. You are connected to all celestial bodies by threads of light and can establish relationships that help you, and your planet, through this evolutionary leap. When you envision your new world experience, consider a deeper connection and appreciation for the far reaches of your universe and an inter-dimensional perspective. Eventually, this deeper link will allow your species to gain knowledge of your universe without even leaving your planet, and will assist in more direct off world travel, when the time is right.

Making light connections with other star systems will also lead to communications with beings from those worlds, and will prepare you for understanding the perspectives of diverse life forms. We mention this as we would like to see you open your minds to the many possibilities that are far beyond what you presently see. Until you can imagine a world with off world interactions, those entities will not attempt to be involved, on a more common level, with your species. An amazing part of your new world experience can be rewarding encounters and collaborations with other-worldly life from throughout your universe and multi-verse. Your species will decide if they are ready for such connections.

As 4D beings, you will have a greater ability to discern the intentions of others as you read their frequency signatures. You will more easily be able to deflect frequencies that try to meddle with your direction. Keeping your focus on higher emotional vibrations will assure that only beings that resonate with your intentions will influence you in your waking and sleeping states. Collectively, you will be deciding over the next several years how much outside communication you wish to pursue in your new world. So, consider this as you imagine the possibilities.

Co-Creating a New World: 7 Considerations

In consideration of the creation of your new world, we would like to make suggestions as to what areas you may want to ponder. We suggest that you fully imagine what your ideal civilization would look like, and how you would all behave within it. What systems do you want to have in place to take care of your major needs? The following are concepts that you may want to think about:

1. **Food**. Your planet is abundant with nutrition. What would you like the quality and nature of your sustenance to be? And, how will you enhance and produce food with a highly efficient nutritional value that is satisfying and also beneficial to the ecology within its ecosystem. Can you imagine a world that feeds all beings with the highest possible quality of nutrients abundantly?

2. **Water**. Your most valuable Earthly asset has far more uses and benefits than you comprehend. Imagine a world in which water purifies and energizes you physically and mentally, to the point where you can live three times as long, or longer, and have much more energy all the while. What if the inherent energy force in water molecules could be tapped as a source of propulsion and electricity generation? Imagine your Earth's water sources as a form of endless life and bounty.

3. **Shelter**. The possible frameworks and styles of shelters are endless. Do you dare go beyond what has already been conceived? Stretch yourselves. Have you considered creating electromagnetic shields for protective shelter? Have you fully recognized

the power of your mental projections to shelter you from storms? What Earthly materials that exist in any given location have you failed to put together in a way that can provide immediate coverage? Widen your views, and options will be seen.

4. **Mobility**. You assume that you must tap into non-renewable sources of energy in order to move objects, and yourselves, at great speeds. What if you could bend time and space, or step out of and back into time and space, by changing your dimensional perceptions? Or perhaps you would prefer to synchronize with the zero point field to power your machines to move. Every invention and physics discovery was first imagined, so start there.

5. **Communication**. The depth of personal and global communication is already beyond what you know. Start by becoming aware of the power of thought transference as it actually exists, and you will be on the way to understanding that you can exchange thoughts consciously, and with intention, using telepathic transmission. And, how rich would relationships be if you could feel and understand the multiple layers of meaning in your interactions and creative expressions?

6. **Resource Exchange.** What if you all appreciated each person or community's gifts, each human being shared their natural talents out of love and grace, and all such resources were happily exchanged? Can you pretend that it is possible that your abilities are the true resources? Once you recognize that your other energy needs are eternally renewable, you will know that creative consciousness is your most valuable asset.

7. **Governance.** You are all slowly, or perhaps quickly, relatively speaking, awakening to the fact that you do not need to be governed by any external force. When you are each following your

soul vision, you are self-governed. And, together you create your world in unison. There is no need for leaders, per se. You are each leaders of you own world, within your collective world. When you think of government....don't. Imagine each person being divinely guided to their highest contribution. Take the power from outside and put it where it belongs, within each individual.

The power to create a completely new, and amazingly rewarding life for all humankind, and your cohabitants of Earth, is upon you. You are living in the most exciting time in the history of human existence on your planet. Take advantage of your individual capability to add to co-creating something beyond what has been dreamed of thus far. The above are suggestions. They are just sparks to get some of your motors running.

There are many among you to interact with. You can inspire one another with your new world visions. Work together to enhance ideas and accelerate the materialization of desired results. There are more possible solutions than you know, and each one of you has answers. Share across disciplines and widen your narrow areas of study. Cross lines of thought and political boundaries and you will find remedies, inventions, and discoveries that will thrust your species into a revolution of creative production and personal fulfillment.

Have no sadness for the loss of the old ways. Allow the past mistakes and rigid systems to fall to the wayside. They may need to entirely crumble and fall to pieces before your eyes, but they will not be missed. Let go of patterns and misguided modus operandi. Do not be concerned that without the old structures you will not be able to maintain order, and people will fall apart, and not be able to care for themselves. Individually and cooperatively you are a hardier bunch than your so-called leaders give you credit for. Humans will be able to go beyond mere survival and picking up of the pieces. They can thrive in the challenges that the new freedoms allow. "Necessity is," indeed, "the mother of invention," and you will have a necessity to establish an entirely fresh way of living together in harmony on this Earth. Keep your thoughts and E-motions as bright and forward thinking as you can. Each of you reading this information is a leader in the force that is driving the soul of humankind to become closer to its origin, in unity with creation. Take on your part and be grateful that you have it within your heart and soul to be a contributor to this great leap.

We, in the seventh dimension and beyond, are enthusiastically awaiting your journey, and its fruition. We are excited to be witness to, and assistants in, your evolution and co-creation with all Earth's beings, in the formation of a new world. When you make the transition, you will be closer to understanding our perspective. And we, along with other higher dimensional entities, will be able to have closer connection with human souls on a more conscious level. We all look forward to an enhanced interaction in your next dimensional plane of existence.

Chapter 13

How We Will Interact
In the New World

As you open your awareness to a new octave, you increase your sensitivity to beings from higher dimensions. There will be fourth dimension entities, and others beyond that, prepared to greet you and or expand your connection to them. Your sphere of inter-dimensional understanding will grow tremendously and allow you to have relationships with a greater galactic assembly. Your species will develop its discernment, and frequency detection abilities, so that you can open communications with a wider array of beings from higher dimensions and other worlds. As light beings involved in assisting evolutionary cycles, we can assist your links with other life forms, and further aid your soul evolution, into and out of space and time. In this sense, we can act as intermediaries and liaisons in your interactions with many beings, if you desire such connections. We will also continue to guide you on your journey in discovering your abilities as creators in the new dimensional realm.

Species Relations Facilitators and Evolution Enhancers

There are other collectives among us that have the sole purpose of facilitating connections between life forms on different planets and in different dimensions. These other light beings, residing in seventh dimensional reality, will be able to greatly enhance and promote consciousness links between you and extraterrestrials. There are many aliens, as you may call them, that will be more able to interact with you when you grow to a less dense form, and are ready to see outside your previously limited views. They will only openly present themselves, and begin a relationship, when you are ready as a species, and when there is benefit to you and them in the transaction. Our 7D light being facilitator collective will assist both sides in developing communications that allow both parties to evolve. Being light grid workers, we always see favor in helping beings to join together in harmonious relations. We are brightened by the brightening of light filaments that are created or strengthened between life forms.

Our evolutionary collective will continue to work with your species as you move into 4D to help you gather your bearings in a less weighty existence. We will encourage communications among your souls and ours, so that your transition and progress will stay on a track of high vibration. It is our delight to see our friends, and fellow creators, move forward in their ability to make worlds that please them. We will come to you with signs, signals, and telepathic messages to guide you to your highest aims. The goals will be your own, but we will infuse your potential with our sparks, just as we suggest you do with each other, and all life on your planet.

More of you will be able to sense our presence, and some may even clearly see us among you. As you learn to accept the visual, intuitive, and all other extrasensory perceptions of your fellow humans, you will be able to have increasing interactions with us in your groups. Certain members of your communities will have deeper affinity with our frequency at first. As the larger group learns to trust and appreciate the abilities of those that sense our presence, more doorways to our world will be opened to yours, and more of you will see and accept us. Eventually, our presence will be as normal to you as the flowers and the trees.

The Appearance of and Communications
With Light Beings

You will see us as shining balls of light in various colors. We will be acting upon the grids of light that connect material forms to enhance their structure and integrity, and help them evolve. Sometimes we will be too luminous for your eyes to manage. When your soul is particularly open, you can take in our energy at its most subtle level and perceive us as glowing orbs. Those that are sensitive to our vibration can communicate with us through the light filaments. This will seem like telepathic communication to you, but for us it is simply the transference of energy that holds information. We are able to transmit large amounts of data in single bursts of energy. Some of you will actually be able to see the sparks of light being transmitted. Such interactions can assist you in developing your creative abilities in the fourth dimension, but they are only offered upon request. This is out of respect and appreciation for your readiness to accept our input.

If you decide you are ready for our help, then we can give you insights and ideas on how to manage energy in your system and balance yourselves with the planet's needs. Since we are able to read energy signatures from a larger perspective, we can give you knowledge as to what is out of balance on a global view and through time, until you learn to do this more easily yourselves. Our intention is not to do things for you, but rather to help you find your way by giving you tools of discernment. We are mentors, so to speak, for evolutionary leaps. Our guidance can save you many years of fumbling around haphazardly. Our methods of assistance are also quite subtle and unobtrusive. We gently nudge, make suggestions, and offer a wider perspective. You can take our advice or leave it, as you wish.

Our communications will occur on an individual and group basis. If a community is open to our vibration then we can transmit a telepathic message to the entire group. Usually, in this case, everyone will also be able to see us. Or, we may come in the form of a collective dream. We use this latter method because you are already in a state of working through dilemmas in your collective subconscious when you dream, and are often looking for assistance. We can then infuse your collective thoughts with our added energy, thereby helping you to draw your own group conclusions. If we come to a group in visual form, then we will have a good reason to do so. It will often be at a time when an important direction is being decided upon, and we feel that our input would be beneficial. This would happen after the community has opened to our frequency and was ready to make such contacts.

We may guide individuals in daily matters that aid in their development. We only take an interest in situations that have creative significance for your growth, because this is our collective mission. We have no interest in your mundane aspects of life. This is not to say that those events are not important. It is just not where our energy is best used. On a personal basis, we may simply show you a brighter path or give you a new idea to pursue. If you see luminous lights, it may be us trying to tell you something. So, you might want to pay closer attention. We can make objects appear brighter by infusing energy into their being. If you see objects light up, it may be us giving you a message. If you are open, you will also hear, see, or feel our telepathic transmission.

Many of your people have already seen us among you. We are often seen in places where there is what you term UFO activity. We are the orbs of light that appear to float in thin air. We are seen in varying colors, which is a reflection of our collective frequency, filtered through your physical dimensional atmosphere and your physical perceptions, in combination. We often accompany UFO contacts as facilitators and regulators. Our energy is protective and regenerative to whoever we interact with. We will often accompany episodes where one world, or dimension, meets another, to ensure that the process is not degenerative.

Our aim is to uplift the interactions between species, and encourage healthy connections. Therefore, if you see glowing orbs of light, rest assured that you are being cared for on a deep energetic level. Since we have the ability to influence the energetic, molecular structure of creations, we are able to inject lower frequency beings with light and alter any motives of destruction. This is not done to manipulate, but rather to uplift, assist in the beings' evolution, and discourage the negative use of force against other developing beings.

We hope you appreciate, by now, that we are all made of the same powerful source energy that made all of the known, and unknown, multiverse. We remind you of this so that you will recognize that our input into your creative structures is a part of the beauty of creation on yet another level of productivity, and that the dynamics of all other beings is also a part of that same creative source. We are all God, if you prefer. It will be crucial for you to have a true understanding that we are all one amazing and vibrant creative force, with various forms of expression of the same source. When you can learn to love and accept that in one another, you will be ready to accept that from the rest of the universe.

When you can send light vibration to those of a lower frequency, even when they appear to have intentions of harm, you will be evolving as creators. True creators can transform, and raise, any energy they encounter into something else. When you realize this ability, you will no longer fear anything of a lower nature. The only thing you should fear is your creation of fear itself. When you fear, you take away your own power to transform frequency.

So you see that our motivation in assisting is to be closer to our source as creators. The more we can uplift, the more we are uplifted. The same is true for you. When your motives are only to raise vibration, then you will be perpetually raised, and will feel the true essence of your creative force. This is the desire and motivation behind all consciousness. It is the driving force that challenges us all, no matter what level we find ourselves experiencing. As you raise yourselves to a lighter density, you will appreciate this fact with more depth. As a consequence, our interactions will become ever more meaningful.

The Nature of Angels Versus Light Beings

We appear to humankind in either our collective form or as what you would perceive to be our individual forms. You observe the energy of the collective as massive and luminous globes of light. When we are seen near or around UFOs we are usually in a collective form. We are often seen elsewhere, on a more personal level, as smaller orbs of light. If you are open, you may detect our telepathic messages. The feeling tone of our transmission is not what you might interpret as emotional in nature. You are more apt to feel sensations of buoyancy, tingling, or heightened senses. We are not emotional beings. We are beings of creative vibration. We are often sensed as an amplification of your own energy. We do not impose on your beliefs; we only enhance the development of your path. Therefore, each of you will interpret our light through the lens of your understanding and beliefs.

We have often been referred to, or labeled, as angels, because your culture has a familiarity with that notion, and we often act in a similar fashion to what you understand to be the job of angels. In a sense, we can be seen as an angelic force in that we are bringers of light. But, we are different from what historically, and biblically, are referred to as angels. Biblical angels are another type of multi-dimensional being. But, their function, or mission, and methods are different than ours. A whole book can be written on the nature, purpose, and behavior of angelic forces. And, that is not our aim in this writing. But, for the sake of clarification, we will offer a simple comparison.

Angels are messengers between the various dimensional expressions of creation, and the ethereal realm between. In other words, they exist as a link between life and afterlife expressions. They assist in the lessons and interpretations during your transitions to the next level, or type of reality. As such, they are assigned to particular beings to help them assimilate what it is they came to do in a given life. They help with the soul's departure from the physical form, and aid them in realizations while in their spirit transition form. Angels are go-betweens. There are angels that assist with all forms of life on your planet, and all others in the universe. They are individual, ethereal beings that can take any particular shape needed to get their messages across. And so they will often walk among you as other humans, animals, or objects that get your attention. Angels will tend to take forms that your minds can formulate and translate.

Angels differ from us in that they do not have the ability to alter or enhance energy expressions. They are messengers, not builders. As such, they are not creators of realities, but are rather pipelines between realities. Specifically, they are the telegraph system between our energy grid creations, and the resting and assessing zone between. We assist you in your journey while you are creating in a so-called physical form, while they keep you on track as to what you were individually intending during this life, and help you build a bridge to the next life. We assist you in evolving as creators, and infuse the entire creative system with energy, while angels relay reminders to your individual spirits regarding your chosen lessons for a given life. So, while we take no offense to being called angels, we are formulators of life forms and are therefore technically quite different aspects of the God force than are angels. We are all different aspects of a greater creation dynamic, and we each have our place in the perpetuation of all existence.

While your interaction with angels has been recognized, for the most part, throughout human history, your association and understanding of our presence has been less predominant. The connection is, however, growing stronger as you become more adept at manipulating the energy grid of creation. As your perception of consciousness and its role in creating your environment grows, so will your associations with our energy. We will become greater companions, as you participate more directly in materializing your thoughts.

Human Relations with the Inter-Galactic Community

Each of you reading this book already has a special connection with light beings, and likely also with other off Earth and future humans. If you have read this far, then there is a strong likelihood that you are linked to us, whether you are aware of it or not. We have already been in touch with your spirit, and you recognize the light within the words. Something in the transmission will resonate with your heart, and activate or accentuate heightened sensory abilities within you. As the transition to your next density accelerates, you will become more sensitive to our frequency around you. Many of you will become leaders in the associations between worlds. We encourage you to allow your imaginations to flow to our realm. When the time is right, many of you will see, feel, and hear us among you.

As aids to evolution, we will be involved in helping you to raise your vibration, so that you will also be able to resonate with, and understand, the many perspectives of other beings of the universe. If your hearts and souls are on a light frequency, you will connect only with other highly developed souls with good intentions. If you are rooted in lower emotional needs, you are at risk of feeding the desires of beings who can take advantage of your newly arising soul. Even as you transition to the new world, you will be responsible for continually monitoring your soul's intentions to assure adherence to a path of light. There is never anything to fear when you come from a place of genuine warmth, understanding, and goodwill to all. When you resonate with those thoughts and feelings, you will attract other beings that have intentions of service to creation as well. Anything lower will not be able to touch your brightness.

When we make contact with each of you, we read your frequency and objectives before making ourselves known. As facilitators, we make recommendations to councils of light as to your readiness to engage in associations. Just as you will be able to read our signals to you, other species will also look for our signs in regard to human interactions. As integral forces in the grid of light, we are always present in major acts of creation, including new meetings between worlds. You can further our aid by requesting our infusion of light into your encounters. A simple acknowledgment of our presence in the universe is enough to warrant our attention. After that, we will be able to offer you a bonus to the direction in which your thoughts are flowing. Clearly, all the tools of self-awareness that we have been putting forth will be beneficial to our communications, and hence to the level of your transactions with other species.

There is literally an entourage of inter-galactic and inter-dimensional beings taking an interest in your planet, and your species' evolutionary cycle. It is an event marked on the calendars of a multitude of advanced civilizations. What occurs in the Earth's sphere of existence impacts not only your galaxy, but others beyond that have an association with your galaxy, as well as other dimensions and parallel futures. As grid workers within the fabric of space, time and beyond, we affect all the interactions of life within the creational structure. We perceive the dance of energy transference that is occurring on multiple levels. Again, it is always our aim to help all species to evolve as creators. Thus, we have an acute interest in spreading wisdom and light to accomplish that. In so doing, we hope that your collective consciousness will embark on a journey to find peace and enlightenment among friends from other worlds.

It is seen that there are many varying views among your species regarding the contacts, types, and motives of so-called aliens. Each of these perspectives can play a role in the nature of what you create, as the transition rolls up on you. There are a majority of humans that are completely ignorant and complacent about the existence of other worldly beings. The energy that such lack of regard infuses is likely to pan out as fear, if and when real encounters are experienced. In other words, the lack of mental preparedness will most likely result in shock and dismay, no matter what the intents of the aliens.

Then there are those who are already of the belief that there are evil or threatening aliens among you, manipulating your outcome. This belief will only serve to attract that frequency of life upon your plane. No being has power over your mind unless you allow yourself to succumb to its tyranny by believing you are powerless. We assure you that no Reptilian can eat you, and no Grey will be able to abduct and experiment on you, if you make your higher intentions known through your thoughts and emotions. Raising your frequency above this fear based creation will rescue you from such a reality.

There are also a growing number of you who are having positive contacts with alien species already. This is the group that can usher in a new era of peace between humankind and the inter-galactic councils, as heralds for Mother Earth. As you rise up, you will be spokespersons for the strength and character of humanity. A victim mentality will not hold up in your dealings with advanced beings. You are not victims; you are creators of your very promising future in a much bigger cultural dynamic. Be not afraid of your encounters as long as your heart is pure. Anything other than purity of spirit will be recognized as such, and will attract a lower spirited interaction. We are here to assist you in creating the best interactions. We have no interest in the creation of more war and destruction. That is de-evolution and not a part of our game plan and neither should it be yours.

In that light, know that all our associations with you are for advancement. If your collective consciousness takes a turn toward destruction, we can no longer assist you. Remember, though, that it does not require a majority of you to change the world for the better. It only takes a strong small percentage to turn the tables enough for a brighter future to be ensured. You are well on the way. The tide is turning in the favor of a light filled future. Keep your chins up and forge ahead with the beauty of peace and prosperity for all in your motives, and the burgeoning force of light will push you through the gateway into an engaging new world of thoughtful inter-connectivity.

Sound, Frequency, and Crop Circle Transmissions

With the acceleration of heightened frequency upon your Earth plane, we are increasingly able to maintain a deeper connection with human thoughts, and their physical reality. As such, we are involved with greater amounts of input into perceivable forms. For example, we are able to have communications with individuals who are adept at sound transference, and have been able to add light to musical compositions. The frequencies in sound can allow a direct contact between emotions and creation. There is a strong potential link between sound patterns and the enhancement of the formation of molecular structure. In other words, the energy inherent in musical frequencies affects matter and all life at the basic building block level. Therefore, sound is an effective tool for enrichment of your environment and health.

Various frequencies, emitted by particular musical compositions, will resonate with cells in the body and molecular structures of minerals and plants, for example. You can learn to measure such affects and fine tune the use of music to uplift life, and the core of all physical objects. As we communicate on this level with many humans that have such interests, we are teaching them the finer aspects of how their music influences the world around them, depending on the vibrations they tap into. This connection will continue in the fourth dimensional experience until unification is created with awareness between the musician, us, and the listeners. All will become aware of the transference of creational light force and will add to the frequency enhancement of the music. In this way music becomes an important regenerative medium for a community. It certainly has a much higher potential than simply acting as a source of entertainment, though it is also enjoyable. Music with connection becomes a means of enlightenment that is shared between groups of beings. It is a method of interaction you will want to enjoy to its fullest as you progress into the 4D perspective.

Specific musical notes and tones in combination are helpful in healing particular aspects of your health as well. There are sounds that affect your respective mind, body and soul levels, and all the layers within those aspects of your being. For example, a piece of music can stimulate the heart physically, while another will change the heart chakra energetically, and yet another will promote the mental projections of the heart. The same can be said for each particular chakra, and other aspects of one's mental and emotional functioning, as well as each body part that makes up the whole human being. Understanding the multiple layers of your nature, and that each has a certain vibration, will assist you in comprehending how musical notes can resonate with, and enhance, these layers.

The vibration of sound is a fluid means of transferring light energy. It is a means of connection that we can bridge with ease. We often do so to make an imprint on your world. We use sounds that are out of your audible hearing range physically, but not for your soul, to make frequency impressions on your planetary plane, in order to awaken aspects of your DNA coding. Sometimes this is done in a way that creates a physically perceivable result, as in the case of crop circles. In this way, we relay a frequency signature to your planet that stimulates your biological essence and encourages connections. They could be compared to the way a Morse code can relay a message by electromagnetic means into a translatable structure. In the case of crop circles, it does not matter whether you can translate the message intellectually, because your body absorbs the frequency into your DNA. You do not even need to visually see the formations. They are merely an image of a frequency that is felt by the entire planet.

There are such signatures being sent, in places that do not necessarily make a physical print as well. One day, as you develop your sensitivities, humans will be able to interpret the frequency that the crop formations emit, and we will have yet another means of interacting. It should be noted that we are not the only beings that use this method of frequency sound transmission. Some of the crop designs are the result of fourth and fifth dimensional cultures' attempts to prepare you for their arrival. They are sending messages that contain their frequency so that you become open to their contact when the time is right.

Mind you, there are also human beings who have created some lovely crop forms. We congratulate those of you involved on your creativity. However, there are electromagnetic residues on crop circles that were created from other than human sources, that can be physically detected, and could not be replicated by human means.

There is much controversy around the formation of the crop circles among you. We assure you that there is no one right answer in this dilemma. In fact, the beauty is that all factions are correct. Every thought related to the topic becomes an aspect of the reality that you create and hence experience in your world. We congratulate those that are able to think outside traditional belief systems, as they provide new hope of expanded views and reality for your species. If no one among you were to imagine that alien beings might have created the circles, then guess what? This reality would never enter into your sphere, and would, as a result, not exist for you. As you explore this option, you create the reality. And eventually, you will create the physical evidence that supports the scenario.

We also know that there are many human crop circle designers, and cohorts, that are beginning to see the potential of using the geometry, and intention behind the manufacture of the imprints, as a means of producing phenomena. Hence, a two-way communication is being developed. We especially promote this as a wonderful step in our relations. You are recognizing that we can relate by means of geometry, mathematical precision, symbols, sound, and vibration. With the use of intention behind these methods, many are seeing and feeling the potential of relaying messages by these means. By doing this, you are opening a channel in both directions, and are learning the impact you can have by using these means of transmitting energy patterns as information, just as we have done. In other words, there are some among you who are learning by the example of advanced beings. You are managing to stretch your reality to venture into the now very real option of extraterrestrial two-way communications. The more you are open, the more possibilities will arise. Remember, our relationship always rests in the minds and souls of each one of you, and your collective dream.

Trust us when we say that we read and respond to all the intentions behind your human crop circle communications. That response includes all those that put their thoughts into the energy of the imprint after it is made. We read the intentions you put forth as a collective frequency, and send our vibration down the threads of light that attach each consciousness to that image in response. In this way, you are creating a bridge between our light and your own soul's light. In this way, all of the crop circles are becoming doorways between our worlds. Thus, we urge you all to continue to focus your creativity, and higher intentions, on the study and creation of crop circles.

Beautifully, other than a few determined debunkers that also play an important role in the urging of new discoveries, those that do not believe beyond the idea that the circles are a simple human hoax, add very little attention energy to the transmissions. It is those of you who stretch the possibilities by searching for more answers, and pondering new ideas, that are adding the richness of the ever expanding connection, elicited through the imprints. Again, it is those seekers among you that are making possible a human future in the intergalactic community.

Receptivity to Telepathy

Given that much of our communications are in the form of information as light transference, we would like to expound upon the nature of telepathy. You are all capable of having telepathic interactions, whether you are aware of it or not. Many of you are having more telepathic communications than you realize already. As you begin to appreciate and acknowledge this natural part of your mental process, you can learn to be more sensitive and become better interpreters of the messages. If you have had moments where you believe you received a telepathic message, be it as simple as knowing who was calling on the phone, or a bright idea popping in your head from nowhere, think about how the thought came into your mind. Was it like a bolt of lightning? Not likely. More likely, it was a subtle and sudden unexplainable knowing. The feeling related is probably not drastic, but is rather calming and relieving.

The frequency on which telepathic communications exist is one that causes the electromagnetic impulses of the mind to be soothed. Such connections are not able to bypass a mind that is too frantic. Messages are more likely to be noticed when one is not thinking or worrying about anything, or is loosely absorbed in a topic. A calmer mind promotes better telepathy. And, when the message is transmitted, it will add to that feeling of calm. This is the nature of the vibration upon which information travels over light strands.

Your guides, angels, higher selves, light beings, and less dense sentient life forms, can make telepathic links to your mental structure. When you are relaxed or meditative, interactions with such beings is easily possible. As you ask for guidance, learn to trust the thoughts that come to you, if you do not already have fluid relations with any of the above. A message that is from a light vibration will make you feel tranquil and even euphoric, not heavy and burdened. A telepathic communication from a denser frequency will be distorted, uncomfortable, and even demanding. Listen to and encourage only sudden thoughts of a buoyant and uplifting quality.

When we communicate with individuals, such as the channel for this writing, we are making a connection with the soul's multi-dimensional being. We relate with the expanded nature of the soul as a multi-dimensional consciousness. Often we are communicating with the soul as it exists in many dimensions at once, or are calling upon higher aspects of the soul's being that can facilitate the telepathic relations. Hence, we filter through higher facets of the soul that are more evolved spiritually. While we are doing so, all aspects of the self are gaining an energy boost from the experience. Since all aspects of the self are evolving out of your concept of space/time, there are elements of your soul that you would see as highly advanced in telepathic, and other, capabilities. You are a part of that evolution as you exist now.

Many of you, like the present channel, also have aspects of your greater soul within beings that reside, or resided at one time or another, on other worlds in your universe. Your soul may exist in a form other than human. This is another way you can help bridge relations between humans and other beings. There are parts of your higher selves, so to speak, that have a deep understanding of certain off Earth civilizations and can allow you to become facilitators, and better telepathic mediums, between humans and those other species.

Many of you have an inherent knowing that you did not come from planet Earth originally. Or, you feel that you are different or do not really belong here. You of course belong here, in that you chose to be here for your evolution. Part of that path is to make connections with the higher aspects of your self, and strengthen those links between the respective beings and current humans. If you can accept that you are a multi-dimensional soul, you may be able to awaken some of the attributes inherent in the portion of your soul that exists on other planets and dimensions. We depend greatly, for example, on the facet of the channel that is living as a highly telepathic being from another star system in your galaxy. This other life form is aware of such interactions and is encouraging to the future of humanity in the process. This energetic link aids the translation from our light energy into your human words.

In the telepathic process, feeling, images, and three dimensional symbols are tools to develop accuracy in transmission. As you evolve your telepathic skills, you will find that thought energy can be more effectively relayed with three dimensional symbols that go beyond the limits of your present language. There is a wealth of information that can be transmitted with a 3D image that includes the emotions that accompany the image. Imagine the difference between hearing or seeing the word apple, and picturing an apple. The latter elicits a much deeper emotional and physical response, and may very well transit space and time. The visual image of an apple can traverse memories of apple experiences, whereas the mere word has limitations in its impact. The adage "a picture speaks a thousand words" applies to telepathic messages as well. Therefore, many cultures that use telepathy have developed 3D languages that they use to communicate more, with fewer transmissions. When you practice your telepathy, try sending 3D images over light filaments while in a relaxed state of mind.

There is much more to be discussed on the topic of telepathy, and a whole book could be written on the subject. We suggest you look into what has been studied on the matter, and begin to trust your own inner soul language. You do have the ability within your human DNA, and the higher aspects of your soul. If you remain open and seek to attune to that which is unseen, and between what is seen and understood, you will be ready when faculties begin to switch on more acutely as you approach the central plane of your galaxy, and your multi-dimensional nature is revealed. Your relationship with us light beings, and others, will be an enlightening experience, and deeply fulfilling for your greater soul. Eventually we will all meet gladly in the spaces between and beyond the envelope of time.

Chapter 14

The Space Between and the Envelope of Time

t is the space between what you perceive as matter that holds the true essence of creation. When you can grasp and feel that the space between really is not space at all, but is the oneness and endless creation with no time frame, you will begin to free your mind from the limits of your illusory reality. For the sake of your understanding, imagine all the space that exists between atoms and particles. Picture yourself being able to walk in and around the particles, and hence perceive how physical objects are actually not solid. As you move around within the object you will no longer conceive of the time in which the object exists. You would be beyond the motion of the pieces of matter and their movement from one place to the next in a relative dance with one another. The space between exists outside the envelope of time. This topic may appear irrelevant to your everyday life. But, in fact, an awareness of where you and your physical creations fit into, and beyond, the so-called fabric of the space/time continuum is of the utmost importance to your awakening soul.

The Singularity of the Space Between

We have discussed the nature of your soul as a multi-dimensional being of source energy, and how your awareness is developing as an expression of creation. We have delved into the grid of light energy and fields that make up your environment, and how you can tap into this core matrix of information. Now we wish to go further into how the matrixes of many physical realities exist, in fact, in a singleness, and outside of the framework of time, and how you can create more effectively by stepping in between the grid fabric to experience the true oneness of everything. Even pondering the notion of the singularity of existence, and allowing your thoughts to be in this perspective, will expand your appreciation of the magnitude and splendor of what we are all a part of as creative beings. While your mind may have difficulty intellectualizing outside your usual material means, your soul flourishes in the spaces between.

Let us take a walk down a sidewalk created by consciousness, and held together by a grid of light fibers. Together we created this sidewalk collectively. We continue to create it as you walk. The thoughts you have as you stroll create ever more experiences for your interaction. Every thought, feeling, and relationship forms more fibers in the grid, and those you come in contact with add to the energy patterns, creating more of the same. The whole system of matter is made up of your thoughts projected as frequency patterns, individually and collectively. When you realize that you create this material energy signature, you can go beyond it by, firstly, seeing that there is a space between which renders the grid illusory.

Your scientific string theories, which suggest the universe is made up of vibrating strands, is on track in understanding the nature of physical existence. However, to grasp the whole of creation one must look between those vibrating strands where it will be seen that the physical frame is not actually there, because the strands are made by consciousness. Without the observer being among the strings, the perception of being in and among objects with reference points ceases to be. In essence, you cannot see what you are creating, until you are able to allow your mind to view the creation from an outside point of view. You may wonder how you can go outside of the material grid with consciousness, if just by doing so you would be observing and hence creating something. The secret of going to the in between world is that it is the birthplace of consciousness itself, and, by allowing your soul mind's eye to venture there, you are experiencing the source of consciousness. This is where true knowing, and the singularity that all realities stem from, can be felt. When you experience this oneness you will not want to leave. However, you cannot stay there, as consciousness inherently desires to get back to expressing itself by creating something within its currently chosen reality. Glimpsing and knowing this source will forever widen your comprehension of the meaning of life, the universe, and everything.

The idea of the space between is actually a misconception in that there really is no space, once you step in between the particles. From your consciousness perspective, though, you will still perceive this zone as having space. But, in reality, space no longer exists in the world of creation's inception. And where there is no space, there is also no time. In your present level of conscious awareness, you will only be able to comprehend the singularity of creation in a limited way. However, by attempting to go between your physical systems, you can glimpse the sensation and gain a valuable understanding of the principles governing ultimate creation. With this knowledge, your species gains an awareness of its connection to all forms of matter, and thus can be welcomed into the greater sphere of life forms that also have this fundamental knowing.

The first step to visiting the in between world is to go there in one's imagination. This is always the first step in creation. After all, you would be creating the ability to view creation. It is within this seemingly empty space that the force exists that forms the energy grids and all that is within and a part of those grids. This force is the essence that creates everything from thought, to the awareness of thought, to the slightest impulse of a one-celled animal, to the motivation for life to grow and a particle to be. All of these aspects of creation affect one another to a degree, based on how aware they are of their interconnection to each other and their acumen at influencing the energy grids. As consciousness units develop this ability, they become more involved in the creation process, as we have discussed. Awareness evolves slowly enough to allow the consciousness to handle each successive leap in the expression of the whole singularity.

How can so much exist in no space and time? Perhaps you can begin to fathom it by imagining how much space your thoughts or dreams take up? Sure, you experience thoughts as taking time and therefore they are related to space, somehow, in your minds. But, are they? The closest thing to pure creation, that you can possibly grasp, is your thoughts. Your thoughts are the first step in your creation process, and thus there is a similarity to the creation of all reality. However, you may ask then, who or what is doing the thinking to create all of creation? This is the big mystery of all time, is it not? It is the question of what or who is God, or the ultimate prime creator? We invite you to make this discovery yourselves, although, it has been said already that we are all God. Does this then mean that the space between matter is the conscious thought of everything that exists?

When you venture to the place of Oneness, you feel that you are all space, all time, all thought and consciousness at once. To feel this ultimate expression of everything is what you would call complete ecstasy. When you are in the state of Oneness, you fully realize that you are it, and it is already perfect. Interestingly, when one knows that they are already evolved, they can get on with the process of evolving. Yes, another paradox. When you evolve to have the awareness of the unity of creation, then you free yourself to continue expressing that creation. With this awareness, the desire follows to be as close as possible to the purity of that ecstasy of expression in all its forms.

Is there, then, one creator of the first unit of consciousness in all of existence? The only answer we can offer, from our point of awareness, is that all that exists including us, you, every planet, every rock, every universe, and each single particle of matter, is in fact the one unit of consciousness of creation, and we see no beginning and no end to this Oneness. We, as in Everything, are God, and we are all The Creator. Therefore, when you are praying to a Creator, it can only be an aspect of you, and everything, that you are praying to. You are created in the image of the Creator because you are the Creator. When you go to the space between, you will reach this awareness that the unity of all forms of expression is formed ultimately out of One Unified Consciousness.

The Subtle Energy of the Space Between

As you venture into the space between, from the point of view of your present level of awareness as 3D beings, and as you evolve to a 4D perspective, you can learn to detect the subtle energy in that so-called emptiness. There is a resonance of consciousness that can be sensed in between what you think is physical matter. It is in this in between zone that the energy of thoughts emerge, before they are then manifested into the matter-energy grid that makes your world appear real. Consciousness, at its multitude of levels of awareness, creates subtle thought vibrations that can be translated into a light grid that represents material forms. The material forms are amplified with the addition of further thought energy. The subtle or fine energy of this space between is the life force of creation. It is the pulse of the oneness and hence of everything.

There are many ways to tap into this sea of subtle vibration, as of yet unmeasured by your sciences. Firstly, know that you are alive and moving because you are made up of this energy, and you continue after physical death because this fine energy does not dissipate upon the collapse of the body. This fine life force is what is real, and the physical vessel is an illusion created by the source consciousness. So technically, everything is plugged into this field of vibration.

As 3D beings, you have fallen head over heels in love with your creations and have forgotten that they are a play. You have forgotten that you have created a sort of hologram that is actually made up of the fine energy, translated into an expression. In essence, it is not a matter of tapping into the energy field as much as it is about recognizing that the energy field is the source of all life, inanimate or not. This force is never ending and continually replenishes itself. If you can put your minds around this idea, then you may be able to contemplate how it is integrated into your present reality, and how it can be blocked by your limited thoughts.

You, along with other creative conscious beings, have created your universal experience based on basic principals which are constantly being altered as you stretch your beliefs about them. When you become aware of your Oneness as expressions of Creation, then you will know that the sea of life energy surrounds and envelops you, and can be used to restore your creations perpetually. Bit by bit, you can expand your accepted principles and alter them to include the zero point energy field that is the space between.

Geometry as a Bridge to Zero Point Energy

Since you live in a geometrical world of your own collective creation, you can use the geometric designs that repeat everywhere in your universe as a bridge to the zero point field. Geometric shapes have the ability to naturally connect with your source energy because the consciousness that created your universe built it with these thoughts. And, you all perpetuate that reality. We have already suggested that geometric shapes emit a frequency. Now we would like to add that they can also extract the vibration that is at the core of creation, and assist in regenerating that which you focus your attention on.

The vibration of the space between is the finest of the fine and is as subtle as it gets. You cannot detect it with physical instruments, but you can experience its effects on the matter-energy grid as you use geometrical configurations to draw its force to particular locations. We suggest you continue your experimentations with these forms and mathematical calculations. Within these studies are many secrets, some of which were already discovered on your planet by previous civilizations, and ancestral visitors. What we are proposing is that you make a link between your physical energy grid and the consciousness field. By making a bridge between your ethereal selves and your creations, you will find that you are closer to the expression of Oneness.

Geometric shapes can also lead you to travel outside the envelope of time, and have already been used in this way by previous cultures on your planet. The shapes become a bridge that allow a flow from the matter grid in your reality, through the ethereal fine energy space between, which is really no space, into other grids of matter in far away realities, parallel dimensions, and moments in time. This is possible because certain sacred geometric patterns have the ability to create links to the eternal no-space zone, and to material grid systems. With the correct intentions, those that have an inclination to explore this area, will be able to find answers to these mysteries, if they join minds and share discoveries.

The use of geometric configurations is not necessary to make a connection with the space between. But, it will allow you to amplify your consciousness and make focused use of the connection in your physical realm. Your consciousness itself is your most powerful force. But, if you

233

use certain geometric structures to intensify its link with source energy, then much can be accomplished. However, your intentions and attention are still of the utmost importance as you delve into sacred geometry energy amplifiers. Using these techniques for destructive ends will create just that for all concerned. If the focus is instead geared toward the betterment of all humankind and the planet, then amazing feats will be attained.

Why and how do you think the pyramids were constructed? These were power houses built for consciousness amplification and travel outside the envelope of time. They were constructed, long before the Egyptian civilization you know of in your historical records, by human ancestors that came from another galaxy. But, where they came from is much less important than the fact that the pyramids are a testament to the power of geometry yet to be discovered by your people.

We leave it to you to go out and explore the potentials inherent in the use of geometric forms yourselves. But, let us say that the powers you can tap into will assist in many areas of life including healing, building, transportation, energy sources, developing psychic abilities, growing foods, and time travel, to name a few. When exploring these ideas, remember that the fundamental goal is to make the connection between your physical energy grid and the source consciousness realm. Both dynamics must be given credence and respect with your best intentions. The idea is to get the most out of the life force of creation for the benefit and uplifting of all concerned.

Meditation as a Tool to Touch the Oneness

Another way that you may personally reach the realm of pure consciousness is through quieting the mind and listening to the vibration of your soul. You can do this through meditation and relaxation exercises. Many of you will find that it is easier to reach the state of Oneness when you are away from the influences of your society, as there are many electromagnetic and frequency interference from mechanical devices and human minds. A place in nature that is relaxing for you can be most beneficial to calming and releasing your mind from outside influences. It is not absolutely necessary, but it is helpful to be in a natural setting or at least away from densely populated areas.

When you do reach the state of Oneness, you will actually feel hugely expanded and vast. Your sensations will encompass All That Is and be overwhelmed with a euphoric feeling of absolute perfection and bliss. Everything will feel dynamic, ever changing, and utterly fulfilled. You will feel the constantly evolving nature of creation and the beauty of thoughts forming realities. When you have these sensations, you can only be in a state of empathy and unconditional love for All That Is. You will feel assured that you are as significant as the most advanced beings of awareness and the most fundamental forms of consciousness.

How do you reach such a state of being? Firstly, intend that you do so. Then, give it a try. There is not one meditative method. There are many ways to reach this awareness. Try different styles of meditation that are designed to be calming and centering for your soul, and use your imagination to take you in between the particles of matter and outside time. As a fourth dimension human, you will learn to see matter more fluidly. And, bringing your soul to this ether zone will be easier and you will gain more acumen at exploring it with your consciousness. Calming your mind and beginning the exploration now will make it a real breeze in 4D. Seeing and feeling this space will free your soul from much of the confines of matter that you are stuck in today. As you move about with your soul's awareness, you will learn to manipulate your physical world using your mental focus and intention.

The art of meditation is a means of practice for your seeing and creating more effectively with your soul mind's eye, by touching the creational space between matter. It is an ability that will be helpful in your 4D world, as it focuses your soul's attention and brings your guidance system into a realm of pure light, which enables self-healing and the elevating of intentions. When you are able to put your mind in a place of unity with the particles of matter and space surrounding them, you gain the strength of understanding how your consciousness creates. We highly recommend that you each make a routine of quieting your mind, in whatever way suits your beliefs and personality. Some of you will respond to the more psychological self-hypnosis methods and others to more Eastern religious meditation practices. Still others will find the many integrations of your New Age guided relaxation tapes most conducive.

Your attempts to reach heightened and focused altered states of consciousness can always be enhanced by the use of sacred geometry, whether by sitting within geometric structures or by directing ones attention to particular mandalas and other universal symbols, such as spiral formations. Again, the shapes can transcend your physical brain and link your mind to your soul. The use of scents, candlelight, and even the creation of an altar of respect to your spiritual journey, will be helpful for many as a trigger to reach a relaxed state of mind. Then, simply sitting within this sacred space or thinking of the scents will bring about the desired calmness. Such tools bridge the gap between the physical world that is most tangible to you, and your more ethereal spirit.

We also recommend that you give due respect and appreciation for your connection and unity with creation as you meditate. Your acknowledgment of your divine link with All That Is will strengthen your awareness of the bond that is inherently there. It is your awakening to this bond that assists in your evolution, and raises your vibration, so that you can more readily see how everything fits into place as a creative construction.

It is also beneficial that you break away from the limits of your cultural and religious beliefs. Recognize them as a part of a created dynamic of life on Earth. Understand that all such ideas are beautiful forms of expression and attempts by humanity to comprehend the magnitude of creation. Give respect and admiration to the variety of explanations. Be willing to see yourself, and others, outside of dogmas and as equally magnificent creative beings expressing different aspects of the Oneness. This is not to say that you should dissolve your religious beliefs. Rather, it will behoove you to recognize that all religious beliefs have a root of absolute love and light. Explore their core teachings with your own heart and soul. Do not depend on others to interpret them for you. Always use your own soul's guidance as your barometer. When in doubt, meditate and follow the sensations of your inner knowing.

The more you practice techniques that take you to the space between, the more you will be able to see beyond the limitations of your creations. And in turn, the more able you will be as creators. Inherent in the exploration of the energy between matter, will be the ability to increasingly step out of the envelope of time, and expand your multidimensional understanding. In 4D, your comprehension of the malleability of time will increase.

Stepping Out of the Envelope of Time

A special quality of your leap to the next dimension of awareness will be your new perception of the illusory nature of time. As you become cognizant of the illusion of space, so you will gain a wider viewpoint from which to understand the relative experience of time. You currently are living in an envelope of time. When you step out of your physical web of creation, you also step out of this envelope. Your soul does not exist in its larger dynamic, within the perimeters of this envelope. And, the less dense your frequency, the closer you are to your true form. Hence, as you step into a less dense dimensional awareness, you become less trapped by the constructs of space and time as they relate to one another. This loosening perspective has many advantages for your creativity as a species, and for your individual soul evolution.

As your awareness develops, so do all the aspects of your soul that are vibrating in different frequency signatures. Therefore, again, as you heighten your awareness, all parts of your soul are influenced and have the potential to evolve in unison. When you are able to lessen your density and see past space and time, you will be more able to recognize other aspects of your soul existing in probable pasts and futures, and possibly on other planets. The grip your mentality and psychology have on the concrete day-to-day existence will expand to include your selves that exist outside of your current envelope of time, and limits of place.

Many of you may already be feeling and experiencing these other aspects of yourselves in the form of dreams, sensations, memories, spontaneous recalls of past lives, or familiarity with communications from outside your planet, through telepathic or channeled means. You are not losing your minds. You are waking up to your multidimensional selves. This will become more commonplace as Earth approaches her final shift. It is evidence that the barrier of the envelope is thinning. It is good that it is occurring slowly, for it is allowing your 3D bodies, and minds, to adjust to the expanded perceptions caused by the weakening of filters that are there to prevent you from having such realizations.

Viewing your own multidimensional reality will aid you in under-standing your larger evolutionary soul, and will allow you to help others in their processes. Many of you will not only find that you see yourselves through time, but that you are able to recognize others that you have a multidimensional relationship with as well. You will sense how you can best assist each other as you interact in this chosen life play. This does not mean that the answers to your connection will be all laid out. But, you will have much greater awareness as to the meaning of your associations, and be able to make more informed decisions as to how you would like to proceed. You will also be able to perceive the effects of your actions energetically, and hence will be able to view the probable outcomes of your actions with more clarity. This will be possible individually and globally.

By stepping outside time restrictions, you have a bird's eye view, so to speak, of how waves of energy may materialize in your own life, and for your species and planet. Obviously, there are advantages in having this awareness. The finer your vibration, the more easily you can see probabilities with clarity, and less fuzziness. The more psychological clutter you have, the more static you will experience in perceiving outside the envelope. In other words, your state of mind, and personal shield of filters, will affect what you are able to view through the time barrier.

The less you allow your present ego personality to influence you, and the more pure soul awareness you activate, the more accurately you will read the patterns of consciousness that lead to various outcomes. In 3D, you have been learning the process of how you mold your experience on a physical stage. As you become more adept at noticing and altering your creations with consciousness, you are elevating your awareness as a creator. Thus, you will be more able to function in the increasing superconductive atmosphere of Earth and see outside the limits of space and time.

When Science Finds the Zero Point Field

As your collective consciousness expands to this new perspective of space and time, your scientific communities will also widen their ideas related to these concepts. They will make many important breakthroughs as a result. The new discoveries and theories will transcend many scientific disciplines, and allow a more cohesive integration of ideas than is currently seen. The awakening of the new perspective will happen in several areas of study at once, including physics, mathematics, biology and psychology. As scientific groups emerge with revolutionary insights and findings that cannot be explained by your currently held beliefs and accepted theories, an explosion of thought will give rise to amazing new paradigms. This process will raise the bar on everything you know, and how it is expressed physically. The new theories will soon lead to inventions that tap into the space between, and transcend the time barrier.

Such discoveries and inventions will forever alter life as you know it. All of this is possible when enough forward thinking minds free themselves from the standard views and norms, and begin to apply these new ideas in all fields of study. The consciousness shift will lead the way for an awareness that sends your civilization leaps and bounds ahead in a short period of time. In your lighter 4D form, thoughts will travel throughout society at an exponential rate, and spontaneous knowing will occur across the globe.

The energy of consciousness will travel at speeds which will cause giant leaps in spiritual, scientific, and technological knowledge. The key to the new ideas will be in the exploration of the space between, and the source energy emitted from it. Following that, there will be discoveries of the nature and flexibility of the constructs of time related to consciousness that will open doors to inter-dimensional time travel. There is much for your species to look forward to as you venture out into the cosmos. When many of you leave your physical body in death, you will be eager to return to play in the evolving Earth plane, as it will represent a new frontier and be the perfect playground for pioneers.

Understanding the space between and time envelope will drastically

240

alter the fields of biology and psychology. This, in turn, will transform the way you view healing, and its relationship to mental health. The inter-connectedness of the soul will also be considered in the holistic approaches to personal and collective health issues. The entire health field will change its focus from physical remedies and intrusive medicines, to that of energy frequency healing as it relates to the mind, spirit, and body connection. Various techniques will be advanced to aid and guide individuals in their self-healing processes. Medical practitioners will become guides in the understanding of causes for disease, and will help in using core energy fields to accentuate and accelerate cellular regeneration. The malleability of time will cause a revolution in your studies of cellular aging, and will allow the possibility of complete physical rejuvenation and slowing of the aging process.

The mental health, and overall psychological state of a person will always be considered before environmental causes. And, the role of the consciousness of a community will be considered in relation to larger outbreaks of disease. Such dynamics of mental health will be taken very seriously as a means of preventing health issues to begin with. Eventually, your health professionals will learn methods of prevention, related to each person and each community's well-being, to keep them healthy. You will then find less and less cases that accelerate to the point of a physical symptom. The health profession will gradually become more focused on detecting and maintaining the spiritual and mental health of individuals first, to prevent outbreaks of any kind. All this will be the result of increased understanding of the universal energy field that feeds all life.

Even when you have accidents that cause physical injury, the deeper mental and emotional causes of the event will be assessed with the assistance of able healers. The cures for such injuries will also advance greatly, when life force energy is tapped to regenerate damaged tissues and organs.

Techniques and technologies will be developed that assist the individual in healing him or herself. Such advances are inevitable once the zero point field is understood, and your society takes on a more balanced perspective that benefits the whole, and is not simply based on financial considerations. The heightened awareness of your species in general will be demanding that these holistic healing methods are pursued.

Likewise, environmentally sustainable systems will take off like rockets when the regenerative qualities of the space between are used for reprocessing molecular structures within your physical framework. Matter can be transformed with consciousness at the seed level of creation. Therefore, you can learn to transform waste materials into something beneficial to the ecology of a given area. Your world can become entirely balanced with nature, once you have the understanding of how the zero point field of energy can be formulated into anything, through the intentions of conscious observers. These observers can then create mechanisms that trigger molecular transformations to continually recur from the energy field.

The ability to manufacture one substance from another will become an art form in itself. It is much like alchemy of consciousness. This is possible by taking physical methods, and injecting them with conscious creation that is linked to source energy. The difference in the way you work today is that you are unaware of the power of the consciousness factor in affecting all creations. Opening that door of awareness will change everything.

The same can be said about leaps in all technologies. Once your physicists wake up, the new theories will push all the envelopes of possibility in how you interact with your physical world. As your reality becomes less solid and time becomes less rigid, much of what your physicists and mathematicians thought impossible will suddenly become very feasible, including transportation across galaxies and through time. None of this will happen without your having a consciousness that respects the unity of all creation, and therefore is not bent on destroying other aspects of creation. Having such abilities and technologies without a certain spiritual maturity will end in destruction of the species, if you are not careful.

Meddling with such matters, without having an appreciation for the effects of the vibration one emits, can cause you to get stuck in some densities that you would not find pleasing. The laws of attraction work on all levels of creation. So, using such advances with a lower density perspective can be harmful to one's health. Beings from other worlds that are on a higher vibrational awareness level will not tolerate interference from dense energies. So, interaction with them would be nil. Such time/space technology can be misused, but it will not be beneficial to your species to do so. If you always aim high in your aspirations and reasons for space and time travel, then you will find a rewarding journey ahead.

As you personally, and collectively, begin to discover the wonders of the space between, we remind you that, in the comprehension that All Is One, there should also be an appreciation that the One has chosen to express itself in a multiplicity for a reason. In other words, you experience singularity of conscious awareness so that you each can bring richness to the One. You are not meant to stay in the state of Oneness between matter. As aspects of Creation, you are meant to, and desire to, continually experience a multitude of perspectives that add to the whole. Therefore, when you look at another life form, be grateful that it is fulfilling another part of the mission of your Oneness. And, be thankful that you are able to share your unique consciousness with all other parts of the whole.

When you are aware of the Oneness that exists in that source field, the beauty of all the intricate bits of consciousness, and their individual contributions to Creation, become truly awe inspiring. Upon feeling this truth, you gain a deep appreciation for yourself, and every living and non-living bit of the creation that surrounds you, and beyond. Also, you will know that this present reality is but a hiccup in the existence of your true being.

Chapter 15

The Hiccup of Existence and the Road Ahead

Your journey to the fourth dimensional perspective will find you vastly more aware of the scope and breadth of your being. The role you have played in this particular life span will be known as a hiccup in your larger sphere of existence, and the road that follows will take on new meaning. Though this life will appear smaller in the scheme of it all, you will also obtain a greater appreciation of the richness that it contains as an expression of your wider multi-dimensional self. The dichotomy of the smallness of this life relative to the depth of its meaning will be revealing in and of itself.

The wonders along the road of soul evolution will be more readily understood as you step through the gateway to the next dimension. In the thinning veil, you will learn to see and feel the subtleties within this existence and better gauge your journey ahead. We will share some ideas as to how this present hiccup in your evolution as a being of light adds to the perpetual path of soul evolution. We will discuss where you will go from here on your fantastic adventures, as individual souls and as collective soul groups, and how that fits into the evolution of the Oneness.

Your Multidimensional Expression and Evolution

While we use terms implying consecutive time, they are only references, as there is no measurement for a hiccup and the road is not actually ahead, but rather is being traveled in all directions at once. The road can just as easily be taken backwards as forwards and you would still be evolving.

Your soul journey is a path of developing awareness of who you are and where you originated from, and allowing yourself to freely express that which you become aware of. This awareness of self is continually changing as your soul expresses itself in a multitude of ways. As this current expression of your larger soul identity becomes more aware, it influences the whole of you throughout time and space at once. It is not as if you change and add to yourself year after year. When seen multidimensionally, this current life is in constant flux. As you seemingly die in this form, you are still evolving in this life, because it is in actuality still occurring, as are all your lives past and future. Therefore, you cannot view your present self as a lower form. You are simply one of your soul's expressions of awareness. The process is not stagnant.

You are not done with this life when you die, because your consciousness does not die. It continues to evolve. You are only experiencing this sequential experience so that you have a means of expressing your consciousness as a creator. Time exists as a means of conveying the creative process of consciousness. How is there evolution if everything is really happening at once? The answer is that though everything happens at once in a singularity, it is in a state of constant change and expresses itself in the creation of constructs of space and time. The Oneness is never the same. Its very nature is a creative evolution.

As you will find, when you step out of existing constructs, the past, present, and future are as fluid as the ocean. If you swirl your fingers through water, ripples will perpetually alter the placement of molecules in all directions. When you travel in time, the history will be different each time you go, as it is never really fixed. You will have to learn to calibrate your consciousness to signature frequencies in order to return to something like the present you left. There are many minute variations that you could synchronize with that would cause you to end up in alternate realities of your present, future, or past expressions.

Free Will Constructs of Good and Bad

It is important, at this stage of growth, for your species on this planet to recognize that you are much greater in scope than you seem, and that there are no right or wrong answers. There is only the matter of more or less awareness, and the observance of consequences. You have the privilege of observing yourself progressing in a linear way so that you are able to make correlations based on your free will. In this physical dimension, you can see how your consciousness affects objects and events.

Your decisions are all displayed in full color before you every day. This is the grace of consciousness, which becomes more fulfilling as you raise your awareness of how your decisions fit into a larger interconnected universe. Physicality is a stage for the play of creation and you have the ability to express yourself within it with awareness and freedom. This is the gift of self-awareness. Species that are less aware have fewer choices and do not recognize the consequences of their actions and thoughts. All consciousness is continuously in the process of evolving its awareness.

The so-called knowledge of good and evil that your soul exposed itself to in the third dimension, is actually the gift of free will. You have been given the awareness to make choices as to what you will experience in this life. This is a blessing. As your viewpoint widens, you realize that good and evil is nothing more than a matter of perspective and each can be changed into the other in a moment. More knowledge allows you to make better decisions for personal growth, not because something you choose is better or worse, but because you learn that anything can be transformed. This growth is about harnessing your ability as an aware being that makes decisions in creating its reality.

When your awareness allows you to acknowledge that being in a state of hate or anger toward something you do not want, only creates more of that or something on a similar frequency, by attraction, then, you stop hating and being angered. When you see that by love and kindness you create everything you dreamed of, you do more of that and become more like your source as a fluid creator. This is the road you are on as an evolving being. The less you are in a dense field of emotional baggage, the smoother your travels will be. Without belaboring this point that has already been made, suffice it to say that the less you perceive the world around you in terms of duality, the more you are able to stay in a place of ultimate creativity, which exists beyond such limited parameters of conception.

The road ahead will always be one of elevating your consciousness to increasing levels of awareness. At this stage, the challenge is to rise above the limitations of lower emotional frequencies and judgments as to good and bad notions. You can view the world and its duality as a testing ground for your free will and creativity as a being. The denser the frequencies you choose to align yourself with, the less effective you will be. And, the less connected you will be to the source of formative conscious creation. Does that mean it is simple? No, and it was not meant to be. The challenge is part of the process of developing your awareness. What use are choices without options?

Sometimes, in order to wake you up, the more drastic the options the better. It is all designed this way, by all conscious life, by choice. So while there is no such thing as one part of creation being more evil than another, all beings have free will as to what they create. Some choose methods and behaviors that are contrary to the ultimate creative energy. You are deciding such behaviors every day as individuals and en masse. It may appear that we are saying it is better for you to choose a path less dense. But there is no judgment in this assessment. We are saying that, while acts are not judged as better or worse, some are in fact closer to what you are as a being of light, which is pure conscious awareness in its most agile form.

It will benefit you to appreciate in this life that all the duality you experience is a means for you to be involved in your own creative process of decision making. It is the process itself that is creative. Creation is a process. If you can learn to admire all the nuances and means of expressing yourself in your most pure form, you will be fulfilling your purpose. You chose to be who you are physically and mentally for particular reasons. Each life is a piece of a larger puzzle that is your higher consciousness. If you can learn to revel in the everyday discoveries and processes of being and knowing your true self, you will be on the road of increasing awareness. You have placed certain hurdles in your way from birth, and throughout your life, that assist you in learning more of who you are. This learning is perfecting the knowing of self and adding to the knowing of the whole.

The Answer is in the Journey Itself

The realization that everything you do is a beautiful poetic diagram for your further awareness can finally allow you to stop worrying and enjoy the flow of living and growing. You are already "there" because the process is the "there." And "there" is "here" already. The evolution of consciousness is creation and vice versa. Revel in your constantly changing self. You are never the same from moment to moment. Every second, therefore, is a new opportunity to be and know another quality of your soul.

The beauty of being a conscious being is that you will always be changing. Sometimes you will do it unconsciously, and other times quite intentionally. That is also your choice. You can allow others to influence your expression of self, or you can think independently. You can try to find out who you are by projecting your problems onto others and by stealing energy from them, or you can reveal yourself by continually reviving your being from the ultimate life force. All these lessons are inherent in all your thoughts and actions toward yourself and everything around you. You have the same ability to create abundance in the world as you do pain and strife. Each is just as accessible. The journey is in discovering your preferences, and learning how to manifest that which is closest to your soul's internal desires.

A part of this process is learning to distinguish between that which you have chosen to internalize from your external world, and that which your internal eternal being is sharing of its true essence. This is not always an easy matter, as you have come to this world with blinders on, and have piled more upon yourself as you have traveled. As you have chosen to pile much on, you also have the choice of dropping your luggage off and starting from your center anew each moment. Every time you drop some of your luggage, your soul becomes lighter and the road ahead becomes freer. Each hiccup that you traverse will seem as a mere pebble underfoot.

We enjoy the expression "Lighten Up," as it says much about how to perceive and embark upon your evolutionary path. As you lighten up your thinking, you in turn lighten your soul and its journey. As you lighten your load and enter a less dense reality, you will be activating a level of your soul that you only have fleeting connections with in the 3D world.

Five Levels of Soul Refinement

There are various soul vibration frequencies that make up your means of input from different densities of existence. These vibrations can be viewed as five levels of soul. For example, you have a physical soul energy that interacts most closely with your body and environment using your five senses. Your physical sensory inputs are an aspect of your soul body. This level of your soul is tuned in such a way that it experiences the particular reality that you are in presently. This soul aspect is the most focused in space and time and it interacts within the grid of molecular life.

Another soul level is your emotional energy form. This frequency is less dense and less focused in space and time frameworks. Your emotional life can transcend the physical grid and guide you in ways your physical senses fall short. The emotional frequencies have various levels of density that are like antennae and radio signals that travel through the matter grid and mold its manifestations.

Even less dense is your mental, thought, or consciousness level soul. This is the awareness that allows you to balance emotional life and physical analysis. This third level is the connection of the first two with the consciousness that makes you an aware being, able to decide how and why it will react to sensory or emotional sensations and events. This consciousness also transcends your physical death. Your emotional and physical memories will follow you, but it is the consciousness level of your soul that synthesizes experiences, and continues onward after this life. This third soul is the one that travels when you have out of body experiences. It is always attached to the physical and emotional souls with a silver energy chord.

The fourth level of your soul is that aspect which understands its full connection to All That Is. This is the spirit, or ethereal, level of your soul that is always linked to the One Unified Soul of creation. It might be called the fine energy form. This is the aspect of yourself that you feel when you touch the space between. As you become more aware, this spirit soul becomes more integrated into your thought level soul, and you become more energized and linked with the creative process. This soul transcends all time and space and communicates with pure intention. Your extrasensory perceptions and intuitive sensitivities tap into this level of vibration.

The most refined vibratory soul level is the fifth. This is the soul self that is completely integrated into the Oneness of eternity. This is the eternal source soul. When this level of the soul is known, consciousness and spirit unify and become fully aware of the source and the evolutionary process. All aspects of creation desire to know this refinement.

All five of these soul levels are a part of your being. As you evolve, you become more attuned to the finer soul vibrations that make you an aspect of creation. You may also look at these soul levels as levels of vibration that vary in density and connection with your source. They are all a part of your being yet your awareness of their vibration varies. The five levels of soul refinement again are:

1. **Physical Soul** (five senses, connected with world of matter)
2. **Emotional Soul** (emotions, transcends matter, guidance system)
3. **Mental Soul** (thought, imagination, creativity, outside time and space)
4. **Spirit or Ethereal Soul** (unified with source, extrasensory, intuition)
5. **Eternal Soul** (all knowing, one with creation)

The awareness of one's true being increases as one connects with each level of soul.

Again, you already have these vibrations within you. You may not be entirely aware yet of the way in which these qualities of spirit interact within your whole being. A part of the evolutionary process is developing yourself to integrate all parts of your greater soul. In other words, the more you function with sensitivity to all five dynamics, the more whole you will feel as a being in tune with creation. Your sense of fulfillment as a creator increases as you align your soul in the process of expressing your particular brand of light energy.

As you approach the time of the energy shift, you will be noticing more of the subtleties in vibration that make up your five soul forms. They are not in actuality separate, but the frequency is different when you are connected with the various levels of yourself. The realization of these subtle energies in yourself, and in the universe, will be a large part of your shift into the fourth dimensional experience. Give due respect to yourself as a multi-faceted being that is connected to a spectacular progression.

The Integration of Spirit

When you finally cross over to the next dimensional octave, the road ahead will be much clearer. You will have a deeper understanding of where you need to go individually, and as a society. What appears to be chaos, mayhem, and opposing ideas, will smooth into clarity of vision for your species' future. The subconscious workings that have occurred collectively over the last twenty or so years will be seen with increased focus. All minds that are on the same frequency will lock into the same channel and communicate ideas over great distances. Much that has a similar objective will appear to happen at once, from one end of the planet to the other. Interference from lower density thought forms that create chaotic manifestations will lessen, opening the way for more vibrant materializations.

Individual souls that are in touch with their fourth soul level will allow integration of spirit into the mental, emotional and physical worlds. This synthesis will completely change the human perspective and potential. The acknowledgment of your unity of spirit will draw profound wisdom into all human and Earth interactions. The 4D reality will bring the spirit soul into deeper focus. You, and the planet, will feel more unified, and closer to that which is your pure creative force.

Whereas now you feel divided and your identities appear separated, as you step into the new octave, you will experience a natural activation of your fourth soul and will automatically sense the inter-connectedness of all. Divisions between nations and neighbors will diminish. Race, color, and creed will fall away in your vision of spirit. The stirring of your ethereal souls will give rise to a powerful sense of unity that will overtake humanity and fundamentally shift attitudes, causing a great awakening.

The blindness experienced by lack of spirit integration will fall away, and as your new eyes see, old ways will crack and crumble. Disillusionment will dissolve, and the way will be made clear. Individual souls will have a sense of where they fit into the unified whole, and will offer themselves in service to the collective growth. The egocentric views will likewise diminish as your spirit soul view allows a holistic perspective. In essence, the soul mind's eye will take over and allow the spirit soul to connect to the unity of creation, and balance your being within the world it encompasses.

The Ascended Afterlife

The clarity of vision of your fourth dimension soul development will open doors to a world only imagined before. If your species can make this leap, your world will be forever changed. As your soul evolution escalates in its physical manifestation on Earth, it also advances the awareness of your soul beyond physical reality. "As above so below," and vice versa, is always true. The leap in awareness that your soul will experience also carries over to your understanding in life after death. After this Earthly endeavor moves forward, your choices will expand in the afterlife. There will be more opportunities of expression available to your more aware self.

A majority of you will reincarnate again on the new 4D Earth so that you can play a further role in the development of a new world vision. Creativity will be enhanced and it will be exciting for your soul to take part in this. The advancement of your awareness will more readily carry over into your next life. You will more easily remember who you are, and be more directed in your mission from a young age. There are already youngsters being born who are more aware. They are precursors to the 4D shift. These advanced souls already have a great deal of 4D awareness, as well as other characteristics that will only be further activated as times moves on.

Many of the souls that are assisting with the shift will choose to be born on other planets where they have a connection. The leap of humanity, and Earth, is affecting many beings. There will be advancements that will also be exciting to take part in on other worlds. Either way, the road ahead is filled with exciting new energy, and enhanced creativity. For souls that choose not to make the shift in awareness, there will be other options for continued development in worlds that are still in a dualistic perspective, including parallel Earth existences. In fact, there may be aspects of you that will exist in a parallel world that does not make it to 4D. But, this will be a hard road, and few will choose to experience the trials and tribulations that occur there.

When parallel realities split off, those aspects of your consciousness will then be experiencing their own awareness that is related to, but in a sense separate from yours, in that they have their own free choice to endeavor within creation. All of your thoughts cause probable realities to spin off from this one. And, the more power they are given, the stronger they become in the sphere of consciousness. While they are parts of you, they are also free expressions of creation. You are influencing each other at all times, but each has its own consciousness. Each develops its own physical, emotional, and mental soul frequencies. Since all is ever changing, some probable selves diminish and others are born, as you evolve together and individually, splitting and reintegrating, continually.

Some of you will join with the energy of beings that will be starting relationships with the human race in future generations. You may even be born into that life knowing that you lived among humans, or as a human. This will assist in your mission to befriend evolving human beings. Your soul attachment to this crucial turning point will inevitably draw you to play a part in this continuing saga, in one way or another. On a universal, dimensional, and soul level, the road ahead is invigorating. Even those that do not leap to 4D will find new challenges on other worlds, so the creative flow of consciousness will continue in its beautiful and miraculous unfolding.

Upon departing from this world, many of you will decide to remain in your ascended ethereal form and carry out tasks within that realm. A consciousness must be developed to a certain degree of awareness to remain in this non-corporeal state of being with intention. There must be a particular sense of purpose for carrying on in the spirit form. There may be lessons or skills to develop by staying among the non-material, or one might become a teacher of the less aware who are merely crossing over between material realities. This ethereal realm exists as part of the space between that we have spoken of, so it is outside matter and physical energy forms.

There is much that occurs at this stage of being, however, and it is just as real, so to speak, as your world appears to be. Existence within the ethereal realm has its particular challenges and rewards. A soul's awareness must be developed enough to be able to maneuver with its own consciousness, and yet be cognizant of its inter-connectedness to all others. When crossing between worlds, angels, and other ethereal souls, will assist those with limited understanding in assessing what they have experienced in their physical incarnation, and where and what they might embark upon next. When your soul ascends to the spirit level by conscious efforts, it will be prepared to move more freely when it crosses over to this ethereal plane, and it may decide to stay and explore this way of being.

There is much to learn in a non-physical state as well. All connections with other consciousness are on an energy level here. Therefore, the effects are not seen or felt in a material way, and one cannot influence the matter world directly from this state. Influences are only instigated through thought and energy frequency. A soul in the ethereal state can only connect with your world, for example, when there is a similarity in frequency and this can only occur by means of the conduit of a consciousness that is presently residing in the physical plane.

From the material plane, you can make contact with the ethereal souls only if you are able to transcend into the spirit soul level and tune into a particular consciousness that is on your frequency. Again this is like tuning into a radio station, but first you need to become an ethereal receiver. Generally the mission of staying in the ethereal plane is not to communicate with material realms, but rather to better understand the dynamics of interconnected consciousness and the dance of evolution from a different perspective. In this state of being your consciousness is still actively creating and furthering its awareness by interacting with other beings of pure energy, including us, in some cases.

Just as there are many dimensions of physical existence, there are also octaves of ethereal realms. The material realities are expressions of the various spiritual planes and vice versa. This again is the meaning of two interconnected tetrahedrons, or the six pointed star as a triangle facing up and one down, that are intertwined. Although one realm is not actually above the other, they are, in fact, intertwined. The realms exist beside or within one another and do so at all levels of dimensional reality. One does not exist without the other and there is always a connection between them. As such you are, of course, always existing in physical and spiritual reality at once, but your focus of consciousness is diverted from one to the other as you experience death in the physical or decide to remain consciously focused in the ethereal world with your developed awareness.

Collective Evolution and Soul-Mates

The journey for each individual consciousness is also linked to a greater collective soul evolution. Your consciousness is a spark created by other sparks of consciousness. And likewise, you create new sparks with your consciousness. There is a never ending conscious creating process, and all the sparks amount to a much greater consciousness that ultimately is a singular sentient awareness. Just as the cells in your body have individual development, yet are aspects of your whole body, your soul is an aspect of a larger soul. Your body would not exist without the involvement of all your cells' participation in creating your body. Similarly, the larger soul would not exist without each of you adding to the whole.

Each one of you has many components or counterparts in various levels of reality that are parts of your greater entity, and these entities are part of larger collective soul groups. Just as individual souls have particular qualities or characteristics, so does the larger collective group of souls that they are related to. This is not a hierarchal system, but rather a layering of consciousness. One layer does not lead over another layer. All parts work together in the formation of the whole. The layers are organically and energetically interlinked, as in the representation of the two triangles forming a six-pointed star. All aspects influence one another and evolve in unison. As your awareness evolves to understand this interconnection, it strives to contribute the best of its abilities to strengthen and enlighten the expanded soul wherever it stretches into the cosmos.

Not only do you have soul counterparts in other realms, you also have many soul connections to others on your planet in a given lifetime. Whether you are aware of these other souls or not, you influence each other. Many have termed these special connections, soul-mates, and this is appropriately stated, as your larger souls have continually split into new sparks of consciousness that are separate, but also remain integral collective energies. These soul-mates can be of any sex, race or species.

There is not only one soul-mate alive with you at the same time. There are likely many, depending on relevant populations being born. However, there are often particular soul-mates that you have agreed to work with during your given life so that you may teach each other, help each other evolve in some way, or to fulfill a mission that you intended for the betterment of your soul group. The more evolved your awareness and sensitivities become, the clearer these interconnections of souls will be.

As you move into the next dimension, you will better recognize your soul-mates as other facets of yourself. You will be able to see that you are offshoots of one another's larger consciousness or soul. With this knowing, you gain an amazing appreciation for the other's journey. You will see that they are expressing something different than you, as a part of your mutual, connected soul creativity.

Again, your whole species is connected in the bigger picture, but there are strands, or fibers of consciousness that are more closely joined within that greater view. Going back to the body analogy, soul-mate groups are like organs of the body, working together with a prime directive to express and maintain that organ so that all the other organs, and hence the whole structure, can continue to live. Soul-mates and soul-mate groups have functions within the creative process of the species and beyond. Your particular soul group may stretch over many planets and galaxies, or it may be mostly focused on Earth. But, its members will usually have similar aptitudes or a common purpose, no matter where the soul-mates are residing, or focusing their attentions. You will often come together to assist one another in various tasks, but not everyone you work with is a close soul-mate. Many of you will join with other soul groups for the sake of unifying and appreciating the bigger picture.

We hope that you can find some solace in knowing that it is not all up to you. You have a tendency, many of you, to take on all the burdens, as if it all depended on your one consciousness alone. There are many of you playing parts in the soul evolutionary process. You have brethren among you on Earth, and elsewhere, who are in on the game and are pulling a lot of the weight by your side. While everything you do helps everyone, know that you do not have to solve every problem alone.

You each do not have to be perfection. Together, you only need to learn that you are perfection as you proceed in your seeking to be perfect. The being is in the seeking. Let yourself be within that state without constantly ridiculing your lack of progress, and understand that you are not doing it alone. What you lack, someone else is accomplishing with ease. The life of discovery does not have to be a struggle. Your heightened awareness comes largely from recognizing that the journey is what you make it, that you always have a choice, and that together you are one amazing, creative expression of that which you are always seeking.

We wish to impress upon you that all of your small acts of kindness, and striving for understanding of your place in the universe, do not go unnoticed. They each have an impact and are changing the world as you read these words. The cells that each of you represent in the wave of consciousness that is arising, are what will make a new day dawn in your corner of creation.

As you each have had moments of rising and falling, the overall trend is on the side of rising. Every time you do a small act of changing your consciousness from the ignorance of darkness to revealing the light of your true nature, you are tipping the world to the light of awareness. Together this ebb and flow moves tides with a potent force. You are each a force that is pushing the wave that will transform life as you know it. One of the most powerful skills you can develop as a creator is how to ride the rising and falling, and ultimately follow the ebb of light.

Chapter 16

The Falling and Rising:
How to Follow
the Ebb of Light

Your lives appear to be a series of ups and downs, like riding in a roller coaster. Some days you are on an upswing and others bring you down. Just when things seem to be going well you are hit with an unexpected crisis. You finally think you have it all figured out and suddenly nothing makes any sense. You are reeling in motivation at the start of a project and slowly the monotony weakens your resolve and the momentum slides. You love your spouse with all your heart and then you cannot stand them. You rise and you fall. Sometimes you do not get back up again and other times you are on a winning streak that never fails.

Life is full of falling and rising events, emotions, and relationships. Mostly, you are busy fighting the falling and painstakingly forcing the rising. Life need not be so dramatic and the ebb and flow can be appreciated more fully. When you learn to have respect for both the highs and the lows, and the process of being within the flow of expression, your flow with the ebb of light will become effortless and rewarding. It is largely a matter of shifting your focus and intention to a state of enhanced awareness of the fluidity of existence, and of falling in love with the creativity of it.

Messianic Elevation of Awareness

The human construction of evil can be abolished in a single moment. The more you fight against evil or what you perceive as negativity, the more you allow it to continue. By fighting something you are giving it energy and are thus creating more of it. When you push against your moments of falling or the obstructions in your path you feed them your precious energy. Negativity only exists for you because you allow it to exist. Your reality can be shifted in an instant by mentally and spiritually removing the concept of evil from your consciousness. You can, in any given second, remove the existence of negativity from your life, by raising your awareness above the concept of bad and good. This is a process that can, and should, be practiced in every moment of your life.

The raising of human consciousness is the second-to-second rising above or transforming the concept of negativity into an awareness of the sanctity of every creation. True free will is choosing what you experience with awareness, and not with blind faith or conformity to mass belief. Your species has been given the gift of the knowledge of good and evil and now it has the opportunity to rise above these constructions. Every falling contains a gift of rising inherent in its being, and vice versa. By shifting ones' awareness past the interpretation and judgment of something as being bad or good, one can choose to see with a clearer vision and ride the wave of light that exists within every single act or thought.

All of your great spiritual leaders were able to see beyond these preconceived notions, and as such were able to elevate the sparks of consciousness within any situation, or soul. This is true mastery of the gift of free will. Unfortunately, instead of following in the footsteps of these leaders with one's own elevation of awareness, most of your religions have chosen to worship these leaders as examples of a distant and seemingly unattainable holiness. However, each of these spiritually advanced individuals spoke of the essence of divinity already within each human being. They all saw the spark of creation within everything and therefore were able to regenerate by sharing their sparks of soul unconditionally.

None of these enlightened beings claimed to be the savior or messiah. Each did state that all humanity has the potential to be the messiah or savior of your collective soul. The coming of messiah is actually the rising of consciousness to a state of awareness that recognizes the divinity and interconnected source of All That Is.

Your spiritual leaders were followed because there is nothing more powerful than connection and awareness of the source energy and the appreciation of that which you are. By worshipping these leaders you are missing their point entirely and give your power of divinity away. This is the farthest thing from what they were sharing. By judging any other beings as unholy, because they do not worship a certain elevated human being alone, is contradicting their messages. On the other hand, by practicing the consciousness that they imparted, which always encompasses accepting and revering all as part of God, including oneself, you are assisting in the coming of the messiah of awareness.

Much can be gained in acknowledgment of the spiritual truths inherent in all the teachings of the great religious figures throughout human history. It would benefit humankind, and its creation of a messianic reality, to appreciate the similarity of vision that advanced souls impart instead of focusing on the worship of one over another. They are guides and examples of what you can reveal of yourselves, and thus should be appreciated as such. No one will attain a higher place in the after world or this world by worshipping any other being. Simply believing in another's divinity does not create that state of mind in oneself. One must be in that state of being to elevate his or her consciousness and assist all of the Oneness in being true to its nature. This need not take a lifetime or many. It already exists within each of you and can be awakened in any given moment. As more of you add to this awareness, the collective soul of Earth and humankind is elevated to a lighter frequency and dimension of perception.

Acting as if You Are Enlightened

Now that you know you are as capable as any spiritual master or guru of attaining a higher state of self and universal awareness, how do you go about it? Firstly, always remind yourself that you are already a being of light and that you chose your journey of challenges for your own unveiling. If you can grasp and appreciate the importance of this truth, then you are already on your way. It is one of the most difficult realizations as it requires you to accept complete responsibility for every nuance in your life and to seek the messages and revelation potential in each happening.

To truly accept that all external occurrences are your energetic doing, and that nothing is either bad or good, is progress for your soul. This does not mean that you should not have compassion for yourself, and others that are in a bind or are experiencing serious obstacles and pain. It simply means that you must take a closer look at why these occurrences exist and what they have to teach you, or what they may reveal about the nature of your soul.

Following a path of light is possible when you can more fully see the potential in instances as they unfold and can make decisions based on conscious insights, instead of programmed emotional reactions. In order to view the happenings of your life this way, you will need to approach everything with a degree of consciousness and intention. This is a skill that takes daily practice. It does not happen to you. You make it happen. However, with the use of your emotions and imagination, again, you have more power than you know.

We ask that you spend a week using your gifts of visualization and mental focus along with your higher emotions, and trust that they will work for you. Sincerely trust in your abilities for one week and see what happens in your life as a result. We see so often that you do not trust yourselves and that to which you are inherently connected. You tend not to believe that you connect to higher frequencies when you attune your thoughts and emotions, so you flounder around and end up back in the muck again. Rather than distrust, try one week of believing that you are already an advanced being with highly attuned sensitivities. This will take some practice and you will likely need to constantly remind yourself to step up and view your circumstances from a higher angle.

Firstly, take a few minutes to envision, and preferably write down, how the elevated, aware you would act throughout the week. See the internal beauty of your potential. How would your integrated five levels of soul confront your daily activities? If you were among the messiah of your age, how would you spend your waking hours? Where would you find and share your true inner bliss? How could you transform those pesky annoyances or daunting tasks into joyous light filled blessings? A big job this is, yes. And, you will not be perfect out of the gate. It is the efforts that count, and the very act of trying puts you in a state of intention that elevates your frequency.

Find inspiration from others that have walked paths of light or offer tools to assist your adventure. Music, art, and nature, all have sacred vibration to synchronize your soul. Listen to what stirs your heart and desires. Listen to all thoughts and ask your soul where they are coming from in your being, and how you can share more of your internal spark of creativity within these thoughts.

Never put yourself down, as that is denigrating the spirit of the One. If you find your thoughts being hurtful to yourself or another, simply observe with detached awareness and determine a finer approach. Putting yourself and others down is denying the divine expression that each one of you is. Every time you catch yourself and reverse your low vibration, a new spark of unity and regeneration is born in the universe and gives strength to overcoming the same hurdle next time, until it ceases to be a problem at all. Take notice of such success and see how you dissipate the need for the lower energy over time. Allow yourself to feel the joy of your spiritual accomplishments and appreciate that you took another step toward the light.

The steps to be taken are unique for each spirit. Therefore, there is no way you can judge another's journey. You can guide and make observations, but each soul has movements designed for their own symphony of expression. What appears small or insignificant to one person may be a huge leap for another. Much of your journey takes place in your thoughts, so there is a lot happening in others and yourself that may be regarded as miniscule, but is actually large. Your journey of enlightenment does not need to be characterized by what you deem to be great feats or masterful external accomplishments. Some of the most masterful developments come in quiet moments when you shift an age old thought pattern. By altering old thought vibrations, you open new doorways through which your soul can express more of its inner being.

Being aware of your veil of darkness and clearing away the debris allows you to gain a wider perspective from which to begin altering your thought patterns, so that you are prepared to make choices as to which ebb you will follow. It is important to take notice of your dips in frequency so that you can make an educated choice to continue downward, or spiral yourself upward. The choice is always a thought away. However, you must be aware of this ability to alter your frequency, and practice it.

Many of you allow external stimuli to govern your thoughts and emotions and hence actions. You can learn to take control of your every sensation, by transforming your thoughts and vibrational output. When you choose to synchronize with particular vibrations instead of randomly accepting your prior programmed responses, you are suddenly able to decide to what and whom you will connect, and how you will interact on a deeper level within the material grid and beyond. The greater your acumen in this regard, the more elevated your choices will become. The paths of light will literally present themselves before your eyes and ears.

Balancing Self Awareness

The opening to the ebb of light begins at the core of your soul in the little moments. These moments will add up until you become a full and brightly radiating being, before you even know how it happened. This awareness state will not occur by acts that stroke your ego. In fact, the more you try to make yourself big, the more your soul shrinks in dismay. It will hide itself to protect your light from yourself.

Do not confuse strength of character with ego actions or inactions. The soul is strong and true. The ego may act like it is strong and true, but is really the opposite. Either way, the difference is in being strong from a core connection to one's inner light versus maintaining a state of wanting to make an external impression. Ego takes the form of either feeling bad about oneself by being depressed and confused, or overcompensating by pretending one is great to hide the feeling of inadequacy that is really underneath. Either way, the soul is denied its depth of character. When your soul genuinely knows the nature of its spirit, it has no need to impress its greatness upon others. It simply is great!

This is not to say that you should hate your ego. It has served a purpose in your spiritual development and as yet still has a role to play in your physical dealings. The evolution of the human species required the self-awareness that created the ego identity. It is not separate from your consciousness. The ego is simply an identity mask that has served you in understanding what it means to be self-aware. Part of this level of awareness involved comparing one's self-perception to that of others. The ego identity served as a platform in which to better understand oneself in relation to the outside world. It was, and still is, an integral aspect of your developmental process.

That said, we are not suggesting you take your ego and dump it into the garbage. However, it has grown out of control in its predominance in your psyches, at the expense of the other aspects of your consciousness. For example, your so-called subconscious does not need to be nearly so sub at all. If you were more balanced in your perspective on your multi-faceted relationship with the universe, you would not need to be hiding so much in the recesses of your mind.

All of the psychological dynamics described by psychoanalysts such as Sigmund Freud were the result of your adaptations to increase awareness and were healthy enough up to this point. It is time to gain a more balanced psyche, especially one that includes the depth of your spiritual existence. Carl Jung was on track in that he grasped the importance of the collective unconscious, and its ability to influence the masses and their symbology. Jung recognized the archetypal images and saw how they crossed cultural and physical boundaries. He was touching on the strength of collective creation and acknowledging the super-conscious self that exists beyond the confines of the ego's needs.

Your ego was a construct of the initial development of human self-awareness. It was the result of your species' becoming consciously aware beings who could knowingly affect their environment and the outcome of events. This awareness placed humans outside of the things that they affect. Now it is time to balance the separate identity of self-awareness with the awareness of the connection of self to a greater reality. A less egocentric awareness will allow for multidimensional sensory input and a connection to all existence that empowers consciousness and its influence on its surroundings.

Self-awareness and individual identity are not what you need to give up when you let go of ego control. Your next step is to integrate a more whole identity into your relationship with the world around you. This more whole identity can only come from your eternal soul that is connected with all other souls. The ego status that needs to be dropped is the one that is hiding your inner truth. The ego that follows the crowd because it does not trust your inner self and light, and acts out of the fear of failure in the eyes of others, can be shed. When you come from a place of true self and interconnected awareness, paths open before your eyes.

Following the ebb of light is a matter of dissolving the self-created veils that hide your way. It is not a matter of fighting evil, but rather of seeing the falling and rising in one's life as energy flow, and choosing what to flow with based on your soul's inner knowing and true identity. As you are confronted with external situations that challenge you, give your ego a check. Begin to notice if it is taking control of your soul vision. Always check back with what you know to be divinely connected to the life force of creation.

You can train your thoughts to create circumstances that emerge from your ethereal soul by keeping your ego identity in check. If you perceive something as good or bad, or right or wrong, you are allowing your protective ego to govern your decisions. Try to take an eagle eye view and ask how your higher level soul perspective would enable you to assess the situation. Where would your higher being flow, given an energetic observation of the dynamics surrounding the event? Believe it or not, your soul can see far beyond the limitations of space and time, if you practice allowing it to do so by learning to trust your imagination and extrasensory intuitive knowing.

Tuning In and Synchronizing with Potential Paths

The task of becoming a balanced soul will become easier as you get closer to the cosmic energy infusion event. All the efforts you make now will allow you to make the necessary frequency modulations to take advantage of the re-coding of your DNA strands. The struggles that you are enduring, to overcome your self-interested focus and expand your mental and spiritual picture, are pushing your envelope of potential. When the time comes for your DNA activation, you will have fused lines of energy that will open you to universal connections.

As you continually clear away the overgrowth in your path to your dream world, each traversal gets less cumbersome. Then, seemingly miraculously, new paths to that vision will be revealed and will already be cleared. The next time the trail may be in a completely different octave. It is not required that you master the art of using your higher faculties now. All that is needed are the intentions to become balanced and to let go of the illusory identities and beliefs that are holding your soul back from seeing its true path.

Your soul is held back from flowing with the ebb of its destiny by any belief that does not encompass your eternal light and inherent divinity as a creator. Each time you are able to see yourself as a being of light that is integral to all creation, you can spread this energy, see with your soul mind's eye, and know which ebb to flow with, and which to let go of.

When faced with a decision, stop and imagine a bright source of energy at the center of your being. Allow that light source to radiate outward into the physical scene. Picture the light finding its way toward one direction or another. Which direction does your spirit choose? Or, allow your light essence to flow to all the possibilities and see which one is the brightest. Which one becomes predominant or gives you the highest emotional response?

Sometimes it is not the path we expect to be the best that our soul actually desires. There are always unseen results coming from situations that you may not perceive in the present moment. But, your soul senses the potential therein. This appears to be a simple exercise. However, it is a powerful action that can activate your higher consciousness, and spirit level soul involvement, in your decision making process. If you practice this method, you will gain aptitude in sensing and interpreting your imaginations and emotional responses.

Eventually, as your DNA strands become active, your practice will pay off and you will know the meaning of the frequencies that you sense all around you. Imagining your light flowing through events, other life forms, and objects, establishes a luminescent connection that makes it possible for you to read the vibration and intentions within constructs. Reading and interpreting vibrations will be your normal way of operating in a 4D environment. Your daily life will be dependent on these sensations and flows.

Following the ebb of light is much like following frequency modulations or deciding what radio station you wish to broadcast in your life. If you can preview the programs offered on each station before committing to a full day of play, then you can make a decision that is most pleasing for you and others. You are, after all, living in a world that is made real by the vibrating strands of energy. If you can see and feel these strands and choose which to materialize, you are more able to create your day and life for ultimate long term satisfaction.

The ability to sense frequency can be called "tuning in". Once you tune in, you must interpret what you are detecting and synchronize with a chosen path. In this way, you are in control of the rising and falling tides that impact your being. As you become less instinctively reactive, and more tuned in spiritually to the tones of the universe, you become a director of energy flow in your environment. In directing your paths, you influence those on your wave length and vice versa. You can learn to be sensitive to the frequency vibrations of everything around you including inanimate objects and all life forms, from the molecular to the giant.

Next time you are sitting quietly in a relaxed mental state, bring your focus to a particular material form. Allow your mind to move into the form. Let yourself sense the nature of things that appear to be outside of you. Let your mind and emotions flow. See and feel where they take you as you project your being into another. Try to take your own identity out of the picture and dissolve into the matter stream of the object, or life form. Allow your mind to fill with colors, feelings, and thoughts as you sense the consciousness underlying the formation of energy.

This may sound a bit wishy-washy, but it will train your faculties to sense frequencies that make up the matter world. Before you know it, you will recognize vibrations that flow with your soul, as well as those that are jarring or contrary to your tone. Remember that it is the soul vibration that you want to be in sync with, and not the ego mentality. This is why a relaxed, balanced brain wave will help you to follow your inner vision, and not your ego constructs.

This way of interacting with your world is quite alien to what you have been taught, and thus will seem contrived and unreal at first. Keep attempting these tools of visualization and expansion and you will rewire your brain functions. Quite literally, new synapses will be formed to open channels of ability. Opening centers in your psyche will assist your soul in shining through in your physical reality. These opened valves will make it possible for you to feel and understand ebbs of energy flow in your matter field, and in turn, be active in creating pathways as you go. The goal is to be a conscious participant in the flow of energy of physical formations by tuning and retuning the frequencies of the matter streams that make up your perceived surroundings.

This talk of frequency modulation may appear rather esoteric in relation to your everyday life. But, in fact, your entire reality is based on such vibrations. Simply being unaware of it does not change the nature of your physical existence. Your evolution lies in your awareness of the vibrations that make up your reality, and learning how to flow with the rhythms that you and your fellow beings create.

Though it may seem distant and unreal to sense frequency, it will get easier, and quite real over time. Your sensing muscles are simply atrophied, but with some flexing you will become strong. Take some time every day to devote to strengthening your soul sensing, and to feeling the energy signatures in various choices you are confronted with. Before you take on any new task, infuse the motivation with light from the core of your being, and intend for that energy to flow through your activities. Imagine it, and make it so. Observe how this infusion affects your experiences, and be keen to notice signs and sensations.

Appreciating the Pure Light in Others

It is also of benefit for you to make a habit of recognizing that all other human beings have a spark of pure source light within them as well, and that they are part of the same Oneness as yourself. No matter how disagreeable certain individual ego portrayals may be, or how much they trigger your own ego reactivity, they are also divine light sources. Train yourself to view the internal radiating source light within each person you come in contact with every day. Acknowledge their light sparks, and offer your love and support to those internally perfect beings before you.

Appreciating the light within others will encourage that ray of purity to shine forth. Seeing their pure potential gives that aspect of their soul an energy boost. They need know nothing, and may feel nothing, as you imagine their light, but it will make a difference somehow in your relationship.

By doing this, you are raising the potential for your relations, no matter how insignificant the act may appear superficially. Seeing the inner spark in others elevates your interactions on a soul connection level. By elevating your consciousness about their being, you open a new pathway for your souls to follow together. This simple exercise can release tensions, and make it possible for you to flow down a new fiber of light on your journey together, no matter how short or long the relationship lasts. You can open doorways of higher potential for each other in this way. Does it appear too basic to be true? We urge you to try this strategy for one week and see for yourself. See the inner radiating light in every person you meet. If you meet the same people several times, see their light each time you come in contact with them. Have no judgments about how much light each person has, merely recognize that they each have the same core source as you, and it is utterly pure, no matter how they act.

Your journey in this life is not alone. All interactions with others offer potential light filled paths. Seeing their light, and your inter-con-nectedness to them, gives you an opportunity to glean the messages and assistance you can offer one another. Within your interactions are gems waiting to be discovered. The more open your soul is to your mutual core being, the more likely you will see, feel, and be guided to raising the bar of your connection in any given moment. This may very well be one of the most important steps to master in strengthening your ability to find the well lit path. Each soul is a link in your journey that can be squandered or fulfilled.

Even if you never see any outcome of your elevation of another's spark, there will be an unseen effect that ripples through both of your lives. As you train your mind in this way, you will have an even stronger sway, and may notice miraculous things occurring as a result. When you see other's light, and even imagine it getting brighter, you are making a connection on a soul level that creates an energy bond, and increases both of your connections to the web of light.

If all humans were to elevate one another in all associations, then your species would ascend. The interconnected flow of your consciousness would reach a higher vibration, and awareness would rise to a new level of knowing. Therefore, if you can do only one thing toward your spiritual progression, make it seeing the spark of light in others, and in yourself, and know that you are linked and united in strength and ability.

You each have personal paths, but together you have a greater path. Through all the trials and tribulations of your lives, there is a singularity that contains the ebb of light. As you connect with that light in others, you access the wiring of conscious energy that is creating in unison. Once you sense this flow, you can add to its direction with awareness. Therein lies the biggest secret to spiritual connectivity and movement.

We congratulate you on every small step you take toward becoming spiritually enlightened beings with true awareness of your light and its connection to All That Is. As your soul makes these realizations, its choices of frequency modulation rise to higher levels, and you become a greater participant in fulfilling the creative process of pure consciousness. When you finally are able to keep your ego in check, and live each moment cognizant of your inner light, and its connection with what it creates individually and collectively, an astounding thing happens; your burdens lift and the weight of matter is lightened. The boundaries between your soul levels and physical creations become more translucent, and melded.

Your awareness elevates to a place that transcends the mere perception of what you create, and finds its way into the patterns of energy that focus matter itself. A finer bridge is made to the space between, where your pure consciousness exists. And, the weight of the world lightens.

Chapter 17

The Lifting of Burdens
and Weightlessness

The coming reward for your lifetimes of seeking and development is obtaining a closer connection to the source of your consciousness, which leads to a life less dense. Just as light lacks mass compared to rocks on your planet, you will be lighter as you radiate more light and have less physical dependency. The mental and spiritual expansion you have been working on for many lifetimes is about to be realized within this cosmic space bulge that is now radiating through multiple dimensions. Your reality is finally stretching to match the progress your spirit has made in lifting its burdens. The lifting of burdens is directly proportional to the brightening of your soul, individually and en masse. From this comes the mental and spiritual sense of weightlessness. This is the ultimate freedom you seek as searchers for light, and the moment is upon you.

Ushering in the Era of light

Those of you alive in this century will become known as those responsible for the uplifting of humankind from the ages of darkness, into the era of light. Not only will your souls be refreshed and replenished by your elevation, but you each will have added to the evolution of the expression of the human spirit in general. You are a part of this profound movement that forever changes the frequency of human DNA in your galaxy.

Your expansion is providing the link of energy that raises your souls in unison to your next octave. Within this new vibration, everything you now see as solid will not be seen nearly as so. Since you will be vibrating at a faster rate, you will see beyond much of the physical constructions, and will move more freely through the grid of matter. The burdens of moving and relating in a material world will lessen with the realization of, and synchronization with, its fluid nature.

Imagine becoming more light filled, or less attached to the atoms and more connected and aware of the space between. What will that feel like? Physical creations will become more malleable, and their connection to consciousness more clear. You will become more like the energy that your thoughts are. As this thought energy, you will move through matter with greater ease. What was once a burden will become a new wave of creation. The sensation of being in a new dimensional awareness is difficult to comprehend when you are still so anchored to your matter expression. But, we will attempt to give you an idea of what it may feel like, to help your mind prepare for the transition.

Your souls have gone through many journeys to find their way to these days of opportunity. The eagerness is thick in the air of planet Earth. Those that are ready for this ascension process are also ready to rise above the turmoil that is taking place on a physical level. This last stand, and demolition of the old ways, is part of your evolution. Welcome the pushing against reform, as this is a sign that the end of the old densities is upon you. The massive arising will completely displace all attempts at the status quo efforts to control and enslave your expanding psyches. En masse the resistance will be so energetically massive that nothing will be able to penetrate its force. What appears as strong government or corporate control will fall apart under the weight of the energy that is coming. Those that are in tune with the lighter vibration will rise to the top of the heap and flow into a new vision. All the wheels are set in motion for the way makers to leap ahead.

Enlightenment and Ascension Sensations

The boundaries that seemingly separate you from the matter surrounding you and the other life forms sharing your space will be less defined as you elevate your consciousness to include everything in your environment. As the burdens you perceive to be shrouding your view dissipate, your soul radiates outward and combines with the energy signatures of all creations in your sphere of reality. This causes a natural unification and empathy with the consciousness that you are attracting into your realm of experience. Your internal source energy literally brightens and expands to fill your aura and beyond once self-imposed burdens are lifted. Your lighter frequency will vibrate through and past the denser tones. This finer self quite literally exists in a separate realm of reality than does the denser self that you will be leaving.

Can you imagine behaving more like light energy? By nature you would regenerate and rejuvenate whatever you came in contact with. As light, you would reflect the colors of your spectrum off of your world. Your environment would be seen as the reflection of your essence and you could make it shine brighter or divert your flow of input in another direction. You would be able to beam yourself with intention and see the reflections of color that radiate back at you. Without blockages of dense form, you could join with other types of energy, and combine to generate more power.

Whereas you will not be pure energy light beings in this next octave, you will be evolving in that direction and hence will be learning to feel your core light influencing what is created. The physical constructions will be seen for what they truly are, consciousness expressed in molecular structures. The more you learn about this dynamic, the more amazing your discoveries and the deeper you will understand the inter-connectedness of what you create.

We cannot help but feel excitement for your development as it is an opportunity for your souls to experience an entirely new perception of reality. There is nothing quite like making such a leap in awareness. It is the ultimate "aah haa!" The term enlightenment is particularly apt for a description of this elevation of perspective. The term works on multiple levels. It describes lightening of density, weight, and radiation of energy, and is "meant" to include the number ten as encompassing a ten dimensional view.

It is one thing for a single soul to make this step, it is quite another for a whole species in creation to make a leap into such an expanded means of expressing closer to the One Creator. Such an evolution resonates from one octave to another and is a tonal chord heard throughout the dimensions. It flows like a wave of energy throughout your physically expressed universe. As you enlighten your own souls, it reverberates into the sea of consciousness and enlightens all.

The finer vibrations of energy that are pulsing into your Earth plane are building. As your soul awakens, so does the DNA that harbors the frequencies that set the parameters of your capabilities as a human form. If you open your soul to these finer vibrations, your physical self will literally become less dense. There will be more space between the physical molecular structures that make up your body. As a lighter being, you will be able to exist on an Earth plane that is also less physically dense. Your lighter existence will be synchronized with a new planet, solar system and universe for that matter, or at least the less dense dimensional version of such. During the transition period, when the Earth is shifting dimensions, there will be a splitting of dimensional realities before your very eyes. This is an incredible event in creation that requires an amazing amount of conscious energy intention from several realms, including our own world of light.

Those that split off into the ascended universe will disappear from the viewpoint of those that remain in the third density world. Many of your great spiritual leaders and cultures foresaw this transcendence and have described it in different, but similar, ways. This rare event is a profound leap that has been building multidimensionally as an opportunity for creation to express a new level of awareness within this universe.

Those that ascend will find themselves on a planet that is less rooted in physical constructs. If this is your path, then your spirit soul will integrate with your mental, emotional and physical souls so that you will feel connected with your environment and have a deeper appreciation for your place in creating a new world. Your new material self will find that its senses reach beyond the mere five that you previously used for assimilation of information. The sensing of your spirit soul will come into play immediately and hence you will experience heightened sensitivity to other life forms and objects.

There will be other, already 4D, life forms to meet you and assist in your transition. Your new sensitivity to frequency will guide you in finding those that are in tune with your soul and can best support your particular avenue of approach. The experience of moving to this next octave will be different for each individual, much like the way the death transition is experienced based on an individual's conceptual understanding and belief system. However, the integration will soon meld together as a collective experience.

Each soul will soon find that they are attracted to others of like interest and natural inclination. There will be many soul-mates joining together to accentuate their energy in the transition. Your soul vision will be turned on so that you will recognize the vibrations of those that are in synch with your wave of light. The joining will be a celebration of your accomplishment in raising humankind to this enlightened dimension.

You will still remain as physical life forms if you have chosen to transcend along with the planet in this way. Some will ascend directly from a death experience, while others will continue in the alternate reality of a 3D Earth. Still others will move to the afterlife and go directly, or soon after, into another 3D world incarnation. Remember, creation is multidimensional and extremely diverse in its expression. Though you may want to make judgments on these various outcomes, everything and everyone is in the perfection of the Prime Creator's expression and, as such, there is no better or worse result. If you are on the path of ascension, you will know that there is no judgment to be made about any of the potential transition experiences.

If you are a soul that is ready for your next octave of awareness, and decide to remain on the 4D physical Earth, you will still experience a body and a separate individual consciousness. However, when you look at your body through new dimensional eyes, you will see a radiant form. You will be able to see the energy that you emit from your core and how all of your cells are connected with each other and their surroundings by energy fibers. In other words, you will be more aware of the actual grid of energetic matter that you exist within. You will be aware of your thoughts as having form and affecting the grid of matter. There will be a greater sense of the illusory nature of the material constructs, and your thoughts will impact matter more rapidly. You will be entering the 4D realm at its lower frequency modulation, and will move into finer frequencies as you learn to control your thought forms.

The ability to see your thoughts and emotions as energy sparks that interact with sparks from others, and the structures of matter, will cause further fine tuning of your processes. When you more readily see the results of your energy projections, you will quickly realize the need to monitor those emissions, if you wish to create effectively and experience your desired outcome.

You will only ascend to this point if you gain a minimal awareness of your energetic impact and interconnected relationship with your world for clear reasons. Firstly, the increased sensory input would cause a complete circuitry overload and lead to insanity if you are unprepared. Secondly, the finer frequency modulation of the fourth dimension would completely fry your physical apparatus if you do not have the ability to synchronize with at least the fundamental tones of the next octave. Therefore, if you find yourself in the new octave, then you were able to hold enough light frequency to maintain form and sanity when your body and mind took in visions that transcended the solid perspective you adhered to in your old life.

Your light body will be turned on and shining bright in 4D, the light body being the ethereal soul integrated into your physical, emotional, and mental soul states. You will feel as if your inner light has been turned up. As such, you will be learning that this radiation impacts the grid pattern and other light bodies in your presence. You will be able to sense vibration with this soul form and translate the sensations into thoughts and images.

Slowly you will learn to interpret these feelings and understand the deeper meaning being transmitted from everything in your surroundings. Also, you will learn to send rays of your spirit body to distant places and people in order to communicate globally and work together by adding to each other's radiance. The exploration of your personal light form will be an ongoing adventure in 4D.

Soul-Mate Communion and Co-Creation

Knowing and sensing the impact you have on one another comes with a new responsibility. Seeing that you can brighten each other or withdraw energy, and knowing where others are coming from by reading their vibration, will change all your interactions tremendously. There will not be much hiding behind a self-made identity. Your true nature and intentions will be seen by all. Hence, our continual reminder to face your self-made façade and become the light channel that you truly are.

In 4D you cannot be anything other than your true self. The challenges will come in sharing this self with increasing effectiveness and delight for all concerned. You will also be able to master the communion with your soul partners, because you will see who they really are, and that they are playing a role that is unique to their expression, just as you are. Together you will develop the ability to accentuate your creations by sharing your special energy signatures with one another. In joining forces you become whole.

Together soul-mates will begin to meld their thought and emotional energy forms and create larger balls of focused light that carry considerable force in changing matter and events. You will be consciously creating by directing your energy in the grid of space and time that you perceive with more clarity. For example, let us say that you and a group of souls come together with an intention to build an energy amplifying pyramid structure for travel to other worlds through transmitting your consciousness. Firstly, you will be able to envision how the structure will be designed in unison through your focused thoughts. Each person will be able to add to the input until you have a precise picture of what you will create. Since you can see and feel the frequency of objects, you will also know what elements to use in your creation to obtain the most powerful results and where to find the materials.

Knowing the true nature and capabilities of others, you will easily determine who in your group, or in another group, will be best to physically construct the design and who will best convey the plans to the constructors. Misunderstandings will be greatly diminished as you learn to read each other and accept your various jobs as specialist creators. The construction crew will work closely with the designers energetically to ensure the vision is accurate. They will be able to sense when the frequency of the creation is in any way out of balance, and what combinations of matter make for the greatest strength. While the construction crew will be making the pyramid physically, they will use their mental and spiritual integration to do so in a way that uses the least energy or makes use of the free energy available in the items being constructed. In other words, you will be integrating your spirit soul into the forms you create. Furthermore, the operation of those forms can be linked to respond to your mind, emotions, and intentions.

Since your self-consciousness has made you feel separate from others and your environment, you have trouble comprehending the idea of being compatibly linked energetically with the souls of others. You have been so rooted in a life of constantly stealing energy from each other, instead of giving and regenerating one another, that it might appear to be an alien concept to be cooperating by joining sparks of consciousness. But as you near the galactic plane and your physical and mental nature "lightens up," you will see that there is no better way to exist. At that point, you will find it tremendously rewarding to calibrate your consciousness with your soul brethren in creating. You will actually be able to recharge each other and mix energy in a way that is fulfilling and invigorating for each soul involved. Your accomplishments will reflect this increased energetic mixing and accelerate your mutual evolution.

Latent DNA Activation

The DNA activation that we have been mentioning will be happening on a physical and spiritual level. There is DNA that is seen in 3D that appears to your science to have no discernible use, but in fact is latent genetic material that was strategically placed in your design by your spiritual parents. The human race is a mix of genetic material from the cosmos, as is all life on Earth. The life on your planet did not originate there, but that is another story. More importantly, the universe is created by consciousness and there exists beings of varying degrees of awareness and ability as creators. There is a higher aspect of your soul that created you, so to speak, and a higher aspect of your unified soul that created humanity and seeded life in this material universe. More of these universal dynamics will become apparent as your mind is expanded and can comprehend creation with a wider perspective.

Everything in your physical world has a spiritual ethereal connection including the DNA codes that are the blueprint of your biological and frequency structure. There is a biological code and various levels of energetic code that allow your soul form to be expressed within certain physical frequencies. That said, there are physical gene codes that will become active and a multitude of energetic codes that will be turned on to allow you to synchronize with the new dimension. With this activation comes a lighter physical body, increased mental and spiritual abilities, and connections to other dimensions and vibrations. Also, when new DNA code is switched on, some old and unnecessary code will become latent over time from lack of use. The new DNA will alter aspects of your brain as new synapses are created with the development of advancing skills. For example, a whole center of your brain will be turned on to deal with sensing and interpreting frequency and become quite active, causing other areas to develop, such as the mental manipulation of vibration.

Abilities in individuals and soul groups will vary depending on particular DNA signatures that exist already and those connected to energy patterns from past soul developments. Therefore, some individuals or soul-mate groups will excel in the vibrations of healing energy, while others may be advanced in multidimensional viewing. Some will find they can manipulate matter grid structures with mental focus, which is akin to what you would call telekinesis. Still others will be visionary seers who are able to grasp and assimilate holistic systems. There will be telepathic communicators and alien life form relations facilitators, among whatever other specialties you can imagine. Capacities will be related to the DNA already in place, personal interest, previous lifetimes, and soul inclinations. There is no doubt that these newfound talents will lift burdens and challenge your souls in wonderful ways.

Each strand of your DNA vibrates at a particular rate and as such can be activated with a synchronized frequency. Some of these frequencies can be created with audible sound, while others cannot be heard by human ears in 3D, because they are above the limited range of your present focus. These will be heard in 4D. We, and other beings, are affecting your species' DNA vibrations by infusing frequency modulations into your realm to begin the step by step process of the awakening of your potential.

The cosmic influences radiating from other celestial bodies are also affecting your activation and will increase their influence as your solar system nears the central plane of the galaxy. The exertion of fine frequencies pulsing through your universe at that time will be potent. The DNA that has been prepared for activation will entirely switch on and you will find yourselves seeing and feeling as if in a dream. Everything that many of you have been dealing with, beginning just before the turn of the 21st century, will all make sense as your fixation on your five sense experience widens to include a multidimensional perspective.

The strands of your newly activated DNA will literally begin to vibrate and change your perception of reality. As we have said, everything will appear lighter in luminosity and weight. The new codes will vibrate with a whole new aspect of creation that was previously closed off to your comprehension. Your brain will quickly accommodate all the new input and fire up neurons that did not exist previously. Suddenly, your consciousness will see and sense beyond three dimensions of space, and the rules of that world will no longer apply with the same limitations. The work you have done in your life to this date has been in preparation for allowing your encoded program to become active. All self-reflection, pushing yourself to view the world beyond the awareness of your identity, and searches within for deeper meaning, will allow you to be open to the finer vibrations and will attune you with what is coming.

For us this is a beautiful image of many strings of energy elevating octaves and singing a new tune with one another in the creation of a balanced symphony of change. This is a grand event. It is the culmination of efforts in many probable realities converging in a great evolutionary shift. The great shift is occurring in the physical DNA and in the energetic codes of all synchronized life and matter in your universe. The wave of music will be heard through all the galaxies and pulse into the multi-verse. We hope that you appreciate the magnitude of this awakening and will share in the excitement of its realization.

Releasing of Burdens or Lightening Up

Many of the burdens you feel weighing upon you, especially in this period of transformation, will be released as you near this great awakening. This "letting go" will be one of the symptoms you will feel when you are ready to move forward to your next level of awareness. If you are feeling particularly burdened with responsibilities and laden with the weight of physical reality, it is a sign that you are ready to shed the last of your personal spiritual hurdles. Rest assured that the weight is a final step to walking away from the burdens you have endured in a third density experience. You will soon recognize all the burdens as the illusions they are and be able to glean the meaning from them and move on. You are on the verge of freedom from the confines of your imposed dense creations. You can now step into a world of richer interaction with your creations.

What does it mean to let go of your burdens? There have been particular aims for your soul's evolution as it exists in the 3D world. Your multidimensional soul has been experiencing the dynamics of a physical life bearing down on it so that it can learn what it is made of. As expressions of the One Consciousness, ultimately, you are each experiencing a part of that whole as you push against obstacles. Finding your source within those obstacles is a way of expressing your strength of consciousness. The journey of pushing and pulling and ups and downs has afforded you much ability as creators. You can liken the adventure to the experience of using heavy weights to work out your body and then putting the weights down and doing the same exercises without them. When you release the weights, the motions suddenly feel easy and your arms and legs feel lighter without the resistance. You have strengthened yourself and therefore usual movement becomes more effortless. You have put yourselves in trial grounds to strengthen your spirit and resolve as creators.

Everything you have endured in many lives culminates in a strengthened soul. What you have experienced in this life is only a small part of who you are, what you have been, and what your soul knows. You may feel as though you have not done much of note in this life, and have lots of flaws that still need to be corrected. However, this is such a small portion of what you have already felt and realized. If you are reading this book, it means a part of your soul recognizes that there is a much bigger picture to your existence than this one life you are living. If you have come this far, then you have come very far in your awareness. Do remind yourself that the personality and life history of the person you are incarnated as now is only a tip of the iceberg that is your multi-layered soul.

The burdens you face in this life are merely a way for you to reflect yet another aspect of the greater you. There is never a right answer along the journey. It is the experience of being you in your journey that is important, and the becoming aware of your divine source interacting in that role that is enlightenment. Your goal is never to be other than what you truly are. Your obstacles are not there to make you different. They are there to wake you up to who you already are and reveal that as yet another spark in creation.

Therefore, letting go of burdens is becoming aware that they are a way for you to reflect your inner strength of being as a source of creation. Yes, you chose certain facets of your diamond to polish in this life. That is why you chose particular events and personality traits to help you reveal something else about your true being. All your burdens are opportunities for you to exhibit more of your personal and particular light in the universe. Letting go of these burdens is lightening up your soul. It is your soul becoming aware of the reasons why you decided upon the burdens. When you see them for what they were intended, you can start allowing them to reveal you. This process will happen individually and globally. The trials and tribulations you are having personally, and around the globe, are reflections of your final hurdles in becoming ascended beings. What you see as darkness in the world, are opportunities for the final redemption, if you will. You are finally at a place where you are able to see the darkness as such, and are on the edge of moving the curtain aside, and showing your true colors as a race of beings and group of souls.

So how do you let go of those last pesky obstacles that hold your soul back? We firstly ask that you once again take a wider view. Imagine that the person you identify with as you in this life is only a piece of a multi-faceted you. Realize that you are all the many people you have incarnated as, and all the possibilities each one of those people or beings expressed in parallel realities. You are all those expressions, lessons, emotions, thoughts, and imaginations rolled into a greater consciousness.

When you come to a big decision or are confronted by something that appears to be going wrong, remember that you are here to experience your inner strength and will, as it is expressed or reflected in that event. What part of you would you like to radiate into the world in that moment? What decision reflects the soul expression that you wish to see in the universe? Letting go is being aware of who you are and making the choice to express your light in the face of struggles, whether they are external or internal. It is time to awaken to this realization and allow yourself to let go of the burdens and shine your expression.

Your burdens will increasingly be revealed to you for what they were intended as you approach a more ascended consciousness. When finally the doorway to the fourth dimension opens, your self-created obstacles will be seen with clarity, and as if by magic, they will drop away and lighten your load. A new era will beckon your consciousness into an expanded perspective in the lighter and extended dimension.

4D Space, Time, and Gravity

The fourth dimension will feel lighter, brighter, and less burdened. It will have expanded horizons that alter the laws of physics that you accept in the third dimension. Consequences of a particular dimensional focus such as space, time, and gravity will be stretched, so to speak. You will find that the laws that governed these factors in 3D do not apply to 4D.

You will find that you must discover the new dynamics that govern your motions and creations in this new world. The effects will be felt by each individual and of course will cause scientists and philosophers to reassess the physical world and its meaning relative to newfound psychic abilities. You will discover that your spatial comprehension has literally been stretched into an alternate realm and experience of time and gravity. With the expansion to another layer of spatial awareness comes a loosening of the confines of time and gravity distortion. All of these factors lead further to the feeling of weightlessness. You see that the lifting of burdens and weightlessness will occur psychologically, spiritually, and physically.

As a 4D being, you will have another whole angle to explore in your universe. With this new perspective, time will be more flexible, and gravity more moldable. All of your senses will also expand to fill the stretched space, time, and gravity. With these alterations, you will gain entirely different viewpoints from which to observe your creations. You may be able to imagine how a flat world extended to a 3D world affords a whole new dimension for the senses to contemplate. This will also be the case as you widen your scope to 4D. Just as a 3D, compared to a 2D world, allows more movement and manipulation of objects, and a very different experience of gravity and sense of time, so will you experience such a jump in 4D. The saying, "thinking outside the box" comes to mind in a literal way.

The elevated experience of fourth dimension will in many ways be like a rebirth. It will feel as though you are just learning to walk, and sense what is in your environment, all over again. It can be disorienting until you acclimate, which is yet another reason for the slow transition, and need for preparations. Like a child, you will slowly assimilate the extra external and internal data that is reaching your expanded brain and newly encoded DNA. You will, in a sense, be retuning your system to the new frequencies. It will be as if a multitude of filters have come down and you must find the order within all the new sensory input. You will slowly adjust and be awakened to an incredible world with much less limits.

Imagine that your house suddenly expanded to include another dimension. You would find you can walk through the walls. You will hear sounds that you never heard before and see extra layers in all the matter around you. You will be fascinated with merely moving through the new dimension and opening yourself to new sensations at first. Then you will try to make sense of what you are processing. You will be moving in more than an up-down manner, and gravity will not necessarily stop you from going there the way you remember it should. Your sense of time will change based on your thoughts, and you will find you need to get a handle on where you are in time as well.

In your 4D experience you will decipher another level of meaning in all your interactions with materials, and will find your minds are open to the ethereal realm as the veil shading you from the space between becomes thinner. This latter quality, incidentally, is not only an aspect of being in a 4D reality, it is a function of the integration of your spirit level soul. Not all life forms in 4D will be privy to the elevations of mind and spirit that humanity experiences. There will be physical forms that transit to 4D from your present world that will take on greater depth as they adjust to living in the new world as well, but their development is not of the same soul function as humankind. However, all life on Earth will benefit from the advancements of the human mind and soul, as humans learn to see and appreciate their fellow inhabitants in a richer way.

New Layers of Life Force and Nutrition

In being able to sense the higher level perspective, you will gain more knowledge of all the matter that exists within this new energy grid. Your deeper comprehension and understanding of your interconnection will allow you to interact with material forms in an exciting new manner. You will find that you can sense another layer of the forms around you. Not only will you be able to touch, smell, see, taste, and hear as you did before, but all those senses will become enhanced as a finer frequency modulation is taken into account.

New senses will be activated to better assimilate the new layer of knowing that comes with your soul view. What you have sensed about a flower in 3D, for example, will expand to include the accentuated five senses and a communion with the flower's consciousness. You will be able to feel the creation happening within the flower as if you are sensing it grow and are aware of its intentions and needs for expression. As such, you will be able to assist its growth by injecting the frequency that it needs to reach its potential. You will be able to do this with all life you come in contact with by detecting its motivation and awareness and using your intention to affect its life force.

With this skill comes the ability to determine which foods to consume based on how the frequency of the plant or animal will impact your energy. You will find that you will prefer to feed on lighter frequency matter and will need to eat much less since you can partake in the most energizing foods for your particular bodily needs. Foods will be grown for their specific energy output and will be enhanced as they grow. You can actually measure the vibration of various foods today, with electronic instruments, and begin eating finer vibration foods. As you measure the frequencies with the machine, try to sensitize yourself to the food's energy and train yourself to be more sensitive to how it is stimulating your system, including your brain functioning. Since each person has his or her own frequency signature, the nutritional needs will vary for each individual and at different times in each person's life.

With the enhancement of the food you are eating, and of your sensitivity in 4D, food will have greater pleasure. While many of you find you desire to eat a lot for a sense of satisfaction, in 4D you will be happy with the exuberance of the tasting experience and desire less quantity. It will require less physical energy to function in 4D because of the release of much of the gravity pull and that you will be literally lighter, therefore, consumption needs will be reduced naturally.

The movement into the next dimensional gateway will be an exhilarating letting go of the confines you have dealt with as a being in 3D. The challenges you confronted physically, mentally, and spiritually will dissolve as your new awareness awakens to a more dynamic realm within which to create anew. The lighter and more spacious existence will feel boundless and free in comparison to the density you fought against in 3D. You will feel and know more inherently, and there will be much to discover about yourselves and your place in the larger universe as a result.

The freedom from your old laws will fire up your souls and inspire you to venture further as creators. The lightness of being is a state to look fondly forward to in your spiritual journey. There is nothing to fear, whether you move to the finer density or venture to other realms of exploration. Your soul knows that all will be well either way.

Those that are ready to ascend in their awareness will not only find they are more buoyant and free of previous burdens, they will also experience a vastly expanded perspective on cause and effect and the sensation of consecutive events will be altered. Your next stop: the zone of experiential time dilation and multidimensional consciousness.

Chapter 18

When Time Stops
and You Keep on Going

*U*pon transcending to the next octave in your evolution, you will find that sequential time as you knew it will seize to be your only mode of experiencing cause and effect relationships. Your increasingly multidimensional perspective will allow your sense of time to stretch beyond the limits imposed by a spatially relational view. Your mental faculties will be able to experience events as probabilities in future time lines as well as viewing their seeming cause related to past events. It will appear as though the limits of time have stopped and your consciousness keeps on going. You will be able to mentally and emotionally assess future probabilities relevant to the moment you are thinking within, and travel to past events that alter both experiences. The cause and effect relationships will take on a depth and a level of discovery that was previously unavailable for your senses to explore.

Envisioning Cause, Effect, and Potentialities

Your new dimensional senses will work on a more visionary scope. Seeing and feeling beyond a moment-to-moment view, you will move with your consciousness based on multiple realizations and potential creations. Human consciousness will expand to include multiple events and situations at once, in a sense. Your minds will learn to constantly filter through potentialities through time to determine significant creation points that can be manipulated to accomplish intentions. Again, this will occur individually and collectively and is only limited by the imagination.

For example, when you awake from a resting state, which incidentally you will require less of, your mind and soul will immediately process the potentials for your day. But, unlike in the third dimension, you will see far beyond a list of goals. You will see the future results of those goals and will be able to alter your past and present according to the perceived desired outcome. So every day will be a dynamic multi-time cause and effect dance of creation. It will appear as if you are flowing through moments, but they will not pile atop one another in a string of sequential events, but rather flow simultaneously based on your conscious focus.

The larger community and global collective will be affected by the intention of each person's frequency, and vice versa. The larger group will shape boundaries of individual potential. The interconnected nature of your souls will be vastly apparent as your existence is altered each day by group intentions. This realization will lead to further cooperation with higher objectives. Individual common will power will eventually propel intentions that benefit the whole.

With an expanded multi-time awareness, your souls will learn to fine tune thoughts and to synchronize them with one another, so that your creations are in tune. You will also learn that your goals are better focused on particular vibrations rather than projections for specific events. If you are too precise about a desired outcome it may block a greater potentiality within a bigger picture. For example, you will learn to focus your consciousness on protection or safety, rather than on having a certain shelter. This allows the greater mass consciousness the opportunity to flow to more possibilities, without being blocked by individual imaginary limits.

As you will see, the cause and effect dynamics will not disappear with your altered time experience, but will rather be amplified and deepened.

Cause and effect will be acutely apparent as will the impact of each individual soul upon the whole group. Those of you who are learning the importance and power of your thoughts, feelings, and imaginations, presently, will find the deepening awareness natural as you will already have practice in attuning your spiritual life.

Instead of waiting for a whole life to be lived in order to be able to more deeply assess the consequences of your actions, you will be able to view your life continually and make adjustments. It will be as if your many probable selves will be joining into a wider and more dynamic consciousness. Instead of every thought or action propelling a new dimensional self that continues in its own time line, each thought will be in constant connection with alternate selves that will access and consciously change one another. In this way, you are creating a more cohesive multidimensional self and collective consciousness.

Multidimensional Self-Integration

As you step through the final gateway into the next dimension, it will be as if the veil of time has lifted and you can sense its illusory nature. Without this sheath, your soul is able to integrate with your multidimensional aspects through time and space. It will be possible for your soul to communicate and interrelate with parts of itself on alternate paths in different realities. It will be more likely for your soul to connect with finer dimensional selves as well. The veil of time and space will be moved aside and your soul will be free to extract from its higher counterparts in a more conscious manner. This will result in a deeper appreciation for your current expression. The sensation of this thinning veil will, not only give you the sensation that you are never alone, but will intensify your understanding of your importance as a segment of advancing consciousness.

The channels will be open so that messages from other times, dimensions and celestial bodies will be felt, heard, and attended to. There will be a sense of knowing and balancing in such communications. Your soul will be able to initiate and commune with other beings and higher relations with increasing ease and comfort. The removal of time constraints literally opens a valve to inter-dimensional comprehension. As you tune your frequency, you will learn to trust your assessments and knowing without restriction. Most of you currently do not trust your inner or higher self and do not understand the sway you have through that blanket of time.

There is tremendous spiritual growth inherent in the integration of your probable selves, multiple soul levels, and physical manifestations, into a more cohesive evolution. For example, without the limitations of time, you will in any given moment, be able to access other potentials that were developed in parallel time lines. Your imagination can tap into those alternate selves and integrate abilities into your present consciousness. As you reach into another reality, you also open a two-way valve so that your other self can, in turn, more accurately integrate various personality developments that you have made. You do not become each other. However, you share your consciousness more readily, and allow for a better understanding of who you are as a whole. The same is true of your soul existing in other dimensions and on other planets. No matter whether a part of your soul exists somewhere in the past or future, or on another planet, you can establish a relationship that transcends these illusory barriers. All your various soul components will become more whole as a result of these communications and will evolve in unison, no matter where and when they are physically attuned.

After the transition, you will also become more open to physically meeting races of beings that you have a soul affinity with. As we have explained, there are many waiting to accelerate relations with humanity. There are many among you who will find they can relate to other dimensional and extra-planetary races, once you remove the curtain that clouds your vision of your soul connection. When you can see your individual and group soul relationship, spanning the annals of time, you will automatically have a deeper understanding of one another. Without the restriction of time, you can see your future or past self within the other race, and could comprehend what your best course of action in working together may be.

The connections to other worldly beings will be varied among you. There are many races represented within the souls of humanity at the present time. This period is a creational intersection for the superhighway of inter-galactic and inter-planetary advancements. It is an exciting time for many beings in many times. The links made with probable human selves and probable extraterrestrial selves will all play a role in your new fourth dimension experience. All will assist in your development of a new flow of reality creation.

We remind you, once again, that everything is related to the frequency tone, and you always have a choice as to what tone you wish to set. All your inter-dimensional selves can be allies in obtaining a future world of peace, harmony, and fulfilling expression. But, even in the next dimension, you can choose to downgrade your frequency in density and disconnect from that ultimate source of life energy. There are those in 4D that struggle to keep their vibration in that flow and find they cannot maintain cohesion with higher vibrations and allow themselves to fall. Even though they see through the constructs of duality, they are unable to continue with the power of the collective force, and are pulled back into a more egocentric dynamic. Although they understand the interconnected nature of their consciousness, some choose to continue feeding off other's energy. So while they have evolved conceptually, they find their focus strays and creations become imbalanced.

Beings that are unable to manage a collective focus that matches the minimal vibration of the fourth dimension are at risk of de-evolution. They can find themselves unable to maintain the octave and become out of sync. Others may be able to assist in lifting them up, but if not, they will fall back into a third dimension of duality. Again, there is no judgment about this. This is only a matter of vibration and each dimensional octave supports a particular range of mental and spiritual focus and oscillation. Often these individuals will find that they simply physically die from the fourth dimension experience and are then reborn in another 3D reality.

Flexibility of Physical Aging and Appearance

The demise of the physical body is also altered when time as you now know it no longer has a grip on your being. The body will no longer be confined to a sequential degradation. In fact, your mind and body soul integration through time will allow you to continually regenerate your manifestation in 4D. There will be no need to see and experience the slow disintegration of your physical form and eventual death. The experience of both birth and death will be a conscious choice.

A soul may choose to be born in the same manner that you experience in 3D, except all beings involved will have a deeper appreciation and knowledge of the entrance of a soul into the world. The soul entering, and the parents, will be cognizant of the meaning and purpose for the soul's journey. This new physical being will learn to process his evolution within the context of a multi-dimensional view of time. Many new lives will be born that come from a third dimensional previous expression. They will, therefore, need to process the experience of growing from a baby to an adult, but will learn quickly about what they can become in each moment by looking through multiple cause and effect windows.

Death of the physical form will only be experienced when a soul decides it is ready to move on and often it will leave the body behind for another soul to use. "Walk-ins," as they have been called, have no need to experience the physical growth process and instead come with a particular mission to be carried out as an adult. Otherwise, when physical death is chosen, the soul decides to allow itself to dissolve its attachment to the form when ready. As your species discovers this ability, you will also create rituals that allow for a soothing transition for all concerned. Since you will have a considerably altered perspective on time, there would be no sadness in this change, only respect and dignity. Your comprehension of the ethereal, afterlife, and in-between zone, will allow a more conscious bridge to form so that the soul can let go of the body, and energetically dislodge from its frequency and the signature of the fourth dimensional grid in general.

The physical age of the form you take during your life journey will depend on your mental, emotional, and spiritual focus in any given moment. You could maintain one particular age your entire life, if it suited you. Many will feel most comfortable allowing an aging process until they become more adept at understanding their own flow through the new experiential time. Eventually, you will each learn to take a form that expresses your development and even mood. Older, wiser souls, for example, may remain as white-haired sages, as an expression of their ages of wisdom. Others may uphold a character of play and joviality and decide to keep an image of youth and vitality. Until you become adroit at manipulating your form, you will appear as what your consciousness naturally projects. In other words, if you feel radiant and strong, you will project that image to others. It will be impossible to hide who you are even in your physical manifestation.

Human physical expression in 3D is almost entirely focused on the ego and most humans are quite out of balance between their emotional and spiritual energies. Therefore, you have little control over your physical body as an expression of your consciousness. But, as you step out of the limits of time and space, you begin to recognize that your body is a reflection of your consciousness and is therefore malleable. The widened view on time will especially broaden your understanding of how consciousness imprints your being at a cellular and even molecular level.

While you will continue to embody a particular human pattern of DNA, your relationship with that material form will deepen. Just as you will learn to sense the frequencies in your environment, you will also attune to your body and will sense when it is out of balance in any area. You will each be able to heal any ailment at the frequency level. You may also have special healing practitioners to assist with blockages. Your vision through time will allow you to prevent or confront misaligned energies before they can overtake your being.

Seeing Probabilities will Accelerate Development

Perhaps the most important development of experiencing yourself through the looking glass of the past and future will be the psychological and spiritual realizations that occur. When you are able to determine the consequences for actions, thoughts, and physical manifestations, in a much shorter period of time, learning is accelerated. Physical manifestations in your body and environment will be recognized quickly as effects of your mental and spiritual intentions. The learning curve will be reduced by thousands fold. What took you a hundred years of figuring through trial and error, will take a fraction of that time, and will be continually advanced in all time frames. In this way, your species can evolve at an exponential rate. In fact, this is what happens to all species as they move up the awareness spectrum. This is why cultures from just one dimension finer, can be light years ahead in spiritual and technological development.

The acceleration of discoveries will also lead to incredible diversity in the manifestation of solutions, as many more avenues of approach will be tested without the cumbersome waiting for time to prove ideas right or wrong. As long as something can be conceived with the imagination, it can be viewed as an alternative possibility. Many ideas will be seen to go nowhere immediately, while some will show potential beyond all expectations. Mind you, since each moment alters the future and past, there can never be any definitive future predictions. Everything is changing everything all of the time.

What you will see through time is waves of consciousness and probable results based on the strength and flow of the collective consciousness. While time in 4D will stop its continuity, there will always be a flexible now in which all time pivots that is based on the predominant consciousness at an individual and universal level. The now you experience will be based on where your attention is placed, and where that attention is focused will permeate all the preceding and progressing moments that surround it. In 4D you will be able to sense those surrounding moments and see their fluctuation based on your intentions.

Let us take a look at how this may appear to you. Imagine you are deciding whether or not to go out to a party. As you have that thought, your consciousness will have access to all the possible outcomes of that decision as they exist related to that pivotal moment. You will be able to read the frequency flow and will see if the path is clear or whether there are interferences in energy. You could see possible collisions along the way, and at the event, given your frequency. You will sense potentially important encounters and see how they may impact your life in sweeping glimpses. Some meetings may show long term impact, while others may be fleeting. The results will be based on a reading of your intentions and the frequencies of others, at the instant you thought about going to the gathering.

If there is nothing in the vision that intrigues, you may have a thought to stay home and meditate or read a book instead. As you have this thought, all the outcomes of this decision will pour forth in your mental picture. Perhaps the consequences of not meeting someone will be more significant than meeting them, for better or worse, for all those concerned. Maybe your meditation will cause a breakthrough in your mental focus and change your behavior for a lifetime. In your mental travels you will sense the meaning of events, for you and those lives linked to yours. If a decision has farther reaching power, the effects may be felt in a global way.

Having such ability to envision or read probabilities has advantages, but as you can surmise, it is not a foolproof means to avoid the challenges of life. Some might even say it could accentuate the challenges of making decisions. Sometimes, not knowing is easier. The more you know, the more you must take responsibility for your actions. And clearly, no peering into time will give you a right or wrong answer, not only because the outcomes can change along the way, but because there is ultimately no right or wrong. As you navigate in this new world of time variants, you discover that the vibrations of your thoughts are more significant than the perception of perceived outcomes as good or bad.

You spend an inordinate amount of time in your present lives worrying about whether your decisions are good or bad, or if they are the best for you or not. In 4D your perspective on time will make you realize that it is not the perfection of the outcome that matters, but rather what you are gleaning from any experience, that offers fulfillment. Explorations in time will reveal that your intention, process, and attention to the elevation of senses, has the most impact on your soul and the web of light. You will learn that keeping your mental state at a certain pitch will bring about the synchronicities that are in tune with the light source of creation.

Once you get the hang of the importance of pitch, you will be able to follow the probabilities that match your intention and will attract those scenarios naturally. When you understand the power of your mental and emotional modulation, you will act on probabilities that generate the most personal and universal power. And, you will have no need to fret over decisions, because you will learn to synchronize and let go of expectations for outcomes. You will do this because you will finally be in a place of knowing and trusting your soul vision.

Manipulation of Experiential Time

A multidimensional perspective of time also allows your soul to experience the timing of events with more fluidity. Even in your present view, you appreciate time differently depending on your mental and emotional processing of circumstances. Scenarios that occur in the same amount of time may not feel that way. Happy moments can slip by and boring situations may seem endless. Experiential time is understood as a psychological interpretation of the progression of events based on perspective. In 4D such perspective may be willingly altered and time can be consciously sped up or slowed down.

Time itself is actually a construct of the spatial grid of matter in which you find yourselves, and thus is only an illusion in the first place. The acknowledgment of this fact will allow personal manipulation of the sensing of how events appear to move through time. Eventually, experts in time manipulation will emerge in your society and sciences will develop around the study and travel of time that go beyond the spiritual sensing of probabilities. This will open the doors for space travel technologies that allow movement through vast amounts of space in no time.

In a personal way, using the manipulation of experiential time for your spiritual growth will advance your soul journey tremendously. In your next dimensional octave, you can change time by changing your mental processing of events, on purpose. You will speed up or slow down the progression of time by altering your emotional expression of experiences. Events will move according to your will with much greater acumen and intention than you currently experience. Imagine actually being able to lengthen events that are rewarding and shorten those that are not satisfying. Immediately, you think of extending pleasure and reducing pain. However, your soul vision will soon outgrow that tendency as you begin sensing the depth of experiences. Surprisingly, you may stay with a painful situation to explore your potential reactions and their meaning for your soul. Since you will be outgrowing the good and bad interpretation, you will see that the pain is as interesting and revealing as the pleasurable moments.

The exploration of experiential time will further broaden your horizons as individuals and collective soul groups. Scenarios of extended time may be accentuated by soul groups in order to access specific growth or learning opportunities. An event lived by many souls may be expanded or lessened by various individuals or groups. One person or group may stay in a situation combing for the meaning, while others may flash by and already be delving into the depth of another matter. There is much to be extracted from this maneuvering in psychological time when it is done with awareness.

You can practice playing with experiential time dilation now by observing the mental and emotional impact of events and deciding to follow their flow to a greater depth, rather than to simply ignore the passage of time. You can choose to mentally extend your experience of an event by purposefully deepening your attention to your sensations within the event, no matter whether they are pleasurable or painful. If you try this, you will find it can be a rewarding, as it forces you to feel more layers within the experience. You may find that you are able to stretch or pinch your involvement with situations at will.

In your 4D mind, the art of manipulating experiential time will become an important part of your reality and will have far reaching implications. It is a wonder as to why your society has not explored this arena more deeply already, but no matter, as you will be forced to discover its power when your perception of time is altered by your octave change. The fact that the normal sequential passage of time will seize, will prompt you to delve into the secrets that time has to offer.

You will no longer take the movement of events through time for granted, but will instead always seek the purpose and cause and effect relationships of scenarios. Seeing through the barrier of time will spur a new appreciation for the construction of your material world and your journey through your creations. You will soon find that extracting the marrow out of experiences, by expanding emotional and spiritual time involvement, will accentuate your expression of creation, individually and culturally.

Spirit and Science Integrated Time Travel

The ability to see through the illusion of time will be a skill that each soul will be capable of. However, there will be some among your people that will become experts at time manipulation. These individuals will gather in groups or will stand out among their soul group to provide the task of envisioning time lines for the larger collective. These people will become time warriors. Their ability will be highly regarded as a tool for the betterment of the species. It will become these gifted humans' job to gauge the flow of consciousness and to report to the collective as to how events may manifest with certain directed focus in past, present and future.

Alongside the time visionaries will be the time scientists that analyze and categorize the information gathered. Some of these scientists will be put to the task of learning to use the knowledge to develop technologies for physical time travel and to break the barrier of traveling long distances over time. The breakthroughs will come firstly from the mental exploration of the new perspective on the illusory nature of time, along with the expanded understanding of space and matter as energy constructs.

The spiritual investigation of probabilities is hugely important in the evolution of your species. Without this elevated comprehension, you would not be capable of or ready for the expansion of consciousness that will come from being able to ride through time physically and organically. Not to mention, all the species that are already riding through dimensions and time would not accept your species into these realms without the proper spiritual development.

It would be far too risky for the state of the universe to allow a species to roam in time, and across the universe, without having the psychological, mental, and especially spiritual knowledge to understand the impact their actions may have on the whole. This is why the next dimensional awareness will act as a classroom, and a filter for the gateway to the manifestation of technologies using spiritual appreciation of time dilation.

Each of the species that you will encounter, or already are encountering in some cases, has a deeper appreciation of time and space and the manifestation of matter therein. In order for these species to manifest in your time and space, they have mastered the manipulation of frequency signature calibration as well as the synchronization of matter vibration in relation to points in time. They have mastered the ability to make themselves a physical space within alternate spatial dimensions and probabilities in any time period. By doing this, they can also travel vast distances in what you perceive as space. When you see UFOs that appear to move in impossible ways, and at impossible speeds, and disappear out of thin air, they are likely alien technologies that alter the space and time within which they appear. In doing this they often affect electronic equipment and can create missing time for those that come in contact with them.

Visitations have increased as your species has developed advanced technologies. There are many extraterrestrials monitoring your development to assure that your spiritual acumen is evolving as readily as your scientific understanding of space, time, and matter creation. Without science and spiritual integration, your species cannot progress to influence other dimensions to any greater extent than it already has. In other words, you are on the verge of going where you may only go if you are able to use your higher consciousness to make wise and connected collective decisions. Without the soul assimilation, you can adversely impact realms beyond your own, and the larger collective would not allow this to happen. The hope is that humankind will join the galactic community in envisioning and creating an expanded Earth, solar system, and universe, via contributions from your advancing souls.

We have devoted a great deal of time, no pun intended, into the subject of time in this book, for good reason. Humans have taken the experience of time so for granted that they have lost an appreciation for its value and have missed the amazingly revealing potential in studying the perception of time. That will all change drastically as you reach the next dimension and shed your current time limits. The halting of a sequential perception will be one of the greatest discoveries of 4D, and will forever alter your evolutionary path, as it has done for other species. How you decide to proceed with this profound knowledge is up to your collective will. There are many willing to guide you in the exploration of your expanded awareness, including us light beings, and our evolutionary counterparts existing in other dimensions and millennia.

One of the most amazing discoveries you will continually confirm as you travel in probable realities is the importance of sharing your light for the betterment and evolution of your larger universal soul community. The more you travel and meet with alternate and advanced selves and souls throughout the galaxy and beyond, the more you will recognize the interconnected highways of light that link every molecule and conscious beings that exist in all dimensions and all times. With this depth of understanding comes the true appreciation of what it means to share your consciousness, and spirit, in brightening the universe for eternal evolution.

Chapter 19

Giving to Evolve

*I*n order to evolve you must give. The universe evolves by giving and the source of everything in the multi-verse, or All That Is, evolves by perpetually giving from its core and expressing it outward in the process of creating. True creating is true giving. The expression of your core consciousness and multi-dimensional spirit is your evolutionary giving to creation. This is your ultimate reason for being.

When we speak of giving, we do not mean giving charity per se. The appearance of true giving is different for each individual, as you are each a unique aspect of creation's means to evolve by sharing what it is. Without sharing your conscious spirit in your special way, you do not evolve spiritually. This is why you all instinctively seek meaning in your lives and purpose for your existence. The very essence of consciousness desires to share its uniqueness. In this final chapter, we will discuss what real giving is and how it spurs evolutionary leaps.

Charity Versus True Sharing

Firstly, you should understand the different types of giving and what type leads to spiritual advancement and deep fulfillment. Much of what your culture considers giving comes from a place of ego satisfaction. Most sharing is done for the sake of some personal gain or approval. Even charity, and often especially charity, is given from a place of guilt or to absolve feelings of impurity. It is often done to appease others, to make one feel special, or to hide feelings of guilt over not being good enough. Charity that comes from a selfless angle is actually rare. When such giving is witnessed, it comes from the expression of pure light. The giver will feel extremely lifted from the experience and not even think of it as giving, because it is a completely natural expression of who they are.

Religions and other organizations take advantage of the innate sense of guilt people have for not sharing to their fullest potential. It is not bad to give charity to the needy, or to spread belief systems, but do not falsely believe that it is true spiritual giving. One cannot even know whether such giving had the desired result. Sometimes giving can have the opposite effect than what was intended. Giving charity can cause weakness where it was meant to make the receiver stronger.

The only giving that you can be assured is pure, is sharing from your soul as a being of light. This type of sharing can only be known individually. When giving from the soul, your heart soars and recipients flourish. However, you will not feel that you gave anything up, because true giving gives nothing up. True giving does not sacrifice; it rejuvenates both the giver and the receiver.

If more of you spent less time pretending to be giving and more time truly sharing your unique qualities, then the world would need no charity. Of course, in order to come from a place of sharing from the soul, you must spend time knowing your own soul and allowing it to be at peace with what it has to give. Is it better then, for you to be selfish and give no charity? In actuality, it would make little difference for you to be selfish and give no charity or to be a giver of charity out of self interest. One is no better than the other. Both come from a place of ego and are therefore ineffectual for assisting evolution. The energy in both cases is being wasted, as it merely bounces around and is not replenished. Giving from the soul requires that you be whole and connected within, so that you are sharing from pure source energy that invigorates others. When we give to you, we do not do so because we will gain from it. We give because it is our expression as creative beings. There is no loss from us when we share. There is only satisfaction and the exuberance of living our purpose. This is what you all seek and can, in fact, find.

Giving from your Central Light

Everything you crave to be and know is answered when you are able to find your true place from which to share who you are with no fear or expectation of particular results. When your expression comes purely from the center of your being, and is not ruled by exterior influences and self satisfaction, you become a whole being in a creative flow. In this state, you are naturally giving to creation, and all your actions become acts of giving. The acts of sharing that you perform are accepted as gifts of light and will add to the evolutionary process occurring all around you. Giving of yourself in this way is the ultimate freedom strived for by each of you.

You all want to be unencumbered by the confines of doing what you think you need to do for survival. To be out of that mind set will make your soul free. The only way to free yourself from the survival prison is to express your soul essence in every moment in every thought and action. This is possible by making the choice with intention and trusting in the validity of the source of your existence.

You did not come to this life to merely survive. You came to express your creative source and share that energy for the evolution of the One. Consciousness desires to be more so that all reality can be more. This is why sharing from an exterior motive does not add to creation. Only sharing from an internal soul motive is truly sharing. Someone who always appears to be doing good deeds may not be doing any more good than someone doing nothing or worse. What is important is whether they are expressing the unique gifts they were given, and are being true to who they are without outside influence. The person that stands up to the beggar and helps them face their fears may be doing more than the person that hands them a dollar bill, or not. It may be the person dancing down the street that gives most to the beggar without even noticing. Why, because the dancer may be dancing an expression of their soul and in that freedom they are sharing energy of creation with everyone they pass.

How do you know when you are being true to your soul? This is a question of utmost importance and you should ask it often. Make it your goal to find the answer to this question in all your actions. Why are you doing what you are doing in this very moment? Why are you reading this page? Why did you do what you did today? Have you acted out of fear or lack? Perhaps you did nothing because of fear or disbelief? Why are you the person you are today? Do you think you are who you were meant to be in this life? Do you feel that you were meant to be something in particular or to act some specific way? To find the answers to these questions you must be willing to go beyond what you think you are, and what you have mistakenly perceived the world to be, for your entire life.

All the tools and ideas we give you to practice and ponder are given to help jar your thinking and open your doors of perception in order to reveal that there is much more, and you are much more, than what your five senses tell you. Your spirit, which is connected to everything, is already a free energy form. It is trapped in self imposed limits that were designed to allow you to burst forth from the cocoon and be the butterfly that you are.

If you could for a moment forget what you think you should be, and stop comparing yourselves to what you think others are, you may give your soul a chance at freedom from the confines of your analytical ego. You each have had glimpses of enlightenment when you have gone outside of ego and simply allowed your soul to shine. Such moments filled you with warmth and spread like a wildfire. At such times you completely lose sight of being self-conscious and are able to let go of your hold on time and space and become a link to your creative soul. Letting go of ego self-interest and expressing your light is true sharing.

You each have gifts that you hide, because they seem insignificant, or you think they cannot make you money, so why bother. Often these gifts, no matter how small, are the angel wings that can help you fly above your fears and envelop the universe. Many of you do not pursue your gifts because you think you are not good enough, as you compare yourself to others. This comparing stops you from sharing your gifts. When you dare to express your soul without fear, you also allow yourself to confront the areas of your life that block you from being your best self. When you stop trying, you never give yourself the opportunity to break through your veils. Many of you fear being what your heart and soul truly desires, and therefore you stop your light from shining. This creates a sad state of affairs for the world.

If you have been working on shedding the veils of your ego, then you are beginning to see your internal diamond. Make an effort every day to remind yourself that your ego is no longer needed, and remember to allow your spirit to shine. It takes a conscious focus to give yourself permission to be the bright spirit that you truly are, and to daringly share that with the world, no matter what others think about your particular brand of expression. This is ultimate freedom and sharing. The diamond you have within is the only one like it. If you do not let it glimmer, then it will go unseen and an portion of creation will be left in darkness. Finding the jewel within is your mission. Sharing it will come naturally once you allow it to be seen. Many of you know of your gem, but have been so programmed not to look at it that you repeatedly ignore its existence, and instead trudge back into old patterns of hiding that do not serve.

The mere act of imagining a bright star of light at the core of your being that is eternally luminescent, will begin to ignite your soul to its true nature. Imagine this central star of light at your core each day, as many times as you can, and see it becoming more radiant. See this core of light illuminating your physical body, and your aura, and radiating outward to the planet and universe. Picture your light connected to all consciousness. See your light sharing its essence. Allow yourself to be at peace with that central star and everything it touches.

Understand that this light is the being that is experiencing physical existence to express itself. Allow this light to guide your heart and mind, through your manifestations. Be the poetic expression of that central star. If your luminous soul were allowed to express itself fully, what would it say to you? What would this central star want you to be and hence share? What boundaries would this radiance pass through in its expression? Give credence to the voice of your spirit and let it be without hindrance from your ego judgments. It is aching to be free from your material constraints.

Accepting the fantastic brightness of your soul opens gateways that allow your essence to be expressed and shared, in a way that fulfills your purpose and spurs your personal and collective evolution. Concentrated focus on that core being, and listening to and seeing its path, will guide you in living your spiritual meaning. Retraining your consciousness to actually trust that inner radiance can transform your being and brighten the universe. Each soul that turns on is another bulb of light that dissolves the darkness and lifts the vibrancy of your Earth. That is true giving. The decision to turn on your light must be made daily. Each day in your realm is a gift your soul is given to brighten the world. Are you being true to that inner spark today? Have you taken a moment to listen? Or are you in robotic mode? The more you connect with the feeling of your central starlight, the more you will recognize that it has no specific agenda and is completely unfettered by notions of should or must. It wants to shine and let shine! It has no judgment of itself or those around it. Your soul only knows to express pure giving unconditionally.

Unconditional Giving

What is unconditional giving? Giving unconditionally does not mean doing whatever everyone else wants to be pleasing. It does not mean that you sacrifice of yourself to make others happy. True unconditional love needs no conditions. It pours forth without expectation. If you are in a place of expectation, then you are not giving from your soul. Giving from your core light will not feel like sacrifice for the sake of another, and it will not be. True unconditional love and sharing has nothing to sacrifice as it simply radiates and replenishes from an eternal connection to the source of creation.

All love that comes from your connection to your source is given unconditionally. There is simply no other way for that energy to emerge. In making the connection to your internal light, you have no choice but to share unconditionally, as this is the very nature of your life force. Your spirit does not have the least bit of concern for what it will get in return for giving or if it gave enough this week. It simply is connected and giving. This sensation is the most fulfilling experience you can have in any plane of existence as it means you are in alignment with your true expressive being, which is synchronized with all creation.

You cannot feel that you are not giving enough when you are in touch with your soul essence. There is no such thing as guilt or self deprecation coming from your soul. When you feel these sensations, then you know you have lost touch with your central starlight. When you lose touch, stop and re-center your attention. There is no reason to feel bad about falling into the trap of your ego gratification. That ego centered view is an opportunity to realize that you have lost your star focus. It is a clear indicator that you are not perceiving with your soul and are therefore stealing energy, or uselessly depleting your own energy, instead of attaching to the universal Oneness, which is always regenerative and giving.

This concept of centering your soul to give from the source may seem esoteric, but this is only because you have been trained to focus your attention on your ego needs and wants, and to ignore the source of your being. It is possible to re-learn to integrate the ego's physical self preservation strategies with a true connection to your spiritual self. This would allow you to become a more whole and energized being that contributes your boundless life to the universe.

If you feel that your ego self has needs or is being imposed upon by others, stop and check with your star center and allow it to shine within the experience. You will likely find that it sheds light on the situation and the desire or imposition is put into a new perspective. The extra light may reveal the situation as being less important or give you a new way to approach the predicament. Basically, you can train yourself to react less from your self-centered survival mode and instead allow your soul to open a new door of sharing, which will be refreshing and freeing. Your ego can then safely express what your soul has to offer.

Sometimes your soul will say absolutely "No" to something that your ego accepted out of fear of rejection or other such victim consciousness. Your soul may say "Yes" to something that you would not have normally done because of a lack of belief in your ability. The inner light will not come from a place of fear or lack, but only express the beauty of the divinity of your unique spirit. It may say "No" to the needs of others because meeting their needs may not be true to your spirit. However, it will never demean another in saying "No" as the words will come with the energy of creation and will be accepted as truth. If your soul recognizes an injustice, it will speak its mind and it will be heard and received. Your soul will not hide its truth in fear of ridicule or to placate. Your soul has strength, character, and courage. When it expresses its truth, it is giving unconditionally, and this is felt by others.

Finding and polishing your inner diamond will lead naturally to a strengthened soul and intuitive sharing. When that spark is gleaming, it will be shared without hesitation and will seek to find ways to be in a constant state of giving. Creation flourishes when it is projected outward to fill space and time in ever changing ways. When you are true to your soul you have a strong inspiration to impart your special means of creating. If you do not feel motivated, then you are not listening to your soul desires.

Before embarking on any task, no matter how mundane, ask your soul for its spark of input and follow the senses that assist. Connecting with your soul occurs by your conscious mental and emotional intentions. Move away from thoughts that direct you to think of "Me, me, me" desires for external stimulation. Instead, focus inward to your eternal energy and awaken your soul's ability to govern your ego mind and share with the world. Be still, imagine, listen, and trust your inner senses. Practice this mind set to become an unconditionally sharing being.

Loving Your Luminous Soul

To be truly unconditional in your loving and sharing with the world, you must firstly accept, love and share with your own being. Opening to and trusting your own light is the only way to find that pure love and self acceptance that will radiate to others. You are not only the physical being you see in the mirror. That material form is only an expression of your soul. Love what you choose to express in this world and appreciate that you have much to share. Being overly attached to a physical image or personality gets you caught in your own shadow web. Learn to appreciate the unique expression that you reveal and what you have to give from your heart. Decide right now that you will accept where you are right now and who you are in this dimensional form. Make a decision that you will share the truth of your soul. Acknowledge that you are not solely the image you have presented to yourself and others and that you are not separate from the world around you. Accept that you are integrated into the web of life and love yourself for your part. There is no reason to demand that you be something you are not. Be content, not with your dissatisfaction, but with your true grace. Be at peace with your being and begin to allow the inner beauty to shine.

Only when you accept that the shadow you cast on the material realm is not the real you, can you let go of the illusions and really be you. Forgive everything you have materialized that you judge harshly, and know that this is not what you truly are. Recognizing your own illusion will free you to transform into a butterfly. Even the acts you judge as your worst can be erased, when you accept that you are more than those acts, and are able to see through their hold on your psyche. Then, you can stop fussing over how bad you are, and start being and giving the light inside.

You can shed all your demons and shine from your center and make every manifestation in your life an act of true sharing from your soul. Allow yourself to fall in love with your special essence, unconditionally, so that just being you becomes an addition to the One Soul evolution. Once you have fallen in love with your soul, you can fall in love with the rest of creation. Everything you experience will become a reflection of sharing that pure energy. And the universe will reflect your giving back to you.

If all humans were to suddenly realize how amazing they are, and fall in love with their souls, then humankind would transcend all its troubles in an instant. Being in love with ones' true individual expression does not mean that you must love all aspects of your ego or its manifestations. You do not have to love that you get violent or that you feel awful because you are overweight. These external manifestations of personality or physical appearance are only a reflection of not loving your true self.

Physical and emotional ailments are signs of the imbalance of your soul levels. A balanced integration of your physical, emotional, mental and spirit bodies will manifest your core meaning. If your eternal spirit connection is running the show, and you release the power you give to your externally focused identity, your unwanted manifestations will seize to carry weight. When you love your inner spirit, the personality or physical flaws become insignificant and eventually will only reflect your true joy. When you love your soul, you accept where you are at present and see the gifts and meaning in what you have created. When you love your soul you can change anything that no longer represents your true nature, and you become a truly giving and evolving being.

In other words, we are not saying love what you would like to change. Rather love your central star connection, and accept your present expression with the knowing that your physical manifestations can be gifts to creation. Love the inherent power you have as a creative articulation and share that love with everyone and everything you come into contact with. You do not have to love everything humanity does, but rather appreciate the power you have as light beings to choose what you experience, and that you can change the playing field from the inside out.

Love that you do not need something outside of yourselves to save you. You are God and can save yourselves as you see fit by believing in your own divinity. It starts with expressing the divine being you already are. The spirit of your religious leaders, such as Jesus Christ, Muhammad, and Buddha all knew the secret of how internal love heals the world. They embodied that teaching and performed what appeared to be miracles as a result. You are each capable of such miracles. You each have that same messiah spirit within you. Acknowledge your beauty as gods and goddesses of creation, and take your individuality back from its enslavement to your externally motivated ego. This is the secret to changing the world.

Learning to love your source also means learning to trust your inner guidance. Some call this listening to your higher self. Whatever you wish to label it, the bottom line is that when you learn to trust your inner knowing, you develop a rapport with that higher self and are guided by light. This light will always be in a state of sharing inherently, which will manifest as a blossoming life experience. Worries of a mundane nature will fall away and paths will open that allow your soul to express itself and share its gifts. The survival needs will be met and then some.

What have you got to lose? Worry, fear, and loathing, have never proved to be creators of anything but chaos and despair. They certainly do not help. Even if faced with a life threatening situation, it will actually serve you best to be centered, calm, and vibrant, rather than strung out with anxiety. You will always have more to give yourself and others if you come from a balanced and peaceful loving centered light.

Receiving, Accepting, and Appreciating

Giving can also be receiving. After all, there must be something there to receive our giving or it will not be giving at all. Therefore, receiving the genuine sharing from others is a crucial part of the equation of evolutionary growth. Although, just as giving can have many self interested attachments, so can receiving. The same rules apply to true heartfelt receiving as do with true giving. If one receives from another with a completely open and appreciative soul, they are allowing the flow of creation. However, just as some giving comes from the ego and is not giving at all, sometimes it is better not to receive from another when one recognizes that the gift is coming from a place of manipulation. If the giving is genuine, so can be the receiving. And this reception is a way to allow the passage of source energy through the universe.

Giving cannot exist without there being a receiver. The fundamental laws of creation are at play with this simple realization. You exist for the purpose of allowing your creativity to shine forth and be shared with other expressions of creation. The multi-verse is a dance of sharing and receiving light for personal and universal growth and expansion. Therefore, being an open, willing, and gracious receiver of the blessings of others, and of all creation, is one's duty as a sentient being. Denying the gifts bestowed upon you, and your planet, is to deny your own light and the source of its divinity. This is why being in a state of appreciation for everything that you experience is one of the most powerful ways to remain connected to the overflowing source of all blessings.

When you remain appreciative, you are opening your portal to be a receptacle for universal expression. If you block that receptivity, you are denying the gifts that are bestowed unto you, and are pushing the givers of such energies away. When you accept the gifts of creation, you are giving back energy to the source of those treasures. Acceptance and appreciation of your personal and external gifts is the other necessary side to being in a state of pure love and higher frequency vibration.

Imagine the difference in energy transference when you give someone something or share of yourself genuinely, and it is accepted and appreciated with a smile, versus with dismissal and lack of care. The latter offers no flow for the shared energy to move through. It is blocked. While your sharing may give you a certain delight, unless it is received and accepted by another, it is not fully realized as a creative force. A receiver has an opportunity to give back to creation by appreciating the shared energy and reflecting it back to the giver. In this way, there is further regeneration of the original intentions being shared. This does not necessarily mean that the receiver must agree with or like what is being given. It simply means that they are open to allowing the gift to flow through them as a conduit of the sharing. The appreciation given back is given for the sake of the sharing, not necessarily for the quality of what is being shared.

When truly giving as a receiver, one expects nothing in return nor feels any obligation to the giver. The act of genuine receptivity is the greatest gift one can return as a true receiver of another's sharing. The same is true of the sharing offered by your planet, and of the grace given by all the universal energies you receive from throughout your solar system every day. Acceptance and appreciation for all the energies that flow to you from your natural environment are the greatest simple gifts you can offer creation. All consciousness has the evolutionary desire to share, and for that sharing to be received. This is what makes the worlds go round. There is nothing more profound than this simple realization. Evolution can only occur when there is a free flow of these components at any level of existence.

Evolution occurs as a process of giving and receiving the source energy of creation. It is the flowing or process of being God, if you will, that causes consciousness to continually grow and develop and perpetually change. God-ing is the process of sharing the light of consciousness. Sharing is expressing that source consciousness in its purity. Receiving source energy is also sharing God consciousness. There exists a beautiful balance in the constant cycling and enhancing of energy as it is moves from one consciousness to another.

As we have indicated, there is no bad or good, only evolution or devolution. In other words, there can be a sharing and regenerating of source energy, or there can be stealing or stagnating of that energy. When one is readily giving from their inner light, and is allowing others to share their light with acceptance, regeneration and evolution occurs. When one is preventing their light from shining or is blocking others' efforts to share, they are causing stagnation in the flow of consciousness. The higher or lighter the frequency of sharing and receiving, the more vibrant and transient the movement of source energy, and hence the faster the evolutionary growth.

Although on the surface, and based on your media reports, it may appear that the majority of humanity is out for themselves, we measure a very different state of affairs on a vibrational level. We are able to detect an amazingly widening scope of awakening frequencies that are disillusioned with the path of self-interest. Many who are completely confused by their lifestyle, are uncertain about how they are spending their time, and are unsettled by the status quo of their lives, are responding to the heightening vibration.

Many of you know there is more, but are unsure what to do about it. Do not fear this sensation. This is a sign that the old ways are falling apart energetically and the new consciousness is upon you. You may be uncertain because, ultimately, the way you are interacting or doing business will become obsolete. The new consciousness of sharing from the soul level is dawning. There are multitudes of you that are aware deep in your soul that there is a wave of humanity that is ready for a new attitude that accentuates the flow of source light in all your interactions, no matter what the mainstream old guard may pretend.

This does not mean you should give up on your present lifestyle. It simply means you are sensing the changes. Allow yourself to feel unsettled and continue to inject consciousness into whatever you are playing at presently. Try, in all sincerity, to remember that you are light and seek to share that source in all your interactions, mentally and physically. Practice caring, empathizing, genuinely listening, and receiving the light shared from others. Even if they appear to be sharing from their ego needs, somewhere hidden in their actions is their true spark. By acknowledging that ray of light behind the façade, you give them a chance to reveal their essence.

What you are going through now is an important part of your process of becoming a being that will evolve into in the next dimension of awareness. Do not deny the aspects of yourselves that feel imperfect. Remember that these imperfections are telling you a story. Pay attention and inject your reality with the intention to express the light that the story is attempting to reveal.

The time is upon you when your species will be aware of the cyclical flow of source energy as the cause of evolution in your world. You will see that you are each responsible for being the conduits of the universal flow of consciousness that creates your dynamic, ever changing reality. A deep understanding that the magic of sharing, and receiving to share, from source consciousness, is the driving force of all creation will propel your soul and species into a new majestic, tremendously revealing, and fulfilling reality. We hope that we have relayed the incredible potential that you each have as bringers of this emerging cycle of soul evolution for humankind, planet Earth, and other beings in your sphere of influence.

The journeys that you have been embarking upon for millennia are coming to a climactic finish as viewed from both consecutive and timeless perspectives. The evolutionary potential has spiraled to a peek in your present signature modulation. Time lines in many realities are converging. The benevolence of extraterrestrial species from many dimensions and time frames are adding to the richness of the evolution of the One, in your now. The giving of source energy from throughout the multi-verse is adding to human efforts. As all receive from one another, an amazing vortex of creative energy is created and realities are propelled upward into a whirlpool spiral of light. In this sharing event, all creation experiences a boost of potential and a rising of awareness envelops manifested worlds within worlds.

Embrace the process of your soul as you flow into the rising frequency. There will be many ups and downs as you learn how to maintain your radiance, and acknowledge the benefits of sharing, as only you can. When you are able to maintain appreciation for the unique sharing of each individual soul, and to graciously receive from their universal light, you will be on your way to expressing your true power. In this state, your species will have no need for stealing any form of energy from each other, or the planet, and you will exist in a regenerating consciousness with endless new tools of creativity. We wish this for your souls from the depth of our own. There is nothing more fulfilling for us than to see another form of consciousness blossom in its expression. This is the greatest joy that we experience as infusers of evolutionary frequencies. As you receive this energy influx from our dimension, you are acting as true givers in creation as well. When you allow the flow of source light from our realm, you are giving to evolve.

We wish to leave you with the notion of your power in choosing what it is you wish to share, and thus perpetuate in the universe, and in your personal experiences, while in your present world. You can and do choose, every day, whether you are going to impose the fears and shortsightedness of your constructed false identity, or whether you will see beyond that illusion and reveal something more from your true eternal consciousness. There is no judgment in the choice you make, but decide which will bring about the creation of a reality you will feel fulfilled and excited within. Which choice takes the fullest advantage of your creative force in this reality?

The greatest majesty of consciousness is that it has free choice in how it will manifest as an expression of source energy. As representations of light that have lived many existences, either on planet Earth or in other 3D worlds, you are adept, and ready to assist in moving the human species to its next potential, and to take part in the intergalactic events of evolutionary change that are occurring. You no longer need the excuses or victimization of Earthly circumstances to hold you back. The dawning of your true potential is awaiting your signal to let go of your limitations, individually and collectively, so that you may embark upon one of the greatest leaps of consciousness of all time. We congratulate you for taking part and meeting the challenges and opportunities as they arise. You no longer need to fear the unknown or confines of your present identity. Let go, have certainty, and take comfort in knowing that you are not alone in this enlightening journey of soul evolution.

For recordings, appearances, and more information about Simion, The Evolutionary Collective, and channel, Jill Mara, please visit their web site

www.simion7d.com

They also welcome your input and questions by email: contact@simion7d.com

Breinigsville, PA USA
09 March 2010

233807BV00002B/1/P